THE **NEW** **INTERNATIONAL STUDIES** **CLASSROOM**

THE NEW INTERNATIONAL STUDIES CLASSROOM

Active Teaching, Active Learning

edited by
Jeffrey S. Lantis,
Lynn M. Kuzma, and
John Boehrer

LYNNE
RIENNER
PUBLISHERS

BOULDER
LONDON

Published in the United States of America in 2000 by
Lynne Rienner Publishers, Inc.
1800 30th Street, Boulder, Colorado 80301
www.rienner.com

and in the United Kingdom by
Lynne Rienner Publishers, Inc.
3 Henrietta Street, Covent Garden, London WC2E 8LU

Library of Congress Cataloging-in-Publication Data
The new international studies classroom : active teaching, active learning / edited
by Jeffrey S. Lantis, Lynn M. Kuzma, John Boehrer.
    p. cm.
    Includes bibliographical references and index.
    ISBN 1-55587-865-2 (hc. : alk. paper)
    ISBN 1-55587-889-X (pbk. : alk. paper)
    1. International relations—Study and teaching. I. Lantis, Jeffrey S., 1966– II.
Kuzma, Lynn M., 1963– III. Boehrer, John, 1943–
JZ1237.N49 2000
327'.071—dc21   99-056615

British Cataloguing in Publication Data
A Cataloguing in Publication record for this book
is available from the British Library.

Printed and bound in the United States of America

The paper used in this publication meets the requirements
of the American National Standard for Permanence of
Paper for Printed Library Materials Z39.48-1984.

5 4 3 2 1

CONTENTS

Part 2   Simulations and Games

Part 3   Technology in the Classroom

Part 4   Afterword

ACKNOWLEDGMENTS

The origins of this project include a shared commitment to active teaching and learning and a good measure of intellectual curiosity. For years, we have been convinced that the many active teaching and learning techniques we use every day in the classroom are effective and exciting educational tools. Our commitment to active learning was further fueled by a natural inquisitiveness about how other teachers developed techniques for student engagement in the learning process. We began the process of sharing ideas about active learning in numerous forums over the last decade: from panel discussions at annual meetings of the International Studies Association (ISA) to the Pew Faculty Fellowship case method workshops at the John F. Kennedy School of Government; from sectional newsletters to e-mail conversations; and from faculty development programs to journal articles. In 1995, dedicated teacher-scholars helped to establish the Active Learning in International Affairs Section (ALIAS) of the ISA, and the seeds of this project truly began to take root.

We would like to express our appreciation to those who made this book possible. First, our contributors represent some of the most talented and proficient teacher-scholars in the country. They are developing and refining innovative, active teaching and learning techniques every day. Their contributions to this book have been outstanding and their dedication to quality education exemplary.

This book also represents a collaboration among three editors. We have truly enjoyed the opportunity to assemble and edit such a fine collection of works. Each of us brought different strengths to the project and different perspectives on international studies. We shared the conviction, however, that a complementary mixture of active teaching and learning techniques can enhance and enliven the educational experience. This has been a successful and stimulating collaborative effort.

Jeffrey Lantis expresses his appreciation to the College of Wooster for providing valuable institutional support for this endeavor. The majority of his work on this project occurred during a leave from the college, for which he is grateful. He would like to express appreciation to his colleagues in the Department of Political Science and participants in the Teaching Matters Program for their support. He would also like to thank his students at the College of Wooster, who have enthusiastically engaged in a range of active teaching exercises and provided valuable feedback. Others who have inspired him to develop active teaching approaches include Charles Hermann, Chadwick Alger, Ralph Carter, Michael Snarr, Thomas Preston, Bill Swinford, Juliet Kaarbo, Karrin Scapple, and Bob Woyach.

Lynn Kuzma gives special thanks to the Department of Political Science at the University of Southern Maine for supplying resources that helped in the completion of this manuscript. Her gratitude also goes to her students, who happily accepted their roles as guinea pigs in her teaching experiments. She has gained valuable teaching insights from numerous colleagues and would like to give special thanks to Patrick Haney, Jeanne Hey, Doug Foyle, Ole Holsti, Margaret Hermann, Howard Tolley, and G. Matthew Bonham—all great teachers and friends.

John Boehrer would like to thank Jeanne Hey for recruiting him to this project, the John F. Kennedy School of Government at Harvard University for the generous institutional support that enabled his participation in it, and the Pew Faculty Fellows in International Affairs for the continuing inspiration of their dedication to active teaching and learning. He is grateful also to Marty Linsky, Lee Warren, Jim Wilkinson, LuAnn Wilkerson, Howard Husock, Kirsten Lundberg, Dan Fenn, Larry Lynn, Michael Nacht, Mike O'Hare, Jon Brock, Marc Lindenberg, Ronnie Heifetz, Mark Moore, Dutch Leonard, Tony Gomez-Ibañez, Steve Lamy, Rita Silverman, Bill Welty, and Tom Angelo, among many others who have contributed greatly to his understanding of case teaching and writing. Finally, he wishes to express his gratitude to Ole Holsti for his unique contribution to this volume, Debby Green for her steadfast encouragement, and his coeditors for their patient and supportive collaboration in completing this work.

Finally, we would like to thank Lynne Rienner and Bridget Julian for their support and patience with this project. Bridget promptly answered the multitude of questions we posed, and she provided needed encouragement along the way. Altogether, it was an enjoyable challenge to produce a book on active teaching and active learning that has exceeded our high expectations, and we alone take complete responsibility for its contents.

—Jeffrey S. Lantis
Lynn M. Kuzma
John Boehrer

1 Active Teaching and Learning at a Critical Crossroads

Jeffrey S. Lantis, Lynn M. Kuzma, and John Boehrer

Active learning and interactive teaching methods are receiving greater attention from faculty who are reconsidering both the process and product of instruction in higher education in the post–Cold War era. Instructors and administrators have recognized that the classroom environment, the nature of social scientific inquiry, and the orientations and interests of our students have changed in the late twentieth century. At the same time, the global political system has undergone a dramatic transformation, prompting those in higher education to review and rethink the international studies curriculum.

This book captures the spirit of change in international studies education by providing a critical reexamination of our method, process, and technique of instruction in the post–Cold War era. In a 1995 article, Robert Barr and John Tagg described this transformation as a move from the traditional, lecture-oriented instructional paradigm to a new learning paradigm. The learning paradigm is a holistic, student-centered approach designed to "produce learning," develop critical thinking skills, and elicit discovery and the construction of knowledge.[1] Barr and Tagg argued that this approach creates powerful and effective learning environments, and they made a convincing case that such a transformation in approach is both appropriate and necessary.

Debates about the best means of instruction in international studies have played out in a variety of interesting forums, including Internet discussion groups devoted to teaching, panels and special conferences supported by the International Studies Association, and

specialized journals of higher education. But this is the first comprehensive volume to examine this topic for international studies in the
post–Cold War era.

It is also important to recognize the broader context of this
exploration of new active teaching methods. The innovative processes described in this book are related to the ongoing transformation in
the content and goals of global education in the late twentieth century. International studies courses began to appear in university curricula many decades ago when social scientists and historians sought to
unravel the tragic puzzles of World Wars I and II. During the Cold
War, political scientists naturally became preoccupied with constructs such as ideology, the nation-state, balances of power, and
arms races. Today, teacher-scholars agree that the complex realities
of contemporary global politics transcend many of the constructs
useful for understanding the Cold War era, and numerous ideas compete as to what new curricular themes are more appropriate for the
twenty-first century.[2] Future teachers in international studies—the
thousands of students enrolled in graduate programs in political science, economics, history, sociology, and related areas—are particularly sensitive to these changes as they approach their teaching
careers with a post–Cold War graduate training. This book presents a
number of innovative teaching techniques that reflect the ongoing
transformation in international studies curricula.

A Learning Paradigm for International
Relations Education for the Twenty-First Century

The chapters in this book promote experiential learning about international studies through new and active approaches consistent with
the learning paradigm. Broadly speaking, this book builds on and
reflects the spirit of recent literature on this shift in international
studies education—a spirit that calls for a transformation in thinking
about international education as both appropriate and necessary. The
chapters focus on new, transnational challenges, including the role of
technology in globalization, competition for scarce resources, summit diplomacy, crisis decisionmaking, international negotiation, pre-
ventive diplomacy, foreign policy goals and strategies for the twenty-
first century, and economic and social justice. These issues are
addressed through a range of teaching exercises that can be adapted

for different class settings—from seminars to recitations to large university courses.

Specifically, these substantive themes are addressed through new techniques in three major pedagogical areas: the case method in international studies education (Part 1), international studies simulations and games (Part 2), and uses of technology in the international studies classroom (Part 3). Chapters present different active teaching and learning approaches in these sections by describing four key design components.

1. *Educational Objectives.* The first step in the application of any interactive teaching tool is to consider specific educational objectives. Clearly, the active teaching and learning approaches discussed in this book can only function effectively when they are employed to fulfill a set of educational goals. Although objectives vary as a function of the design and setting, the exercises discussed in this book serve as strong vehicles to move students from theoretical discussions in the classroom to real-world experience and learning. Generally, the authors presented here contend that active approaches enhance knowledge and promote learning, and they consider assessment of the effectiveness of the exercises in these areas.

2. *Design Parameters.* All interactive approaches have specific design parameters. Instructors seeking to integrate the exercise into a course program should be concerned with the time length and intensity of the exercise, the amount of background historical information required for a successful run, the selection of appropriate technologies, and related resource concerns. Put simply, these parameters represent guidance for setting up the active learning exercise. For students, design parameters may include a review of background historical information, role descriptions, research areas, and skills training. Specific design parameters in role-playing simulations, for example, include role assignments and background research that are a direct extension of educational objectives. In case teaching, design parameters often include advance reading assignments and the preferred method of case analysis or discussion. Technology applications also have clear parameters depending on the assignment (i.e., how much information is required, what technologies are appropriate, and how instructional approaches relate to educational objectives). In sum, design parameters are extremely important for both the students and the instructor.

3. *Procedures.* Experts on active teaching stress the importance

of a set of procedures that guide instructor and student through the experience and toward educational objectives. Procedures may include a list of questions to consider in classroom discussion, protocol or a set of rules of procedure in a role-playing exercise, a list of required Web sites in a research project, or an essay assignment to guide students in reflection on lessons from a contemporary film. Procedures not only help to guide participants toward educational objectives but also simplify and order the exercise. In many exercises, these procedures may reflect basic guidelines to keep participants within the proper intellectual boundaries.

4. *Assessment and Debriefing.* Each of the active teaching approaches discussed in this book offers the opportunity for an enhanced, interactive educational experience, but none is sufficient in itself to achieve educational objectives. Experts stress the need for student-centered debriefing as well as periodic review of the effectiveness of the exercises by the instructor. Debriefing and reflection often provide necessary closure and an opportunity to discuss individual and group experiences. Scholars note that this type of analysis is particularly important because experiential learning frequently occurs after, rather than during, an exercise.

As the discipline considers a variety of innovative educational tools for the twenty-first century, it is essential that we develop more systematic assessments of the effectiveness of these efforts in the classroom. Scholars interested in the use of role-playing simulations, for example, are aware that few comprehensive studies confirm their experiences (and convictions) that such exercises are truly effective. Therefore, we hope that the active learning approaches considered here will serve as a foundation for a more serious movement beyond observation, class discussions, and written evaluations to a more rigorous assessment of these means of instruction. Such efforts would clearly be in the best interest of the discipline. More systematic presentation of evidence that active learning promotes the retention of knowledge about international affairs will underscore the need for a paradigmatic shift in the means of global education.[3]

We are confident that the reader will find in this book a number of interesting applications that relate well to contemporary developments in international studies theory and practice. Chapters feature a practical orientation toward these approaches—with an emphasis on curricular linkages between theory and experience and with classroom objectives such as historical analysis, student interaction, writing, and critical thinking. Furthermore, the range of teaching exercises presented here has been developed and tested in different classroom settings, and many of these innovations can be applied in courses in a variety of institutions.

Major Approaches to Active Teaching and Learning

The Case Method in International Studies Education

Case teaching rests on the idea that students learn effectively through active engagement in real-world problem solving from the perspective of central figures in actual events. Case discussion, the defining classroom manifestation of this method, is a collaborative exercise in wrestling with the dilemmas, issues, and implications of a compelling story. International studies cases are concise accounts of pivotal events, key decisions, important negotiations, historical turning points, development efforts, environmental quandaries, and related challenges. Cases usually consist of written texts, but they can also take the form of oral presentations, film or video clips, newspaper articles, and CD-ROM and Internet sources. The commonality is student-centered, interactive analysis and decisionmaking that stimulates vivid recall and grounds abstract concepts in the specifics of real situations. In the classroom, the professor's role as supplier of facts and wisdom gives way to that of discussion facilitator.[4] Case teaching thus becomes a signal expression of the learning paradigm discussed above.

The case method is already a well-established instructional approach in several disciplines, but its growing application in international studies is relatively recent. This trend is partly because more and more faculty are finding that cases activate student participation and make theory accessible. The increasing visibility and popularity of case teaching in this field also result partly from the Pew Faculty Fellowship in International Affairs. During the early 1990s, the Pew Charitable Trusts funded a large-scale effort to equip international affairs professors to teach and write cases. Over five years, 120 outstanding teachers from across the United States and Canada participated in intensive workshops at Harvard's Kennedy School of Government and returned to their campuses to apply the case method broadly in their courses. These Pew fellows are not only active case teachers themselves; they have spread their enthusiasm for cases to colleagues and graduate students around the world.[5] Indeed, all of the chapters in this book on case teaching are written by veterans of the Pew fellows program, and they present exercises that can be applied in a range of classroom settings.

In Chapter 2, "Teaching Introductory International Relations with Cases and Analytical Exercises," Steven Lamy describes the nature of the case teaching method and potential applications for the international relations classroom. Lamy, a founder of the active learning program at the School of International Relations at the University of Southern California and director of the Pew Initiative in Diplomatic Training program at that university, draws on his expertise to introduce the case method and its value in promoting student participation, intellectual risk taking, involvement, and inter-activity. Lamy describes how case teaching can facilitate the opera-tionalization of key concepts, theoretical arguments, and debates in the discipline, and he goes on to link these educational objectives to specific blueprints for course design.

Joe Hagan argues that the case method serves as an excellent active teaching approach for international relations theory. In Chapter 3, "Teaching International Relations Theory Through Foreign Policy Cases," Hagan points out four ways in which tradi-tional (and nontraditional) cases support the study of international relations theory. (1) Cases present substantive historical materials quite efficiently and thus provide more class time for theoretical dis-cussions. (2) Cases illustrate core concepts in theories of internation-al relations and the foreign policy decisionmaking process. (3) Cases often explore interesting and complex domestic sources of foreign policy behavior. (4) Cases may provide an empirical basis for testing state- and systems-level theory. Hagan provides compelling and thoughtful illustrations of each of these arguments, and he offers a series of recommendations for course design based on the case method. He concludes that cases can be used in a range of interna-tional relations courses to link theoretical frameworks with global political realities.

In Chapter 4, "Teaching About the Third World with Cases," Jeanne Hey supports the themes raised by Lamy and Hagan and argues specifically that the case method can promote a deeper under-standing of international relations and foreign policy in developing countries. Hey presents case teaching applications to confront the "academic problem" of a lack of understanding of the developing world and the "theoretical problem" of humanizing the policy process in developing countries as it relates to ongoing debates in the foreign policy analysis subfield. Hey describes how she has successfully integrated two teaching case studies—one on U.S. military intervention in Ecuador and the other on Brazilian foreign debt—into an advanced course on foreign policy development in the Third World, and she provides ideas for related assignments and role-playing simulations. Hey's classroom experience shows that the case method can truly deepen and broaden student understanding of developing countries and their foreign policy behavior.

David Schodt, in Chapter 5, "Using Cases to Teach Analytical Skills," describes an innovative and thoughtful approach to case teaching for advanced international studies courses. Schodt, a professor of economics at St. Olaf College, contends that cases bring reality to the classroom and provide necessary context for theories of international development. Schodt argues that cases encourage non-linear, "spiral" learning processes in which students gain a deeper understanding of complex political and economic problems. To achieve educational objectives for a course on economic development, Schodt has assigned cases focused on poverty and development in Panama, the Brazilian "economic miracle" of the 1960s, and a development model of Taiwan. By comparing theories of economic development with real-world models and practices, students gain valuable insight into development challenges.

In Chapter 6, "Case Teaching Without Cases," Maryann Cusimano describes alternative active learning approaches that are based on the principles of the case method but that apply nontraditional materials. Cusimano discusses a number of promising applications of "noncase case materials" in the international studies classroom—including everything from newspaper articles to edited volumes, government documents to works of fiction, and television news clips to empirical data. Like formal cases, noncase materials can be used to achieve educational objectives by drawing students into political stories and engaging them through focused lines of questioning, role-playing simulations, group exercises, and debates. In addition, this chapter provides valuable tips for selecting noncase materials and for integrating them most effectively into course designs. Cusimano concludes that noncase materials prompt students to ask critical questions and to take ownership of the learning process, valuable skills that go beyond cases and beyond the classroom.

In summary, these chapters on the case method in international studies education represent the most comprehensive treatment of case teaching in this field yet written. They detail a breadth of case method applications, from introductory to advanced courses, from foreign policy to international development, from political to social analysis, from national to global perspectives, and from formal to informal cases. In so doing, these chapters express both the changing content and goals of international relations teaching and provide the most detailed guidance yet available to faculty who have expressed a growing enthusiasm for case teaching.

International Studies Simulations and Games

Simulations and games represent the virtues of Barr and Tagg's learning paradigm and have produced impressive educational results. These exercises are often structured games that involve negotiation and the allocation of scarce resources. Student participants try to "win" the games by garnering political support for their preferred outcome, but scholars emphasize that such experiences rarely produce clear winners and losers. The real measure of simulation success in the classroom instead depends on two key factors: (1) a willingness on the part of student participants to take their adopted roles seriously and (2) the achievement of specific educational goals. Together, these factors promote a special, experiential learning process that can generate a foundation of knowledge and the motivation for critical thinking.[6]

The use of simulations in the international studies classroom is not new. Indeed, the modern development of these exercises is rooted in the history of the discipline. In the late 1950s, Harold Guetzkow and colleagues in the "Company" at Northwestern University created one of the first international relations simulations, the "Inter-Nation Simulation," which included rules and specific formulas for state behavior—and which sparked wider scholarly interest in these exercises as research and teaching tools. William Coplin, another pioneer of simulations, created a computerized "PRINCE" model in the 1960s that represented an interesting attempt to generalize and mathematicize the foreign policy decisionmaking process. By the 1980s, scholars had accumulated a number of sophisticated simulations of international politics, with names like "Crisis," "Grand Strategy," "ICONS," and "SALT III."

Instead of diminishing scholarly enthusiasm about simulations, the end of the Cold War actually has prompted a renewed interest in role-playing simulations as innovative teaching tools. Although clearly related to past efforts, the new level of interest in simulations and other active techniques is distinct from Cold War approaches in several ways. First, many of the most popular simulations of the past now appear to be time-bound, static creations that could only capture specific sets of conditions such as rigid bipolarity. Second, scholars now charge that many commercially available simulations of the past were simply too time intensive to be incorporated easily and successfully into classroom instruction—with some requiring as many as forty hours for full play. Thus, new attention and effort have been devoted to diversification of the type, scope, and nature of simulations.[7]

In Chapter 7, "Coalitions, Motives, and Payoffs: A Simulation of Mixed-Motive Negotiations," Mark Boyer describes an exercise designed to promote experiential learning about international relations concepts. This simulation illustrates general themes of conflict and cooperation in world affairs, and it is adaptable to focus on more specific themes, including relative versus absolute gains, international development concerns, zero-sum versus non-zero-sum games, alliance formation, distributive justice, and coalition formation theory in legislative settings. Boyer's simulation is unique in its adaptability and application in short-duration classroom settings. In all runs, students are divided into teams and presented with structured, simple-choice games that produce set values according to a computerized spreadsheet formula matrix for payoffs. These values can be interpreted as power, prosperity, or wealth, depending on the educational objectives of the exercise, and they can be directly related to international relations theory.

Chapter 8, by Thomas Preston, "Securing Tomorrow: A Simulation of the National Security Policy Process," presents a contemporary exercise in foreign policy design. Preston combines his experience with simulation design and his path-breaking research into presidential foreign policy decisionmaking to create this exercise. Preston's role-playing exercise was originally developed for his introductory U.S. Foreign Policy course at Washington State University, and it is designed to educate students about the foreign policy dilemmas faced by decisionmakers in the post–Cold War era. The "National Security Policy Simulation" places students right in the middle of political action. On the first day of the course, students are recruited into service by a new, independent president as "the best and brightest" foreign policy staffers of the Departments of Defense and State and the National Security Council, tasked to make good foreign policy for the country. At various stages of the exercise, students complete written and oral presentations for the fictional president in which they must confront serious, real-world policy questions related to U.S. security requirements, threats, and strategies in the post–Cold War era.

In Chapter 9, "The United Nations Security Council Restructuring Summit," Jeffrey Lantis describes a simulation that captures the spirit of changes in world politics in the 1990s head-on. Originally designed for an introductory-level course in international relations, the exercise illustrates the dynamics of international cooperation and allows students to critically examine the role of international organizations in world politics. Students are assigned roles as diplomats representing key countries engaged in negotiations to create a restructuring plan for the United Nations (UN) Security Council that will best represent the global political climate at the dawn of a new millennium. Student diplomats debate new membership and voting arrangements for the Security Council in formal and informal settings. This simulation has proven to be very effective in multiple runs, and the design can be adapted for a variety of courses and levels.

In Chapter 10, "Bureaucratic Bargaining Revisited: A U.S. Foreign Policy Simulation," Heidi Hobbs and Dario Moreno describe a crisis decisionmaking exercise that provides students with a deeper understanding of bureaucratic bargaining theory and the foreign policy decisionmaking process. Students are assigned roles as bureaucrats representing various actors engaged in governmental bargaining and are then presented with a timely scenario: a crisis fueled by rapid expansion of the North Atlantic Treaty Organization and Russian revanchism. Students must avert a new Cold War through careful policy review and planning, and a solid battery of research and writing assignments is connected with this exercise. The simulation is designed with three decision phases: intrabureau discussions where students meet in their respective groups to develop positions and work toward policy agreement, intergroup meetings focused on bureaucratic bargaining, and White House presentations and debates leading to the development of a foreign policy solution to the crisis.

Finally, Michael McIntyre and Patrick Callahan describe an intriguing, historical role-playing simulation of international relations in Chapter 11, entitled "Constructing Effective Systems: Simulating the Paris Peace Conference." This peace conference simulation is designed to achieve multiple educational objectives by providing lessons about national security, great power politics, and the role of law and morality in world affairs, colonialism, imperialism, and self-determination. Students also gain valuable skills through critical readings of classic international relations theory and primary historical documents. McIntyre and Callahan describe a bold effort to place the Paris Peace Conference simulation at the center of classroom activity for an entire term of the authors' advanced international studies course. Students are assigned roles as historical figures engaged in the challenging task of constructing a more peaceful world order at a critical moment in world history. Student participants re-create the final stage of the Paris Conference of victorious allies at the end of World War I by designing sections of the Treaty of Versailles and the Covenant of the League of Nations. Also unique in the simulation is the means of communication—all group discourse is written, and a drafting committee reviews each phase of written communication. Student participants in this simulation have the opportunity to confront what McIntyre and Callahan appropriately label "a mother lode of dilemmas and conflicts over the design of an effective international system."

In summary, all of the chapters in Part 2 feature simulation designs for the post–Cold War era that present instructors and students with background information, specific roles, and basic rules of procedure. Each exercise can be used to model contemporary global politics—from alliance formation to foreign policy design to a critical review of international organization structures and processes. Many are quite adaptable to large and small classroom settings. Combined, these chapters offer an exciting and diverse set of applications for educators.

Technology for the International Studies Classroom

Technology has grown increasingly important for the study (and practice) of international relations. The 1995 National Survey of Desktop Computing in Higher Education, a survey involving more than 650 institutions of higher learning, revealed a 50 percent increase over the preceding academic year in the percentage of courses using e-mail, advanced computer software, multimedia, and the Internet.[8] Part 3 features innovative presentations on how various technologies have become tools for active learning in the international relations classroom. Several authors discuss direct linkages between active learning exercises such as case studies and role-playing simulations and new instructional technologies. In addition, chapter authors critically examine the question of whether these new utilities offer real advancements in a globalized educational environment for the new millennium.

Lev Gonick provides an introduction to Part 3 in Chapter 12, "Creating Active Learning Spaces in the Digital Age." He explores the philosophical and pedagogical implications of technological advancements for international studies. Focusing attention on the potential of the Internet for active learning, Gonick explores the capacity of new technology to support asynchronous, nonhierarchical, multisensory, and democratized learning environments. He believes that new technology has contributed to a paradigmatic shift in pedagogy, challenging traditional linear approaches to teaching, learning, and knowing. He argues that new approaches are more intensely individualized—saying that "learning in a hypermedia world is now, more than ever before, the challenge and responsibility of the learner"—and that hyperlinks have dramatically broadened our learning environments by creating "a technological bridge joining the monochronic world of the west to the polychronic world of the rest." Building on Chickering and Gamson's seven principles for good practice in undergraduate education,[9] Gonick also examines ways that technology may serve as a lever to promote student-faculty contact, encourage cooperation among students, communicate prompt feedback and high expectations, and bring needed diversity to the learning environment.

In Chapter 13, "Face-to-Face in Cyberspace: Simulating the Security Council Through Internet Technology," Lynn Kuzma describes innovative linkages between technology and active learning. Kuzma presents a course design for an advanced offering on international organizations that includes interactive exercises on the World Wide Web and videoconference role-playing simulations of the UN Security Council. Students gain firsthand experience with international diplomacy and a deeper understanding of global political challenges. At the same time, they develop valuable research skills on the Web, and they sharpen their critical thinking and writing skills. Kuzma concludes with some thoughts on the virtues and vices of videoconference technology and the Web for international studies education today.

Jeffrey W. Seifert and G. Matthew Bonham present a powerful survey of the ways in which digital technology have been incorporated into international studies instruction in Chapter 14, "Learning Through Digital Technology: Videoconferencing, Text Chat, and

Hypertext." Seifert and Bonham recognize that the technological revolution of the past decade has provided instructors in international studies with unprecedented opportunities for applications of digital technology to the classroom, but they question the nature and effectiveness of these applications to date. For example, Seifert and Bonham contend that "Webified" courses (those that convert "printed materials such as syllabi, handouts, and readings into basic HTML documents with little interactivity") do not significantly enhance student learning. Instead, the authors suggest that three forms of active learning—incidental and contextual learning, independent and active learning, and collaborative learning—may be enhanced through applications of digital technology to the international studies classroom. On the basis of these objectives and a postmodern theoretical perspective, Seifert and Bonham describe learning environments that they have designed to become progressively more contextual, active, and collaborative. In so doing, they present a blueprint for the creation of a successful virtual learning experience through third-stage international studies cybercourses.

In Chapter 15, "Teaching Human Rights Online: The International Court of Justice Considers Genocide," Howard Tolley describes a set of approaches to instruction about human rights, international law, and international organizations that are based upon emerging technologies. Tolley's chapter describes both the parameters of the Teaching Human Rights Online Project and a specific prototype interactive exercise focused on International Court of Justice (ICJ) review of war crimes and genocide in Bosnia. The exercise is based on a real-world case brought to the ICJ by Bosnia in 1993, which charged Serbia with genocide, called for an end to the international arms embargo, and sought monetary damages. Students play roles as justices of the ICJ through interactive Web sites designed by Tolley, where they review the facts, research the law, and consider opposing legal arguments. Tolley concludes that Web site interactivity has helped students learn more about contemporary problems with human rights violations and develop critical thinking and writing skills and has stimulated student interest in international law and organization.

In Chapter 16, "Learning About Foreign Policy at the Movies," Patrick Haney describes ways in which movie clips, documentaries, and television news segments can be incorporated into courses on U.S. foreign policy. As Haney argues, videos provide a way to engage students, in an "unintimidating way," in a critical analysis of the actors, conditions, and institutions that influence the policy process. Furthermore, the use of movies fits with the emerging learning paradigm, given that video technology has become effectively a part of the lived reality of students. Haney describes his efforts to apply video technology to achieve educational objectives in a course on U.S. foreign policy and national security. Haney helps students to make theoretical connections between *The Mouse that Roared* (1959) and the scholarship of George Kennan and Madeleine Albright; and from *Dr. Strangelove* (1964) to Senate debates about the ratification of the Chemical Weapons Convention. This fascinating chapter will encourage the reader to think critically and creatively about course design using video technology.

In summary, all of these chapters recognize the value of technology as a tool of active learning. Authors show that instructional technology can deepen and broaden active learning both inside and outside the classroom.

Conclusion

The authors in this book explore the paradigmatic shifts under way in international education today. In so doing, they capture the spirit of a new generation of teaching and scholarship.

The final chapter of the book places these approaches in valuable perspective. Widely regarded as one of the foremost teacher-scholars in international studies today, Ole Holsti of Duke University draws together a number of themes from the book in his chapter, "Reflections on Teaching and Active Learning." He provides observations about the rich diversity of ways to get at active learning that have been demonstrated in the book and discusses three essential elements of effective teaching. Consistent with the theme of the book, Holsti then provides an example of his favorite active teaching approach that draws students into the study of international relations, promotes critical inquiry, and helps students become active rather than passive participants in the learning process.

We believe the book will initiate a critical dialogue on the paradigmatic shift under way in international studies education today. We hope that readers will share our enthusiasm about these methods and consider their application to enliven the classroom and enhance the educational experience. The accompanying Table 1.1 offers a concise summary of the book chapters.

Table 1.1   Summary of Active Teaching and Active Learning Approaches

Chapter and Author	Focus	Nature	Course Levels	Duration[a]
2. Steven Lamy	International Studies	Case Studies	Introductory and Advanced International Studies	Open
3. Joe D. Hagan	International Relations Theory	Case Studies	International Relations Theory and Advanced International Studies	Open
4. Jeanne A. K. Hey	International Development and Regional Foreign Policy	Case Studies	International Development and Advanced Foreign Policy	Medium
5. David Schodt	International Economics and Development	Case Studies	International Development and International Economics	Medium
6. Maryann Cusimano	International Studies	Noncase Case Studies	Introductory and Advanced International Studies	Open
7. Mark A. Boyer	International Relations, Negotiations, Security, and Global Issues	Simulation	Introductory and Advanced International Relations, International Relations Theory	Short
8. Thomas Preston	U.S. Foreign Policy and National Security	Simulation	Advanced U.S. Foreign Policy and National Security	Open
9. Jeffrey S. Lantis	United Nations and International Organizations	Simulation	Introductory International Studies and International Organizations	Short
10. Heidi Hobbs and Dario Moreno	U.S. Foreign Policy, Bureaucratic Politics, and Crisis Decisionmaking	Simulation	Advanced U.S. Foreign Policy and International Security	Medium

continues

Table 1.1 continued

Chapter and Author	Focus	Nature	Course Levels	Duration[a]
11. Michael McIntyre and Patrick Callahan	International Negotiations	Simulation	Advanced International Studies, International Relations Theory, and History	Long
12. Lev Gonick	Technology and Active Learning	Instructional Technology	Introductory and Advanced International Studies	Open
13. Lynn M. Kuzma	United Nations and International Organizations	Internet and Videoconference	Advanced International Studies, International Organizations	Open
14. Jeffrey W. Seifert and G. Matthew Bonham	International Studies	Internet, Text Chat, Videoconference	Advanced International Studies	Open
15. Howard Tolley	International Law and Human Rights	Internet	Advanced International Studies, International Law, Human Rights, and Security	Open
16. Patrick J. Haney	U.S. Foreign Policy and National Security	Video	Introductory U.S. Foreign Policy and National Security	Open

Notes: a. "Open" indicates flexibility in the design of active learning exercises to allow the instructor to choose short- or long-term applications—from single class meetings to full academic terms. "Short"-term application denotes a single class meeting to one-week duration. "Medium"-term applications could last several weeks. "Long"-term suggests possible applications of, or connections to, the exercise throughout the academic term.

Valuable related information on active teaching and learning—including course syllabi, teaching materials, case studies, and teaching tips—can be located through the official Web site of the Active Learning in International Affairs Section of the International Studies Association at http://csf.colorado.edu/isa/sections/alias/index.html.

Notes

1. Robert Barr and John Tagg (1995), "From Teaching to Learning—A New Paradigm for Undergraduate Education," *Change*, no. 6, pp. 13–25.

2. See Ole Holsti (1993), "Teaching International Relations in the Post–Cold War Era," *International Studies Notes* 18, no. 3, pp. 1–4; John S. Applegate and Douglas J. Sarno (1997), "FUTURESITE: An Environmental Remediation Game Simulation," *Simulation & Gaming* 28, no. 1, pp. 13–27; Joseph G. Bock and Dean Dunham Jr. (1992), "An Active Approach to Teaching the Political Economy of Development," *PS: Political Science & Politics* 25, no. 3, pp. 538–541; Gary Buckley (1993), "Rethinking the Teaching of Security Policy in a Post–Cold War Environment," *International Studies Notes* 18, pp. 5–7; John K. Butler (1996), "After NAFTA: A Cross-Cultural Negotiation Exercise," *Simulation & Gaming* 24, no. 4, pp. 507–516; Ilan Fischer and Ramzi Suleiman (1997),"Election Frequency and the Emergence of Cooperation in a Simulated Intergroup Conflict," *The Journal of Conflict Resolution* 41, no. 4, pp. 483–502; Urls Rosenthal and B. Pijnenburg, eds. (1991), *Crisis Management and Descision Making: Simulation-Oriented Scenarios* (Dordrecht, The Netherlands: Kluwer); Jürgen Rotmans and Bjorn de Vries (1997), *Perspectives on Global Change: The TARGETS Approach* (Cambridge: Cambridge University Press); Stanley J. Heginbotham (1994), "Shifting the Focus of International Programs," *The Chronicle of Higher Education* 10, no. 19, p. A68; John Lewis Gaddis (1992), "International Relations Theory and the End of the Cold War," *International Security* 17, no. 3, pp. 5–58.

3. For a discussion of the effectiveness of active teaching and assessment, see Elizabeth T. Smith and Mark A. Boyer (1996), "Designing In-Class Simulations," *PS: Political Science & Politics* 29, no. 4, pp. 690–694; Barbara Steinwachs (1992), "How to Facilitate a Debriefing," *Simulation & Gaming* 23, no. 2, pp. 186–195; Lea P. Steward (1992), "Ethical Issues in Postexperimental and Postexperiential Debriefing," *Simulation & Gaming* 23, no. 2, pp. 196–211; Sivasailam Thiagarajan (1994), "How I Designed a Game—and Discovered the Meaning of Life," *Simulation & Gaming* 25, no. 4, pp. 529–535; Sivasailam Thiagarajan (1992), "Using Games for Debriefing," *Simulation & Gaming* 23, no. 2, pp. 161–173; T. A. Angelo and Kevin P. Cross (1993), *Classroom Assessment Techniques: A Handbook for College Teachers* (San Francisco: Jossey-Bass). See also Chris Bell, Mandy Woden, and Andrew Trott, eds. (1997), *Implementing Flexible Learning* (London: Kogan Page); William Carr (1986), *Becoming Critical: Education, Knowledge, and Action Research* (London: Falmer Press); Arthur Chickering and Zelda F. Gamson, eds. (1991), *Applying the Seven Principles for Good Practice in Undergraduate Education* (San Francisco: Jossey-Bass); George Gibbs, ed. (1995), *Improving Student Learning Through Assessment and Evaluation* (Oxford: The Oxford Centre for Staff Development at Oxford Brookes University).

4. John Boehrer and Martin Linsky (1990), "Teaching with Cases: Learning to Question," *New Directions for Teaching and Learning* 42. See also John Boehrer (1994), "Teaching International Affairs with Cases," Web site http://sfswww.georgetown.edu/sfs/programs/isd/files/cases/boehrer.

html; Karen Mingst, ed. (1994), *Special Issue of International Studies Notes: Case Teaching in International Relations* 19, no. 2.

5. William J. Long (1993), "The Pew Initiative: Case Teaching in International Affairs," *International Studies Notes* 18, no. 3, pp. 36–40.

6. Leonard Suransky (1983), "International Relations Games and Simulations," in *The Guide to Simulations/Games for Education and Training*, ed. Robert Horn and Anne Cleaves (Beverly Hills, CA: Sage), p. 163. See also W. Robert Gump and James R. Woodworth (1987), *Atlantis: Role Playing Simulations for the Study of American Politics* (Chicago: Nelson-Hall).

7. For more on the development and diversification of active teaching exercises, see Juliet Kaarbo and Jeffrey S. Lantis (1997), "Coalition Theory in Praxis: A Role-Playing Simulation of the Cabinet Formation Process," *PS: Political Science & Politics* 30, no. 3, pp. 501–506. See also J. W. Endersby and D. J. Webber (1995), "Iron Triangle Simulation: A Role-Playing Game for Undergraduates in Congress, Interest Groups, and Public Policy Classes," *PS: Political Science & Politics* 28, no. 3, pp. 520–523.

8. Kenneth Green (1996), "The 1995 National Survey of Desktop Computing in Higher Education," Web site http://ericir.syr.edu/Projects/Campus_computing/index.html. (July). See also William Ball (1995), "Symposium: Using the Internet in the Political Science Classroom," *PS: Political Science & Politics* 28, no. 4, pp. 718–730; Lee R. Alley and Philip C. Repp (1996), "Technology Precipitates Reflective Teaching: An Instructional Epiphany and the Evolution of a Red Square," *Change* 28, no. 2, p. 48; Robert Armstrong, Fred Percival, and Danny Saunders, eds. (1994), *The Simulation and Gaming Yearbook*. Volume 2: *Interactive Learning* (London: The Society for Interactive Learning); Adele F. Bane (1994), *Technology and Adult Learning: A Selected Bibliography* (Englewood Cliffs, NJ: Educational Technology Publications); A. W. Bates (1992), *The Role of Technology in Distance Education* (New York: St. Martin's); A. W. Bowers Jr. (1994), "Using Prodigy and Other Online Services in the Political Science Classroom," *PS: Political Science & Politics* 27, no. 4, pp. 702–710; Diane M. Gayeski, ed. (1993), *Multimedia for Learning: Development, Application, and Evaluation* (Englewood Cliffs, NJ: Educational Technology Publications); Lynn M. Kuzma (1998), "The World Wide Web and Active Learning in the International Relations Classroom," *PS: Political Science & Politics* 31, no. 3, pp. 578–583; Richard J. Harknett and Craig T. Cobane (1997), "Introducing Instructional Technology to International Relations," *PS: Political Science & Politics* 30, no. 3, pp. 496–500.

9. See Arthur W. Chickering and Zelda F. Gamson, eds. (1991), *Applying the Seven Principles for Good Practice in Undergraduate Education* (San Francisco: Jossey-Bass).

Part 1 | THE CASE METHOD

2 | Teaching Introductory International Relations with Cases and Analytical Exercises

Steven Lamy

Fred Friendly, a pioneer in broadcast journalism in the United States and a professor of journalism at Columbia University, is often remembered for his case teaching on public television in the Columbia University Media and Society seminars and his challenge to all of us who teach future decisionmakers. Friendly stated: "Our job is not to make up anybody's mind but to make the agony of decision-making so intense you can only escape by thinking."[1]

This thoughtful dictum clearly presents one of the major challenges faced by instructors who are asked to teach large introductory courses in any discipline. How do we motivate participation, intellectual risk taking, involvement, and interaction? How do we encourage our students to think critically and creatively as we discuss international issues and events in a discipline in which controversy rules?

Experience suggests that students who are engaged and involved in their classrooms learn more and remain more interested in the subject matter. Lectures and traditional texts need not be abandoned. In fact, these sources of information are usually more relevant to the student when they are operationalized by cases and other active learning exercises. Engaging in these courses, students must use readings and lecture notes to clarify complex issues, evaluate and compare arguments, explore the consequences of decisionmaking, secure evidence to support their own positions, and craft solutions to complex problems.

Active learning exercises, such as case discussions, work best if students are forced to take risks by expressing their views and discussing complex and controversial issues. This is one way to help students develop confidence in their ability to think. Lectures alone may not be enough: "The most conclusive argument against the lecture system is that all true education must involve response. If there is no dialogue, written or spoken, there can be no genuine education. The students must be lured out of their passivity."[2]

Cases tell engaging and dramatic stories that address important issues or introduce students to the complexity of the decisionmaking processes in public and private organizations. Cases provide a meeting place for competing theories about what is real in the world and contending images and explanations of the behavior of state and nonstate actors. Since teaching cases, unlike research cases, leave analysis and evaluation to the students, almost every case discussion will encourage students to think independently, develop intellectual confidence, and become more accepting of the need to find competing explanations of controversial events. As students "inhabit" a decisionmaking situation in a case, that is, put themselves inside the situation and confront the problem as if they were the decisionmaker, they have an opportunity to practice skills that are essential for leadership in public and private organizations.

Students completing course evaluations in one case-based foreign policy class suggested that they were more confident about their capacity to identify the specific differences in policy or theoretical perspectives; compare beliefs, assumptions, and policy positions; identify the sources of societal problems; recognize contradictions in the facts or logic employed by decisionmakers; distinguish relevant from irrelevant information; listen to others and connect ideas and arguments; and consider options and make decisions.

Emphasis on the development of critical and creative thinking skills is an important element of all case classes. This raises some obvious challenges for instructors who are wedded to the traditional examinations and assignments that are more appropriate for courses based on texts and readers.

Creating an Active Learning Environment

Two factors prompted faculty in the School of International Relations (SIR) at the University of Southern California during the 1980s to consider taking more of an active learning approach. The first was declining enrollments in the SIR's general education courses. It was becoming clear to those reviewing course evaluations that the only "agony" experienced by our students in these large classes was attributable to long and boring lectures. The second was an invitation to participate in the Pew Initiative in Diplomatic Training, an effort to introduce the case method of instruction into leading U.S. graduate schools of international affairs.[3]

Our first response to the problem of declining enrollments was to develop a collection of analytical exercises for instructors or teaching assistants to use in conducting lectures and discussion sessions.[4] These exercises encourage students to think again about readings and lecture materials, to work cooperatively with fellow students to explore ways of solving complex international problems, and to participate in simulations and role-play exercises in which they practice diplomacy and statecraft.

Through the school's participation in the Pew Initiative, a significant number of our faculty became familiar with cases and case teaching and saw how case materials and disciplined, focused questioning techniques could transform a passive lecture course. In addition, we learned that many of the analytical exercises worked well as pre-case lessons or as follow-ups to case discussion.

A core group of SIR faculty became committed to the case approach and added introductory undergraduate case-based courses in foreign policy analysis and international political economy to the curriculum. We also developed two new introductory courses. Both courses link case studies with analytical exercises. For example, students explore a case about the illegal dumping of hazardous wastes in a developing country that reveals the complexities of globalization.[5] The case illustrates issues and concepts discussed in readings and lectures, such as sovereignty, uneven globalization, delocalization, competing national interests, and the role of nongovernmental organizations (NGOs). In the analytical exercise that follows the case discussion, the students explore how their daily activities might influence the quality of life in distant communities and the reverse.[6] Each course usually includes five or six cases, frequently using short case studies to encourage participation or to enliven an important concept or issue.

In these two introductory courses and in our other case-based classes, active learning strategies provide a variety of opportunities for students to practice critical thinking. Not only are students encouraged to consider contending perspectives, but also they must find answers to such complex and intellectually sophisticated questions as: Why did that happen? What options did the decisionmaker have in that situation? What was done? Was it a good choice? What would you have done?

Students recognize the importance of this approach to teaching and learning: "Case teaching encourages critical thinking, good analytical skills, and promotes intellectual courage, which is something I lacked . . . the knowledge that I gained discussing the readings in the context of the case made me want to do the readings and to more carefully analyze them."[7]

Two Case-Based Courses

Introduction to International Relations

Introduction to International Relations (IR 101) is a general education course that introduces students to the "four worlds" of international relations: a global economic world, a transnational cultural world dominated by materialist Western popular culture, the world of social activism and social movements attempting to create a global civil society, and a persistent and dominant state-centric political world. Readings introduce students to issues, actions, controversies, and future concerns in each of these worlds, and cases and analytical exercises provide an opportunity to critically review the issue agenda defined by the interaction of actors in each world.

Using the reading "The G-7 Negotiates Soviet Aid,"[8] for example, students explore problems associated with political and economic reform in the former Soviet Union. They also become familiar with multilateralism, summitry, and arguments for and against more support for the former Soviet Union. The pre-case discussion focuses on the question of who won the Cold War. In the post-case exercise, "International Priorities," students evaluate contending arguments for giving aid to several developing countries and make a case for or against giving assistance in several categories.

Case studies and analytical exercises are effective ways for students to practice the basic skills of analysis, evaluation, and reasoning. In IR 101, the emphasis is on learning skills that make it possible for students to analyze complex and controversial issues. Case questioning and writing-research assignments require students to consider contending images or perspectives. In every case discussion, students practice *DEPPP* skills: as they consider and evaluate how different actors with competing worldviews might *describe* issues or events, they *explain* policy behavior, *predict* future trends or outcomes, suggest or *prescribe* policy options, and consider how they might *participate* in a specific policy issue area.

After each case and analytical exercise, students are required to answer several analytical and evaluative essay questions that help them link the case or exercise to readings and lecture materials.

Introductory Theory and Analysis

The second case-based course, Introductory Theory and Analysis (IR 210), is a comprehensive review of theoretical and analytical developments in the field of international relations. As stated in the syllabus, the course learning objectives are to (1) develop a more comprehensive understanding of the various theoretical positions and the roles these theories play in our understanding of the international system (knowledge building); (2) understand the relationship between theory and policymaking in the international system (problem solving); (3) develop an appreciation of other worldviews or perspectives and theoretical assumptions (values and attitudes); (4) explore strategies and opportunities for enhancing one's capacity to participate at various levels in the international system (informed activism).

Cases are a major part of this course. As in IR 101, five to eight cases are linked with analytical exercises. Most of the lectures begin with a short case or problem-based exercise to stimulate class discussion. For example, students might read a brief account of George Kennan's views of the Soviet Union before the class discusses the resurgence of realist thinking in U.S. foreign policy after World War II.

The cases open up both theoretical and policy debates. Before discussing the influence of domestic attributes in shaping foreign policy priorities, for instance, students read and discuss a case that compares the human rights policies of the United States and Canada in Nicaragua. In their analysis of "Confronting Revolution in Nicaragua: U.S. and Canadian Responses,"[9] students consider how the Reagan administration's Cold War belief system and Canadian middle power internationalism influenced eventual policy positions. The analytical exercise that follows the case involves the students in a discussion of worldviews and the operational codes of key decisionmakers. Students are divided into discussion groups and assigned one of five operational codes. After a review of possible foreign policy priorities, the students attempt to create a common foreign policy agenda.

Selecting Cases for Introductory Courses

Most instructors think carefully about why they plan to teach specific materials: What is the critical knowledge to be learned? What skills should be emphasized? Instructors should select cases with an eye toward these same questions, keeping in mind also that cases are not substitutes for texts or research articles. They are supplemental teaching vehicles that enable exploration of theoretical claims, yield insights into the idiosyncrasies of policymaking, and give students a chance to critically analyze evidence and creatively respond to policy challenges. Cases provide the laboratory work that students in introductory courses need to understand new concepts, complex issues, and confusing policy and theory debates.

It is not wise to select a case only because the topic matches some research or teaching interest. Case instructors must carefully consider the specific affective and cognitive skills they would like their students to practice and select the case for the relevance of its story and the quality of the engagement it offers to a particular class. A good case may open up an important debate, provide grist for theoretical arguments, or give students an opportunity to analyze the behavior of important state or nonstate actors.

A good case should make the most complex and controversial situation translucent, if not transparent, presenting all relevant voices, never reflecting the views of just one actor. This is not possible unless the case is well researched. The instructor needs to determine whether the case draws on primary and secondary sources that introduce the readers to all major participants, their perspectives, and their policy prescriptions for action.

It is important to read a case carefully, perhaps twice, before selecting it. The ideal would be to actually participate in a discussion of the case first. In considering a case, the instructor needs to assess its appropriateness for the class. Beyond topic, length, and background issues, the instructor should decide if there is enough information in the case to support the desired analysis. For example, if students should discuss a case in order to examine how belief systems influence decisionmaking, they must be able to read the case and identify attributes of the actors' belief systems and connect those beliefs with eventual policy choices.

In selecting cases, one might consider three categories. The first is *decision-forcing cases,* which present a problem or issue that must be resolved, leaving the story incomplete. This type of case is particularly useful for preparing students to make policy decisions in complex issue areas. A good decision case provides the reader with a thorough review of the problem, a discussion of what has occurred so far, and a full review of possible options; students reading it have enough information to assess the costs and benefits of contending policy strategies. The decision might concern the most cost-effective way to protect an endangered species or the best strategy for dealing with a trade dispute between strategic allies. Many decision-forcing cases present students with moral or ethical dilemmas. For example: Should a soldier be loyal to his unit and disobey an order from a superior officer? Is it a moral policy if you send food to a drought-stricken region and do nothing to remove the repressive government that perpetuates conditions of poverty?

A good case in this category generates a great deal of discussion. The goal is not to reach consensus but to encourage a critical review of relevant options. Students learn that leaders are rarely presented with simple situations that they can resolve by the application of instrumental thinking, for example, cost-benefit analysis. These cases force students to consider their own interests and values, and the values and attitudes of others, before making a decision. They come to realize that decisionmaking is rarely easy and that it involves trade-offs between positions that might have equal moral standing.

Cases in the second category, *analytical-theoretical,* are typically retrospective: presenting the history of an important issue, conference, or event; completing the story; and focusing on the often contending positions of all relevant actors. The drama of such a case emerges from a careful discussion of the competing interests and the difficult choices faced by decisionmakers. A good analytical-theoretical case provides students with enough information to identify key factors that influenced the decisionmaking process. A detailed description of a crisis situation, a trade negotiation, or coalition-building diplomacy gives students an opportunity to explain the actions of key players in the story. Typical questions in such a case discussion might be: Why did the Bush administration object to the French position? How do you explain the French views? One might also ask questions that encourage students to speculate about future or hypothetical scenarios. For example: Given the information presented in this case, what do you think might happen next? What would have happened if the British had taken the minority position? Students with a good understanding of the present, as revealed in the case, develop confidence about predicting the future.

Cases in the third category—*policy process cases*—are also typically retrospective. They provide detailed accounts of how various public and private actors made decisions. These cases are particularly useful for courses in comparative politics. For example, a well-researched case might present a chronological description of how a position promoted by an interest group became a policy and was eventually implemented. Debates about the problems of implementation and concerns about the consequences of the decision are well documented in the best of these cases. Cases from the Kennedy School of Government at Harvard are particularly useful here.[10]

Most of the cases available for classroom use, however, focus on the U.S. foreign and domestic policy processes. To provide a complete picture of the policy story, the instructor might supplement a case with articles about the history, culture, politics, and economics of other countries that are important players in the case. For example, one case on how states reacted to apartheid in South Africa presents only the debates in the U.S. government in detail.[11] Yet the case mentions the different positions taken by Canada, the Netherlands, and other countries. It is often necessary to provide several short articles as pre-case materials to help students compare policymaking processes and foreign policy behavior.

Finally, a good case does not have to be very long. Students tend to like cases that are between ten and fifteen pages, not including charts, supporting documents, and references. Students may read cases two or three times to prepare for the class discussion. A shorter case simply means the students are better prepared. Shorter cases also work better in undergraduate classes that are only fifty minutes long.

Preparing Students for Case Classes

In a case discussion, every student knows that he or she could get the next question. "Staying involved is critical," one undergraduate student observed. "You have to sit on the edge of your chair ready to pounce on the question, and you cannot let up if you are not called on, because the next question could hit you between the eyes."[12]

Most of us work in a noncase teaching and learning culture, so we need to see to it that our students receive proper advice about what to expect of a case course. We need to brief those responsible for advising students about what goes on in one. To this end, our advisers have sat in on case discussions and given students videos of case classes to review before they decide about taking these courses. Students need to understand the rules of the game in a case class: that there may be attendance requirements, for example, that reading assignments are extensive and need to be well prepared, that there are high expectations for class participation, and that case discussions frequently lead to writing assignments.

A case course might be described as a self-service learning environment, in which the instructor facilitates the students' learning and guides them through the cases. Many of our students are not ready for the responsibility of being active participants in their own education. Some are caught off guard—for example, when they find that their lack of participation in one class costs them 5 percent of their grade or that they are locked out of a case discussion because they are two minutes late to class. Such procedures may seem overly stringent, and an instructor may choose to adopt others, but it is critical to communicate with students about their responsibility for their own and others' learning and to set clear expectations about preparation and participation.

It is a good idea to start a new case course with a few short cases. Walk through the case; discuss what is relevant and irrelevant information, what the questions mean, how to respond clearly and concisely, and how to listen to questions and other students' contributions. Give students a few study questions before each case and share ideas on how they can use these questions to read the case and prepare for the discussion. Encourage them to form study groups, as well. Meeting with a few other students to complete their preparation reliably enhances their participation.

Since a good percentage of a student's grade usually depends on the quality of his or her participation, it is important to set out the expectations and the criteria for evaluating it and to be clear that points for participation will be awarded according to a set of measurable indicators. In our case courses, each student receives a scoring sheet that specifies the following criteria:

Substance. Is the answer correct? Does the response clearly address the question with information from the case? Does the student understand the case? Does the response link information in the case with other readings?

Critical Listening. Does the contribution advance the discussion by building on previous remarks? Does the student link his or her intervention with points made by fellow students? Is the contribution a positive addition, or does it pull the discussion back?

Creativity and Critical Thinking. Does the student take the discussion into unexplored and unexpected territory? Does the student think carefully about points of controversy in the case?

Clarity. Is the response understandable, clear, and concise? Does the student use polite and appropriate language?

No student is denied admission to a case class in the SIR; we do try, however, to promote the idea that these courses are for the highly motivated. Yet, they fill before all others. These courses tend to attract the best and the brightest, to receive very high evaluations, and to generate student demand for more case-based classes.

Instructor Preparation

What students learn from a case depends significantly on how their reading of it is prompted or shaped by the questions asked before, during, and after the discussion. Since well-written cases do not include analysis and evaluation, instructors must ask questions that encourage students to think, for example, about why something happened or about the relative value of a certain decision.

In preparing to lead a case discussion, you might start by developing a list of questions that you could ask about the case. Structure the questions to encourage participation from students with divergent learning styles, for example by asking the following six varieties of questions:

Knowledge/inquiry questions. Who made the decision?

Comprehension/translation questions. What actions led to the failure of the policy?

Application/acquisition questions. How do you deal with conflict at work? Did the participants in the case do similar things?

Analysis/comparison questions. Have you ever been in a developing country? What was it like? What are the similarities with the countries in this case?

Synthesis/influence questions. What impact do you think Bush's success in the Gulf War will have on Clinton's actions?

Evaluation/interpretation questions. Do you think that was the best policy choice?

The next step in the process of preparing to teach a case is the development of a teaching script. This is where the instructor must map the case discussion, linking questions, and being sure to cover key issues raised in the case. Select questions that enable students to take the situation apart, critically examine the pieces, and put it all back together again or that suggest alternatives based on the students' analysis and evaluation of the case. Opinions vary on this, but many experienced case instructors expect to have time to discuss only four or five core questions. Other questions will emerge from the discussion.

Try to anticipate the different directions in which the students might take the case with their interventions. Recognize that the instructor manages the discussion with the questions but that it is also important to encourage students to continue a fruitful and engaging discussion that may not go in the intended direction. If the NGO discussion generates more interest than your questions about the bureaucratic battle between the Environmental Protection Agency and the Commerce Department, let the discussion move in that direction but be prepared with questions. If the students are going to hijack the case, be prepared to work with them and direct the discussion in productive ways.

The opening question is always an important one. It is an invitation to all to begin a conversation about an important issue or event. A question that is too narrow, obscure, or difficult may intimidate students and will probably constrain the rest of the discussion. This is not a quiz show, so avoid starting a case with a question that requires a specific right or wrong response. Some opening questions that work well are the following: What surprised you most about Y's position in this case? Have you ever been in a situation like this? If you were X, how would you describe the major problem in this case? Does this case remind you of any current events?

Make certain that anyone who has read the case will feel comfortable with a cold call. Note that a question that is too broad, however, might encourage participation from students who have not really prepared.

Additional Considerations for the Instructor

The actual teaching of a case class takes a tremendous amount of energy and commitment. To be successful, an instructor must pay careful attention to all students during the discussion. It is important to listen and respond to the majority of the students' interventions. An effective case instructor must link responses and questions, rephrase important points, periodically summarize the discussion, and keep the discussion on track.

It is important to honor all relevant contributions; an instructor must be honest and direct, however, with students whose responses are unsound. This has to be done delicately to make certain you don't discourage the risk taking and creative thinking that case teaching promotes. When a response is ill founded, you can rescue the interchange by helping the student dissect the thinking process that led to his or her confusion. A response such as "How did you reach that view?" or "What information in the case supports that position?" continues the discussion and keeps the contributor in the case. Try not to let students retreat because they misstep once or twice.

Encourage students to talk to each other and not only to you. Ask them to learn the names of their fellow students. Name placards help here. Students are not just numbers; in case discussions, they see themselves as members of a community of young scholars with a common task. It is a collaborative learning process; students depend on each other to reach an understanding of the situation described in the case.

Keep track of the time. Move the discussion forward. The pace should be a brisk walk, neither a sprint nor a leisurely stroll. If the case begins to slow down, and only a few students seem to be participating, break the class into small groups and give them a question or two to brainstorm. Role-play exercises within cases often promote more discussion. In a particularly controversial case on the Gulf of Tonkin incident that led to the intensification of the Vietnam war, for example, students took on the role of advisers to President Johnson and explored arguments he might use to make his case to the U.S. public.[13] Another group expressed the opposition's position. The discussion took off after this exchange. Enhance discussion also by introducing additional materials that complement case themes and issues, an audio tape of a speech referenced in the case, for example, or a video of interviews with key actors.

Instructors and students will find that case discussions improve with experience. Post-case debriefings and written feedback from students, however, can enhance the quality of the discussion even more. The instructor has a responsibility to listen to students and learn from their comments. After each case discussion, spend fifteen minutes or more debriefing the case and the actual discussion process. My students are free to make comments about how well they thought the case was written or whether or not my questions clarified or confused the situation described by the case. Before long, students are making suggestions on questions to ask, learning objectives, and more effective teaching cases. Record this session and use the comments to review teaching notes and make decisions about which cases to use the next semester.

Conclusion: Why Case Classes Work

Case teaching is a low-cost method of creating a highly interactive learning experience that energizes both students and instructors. Reports from our recent alumni suggest that case classes have contributed to their success in law school and other graduate programs as well as in their careers. Student evaluations of case courses have also been generally very positive: "In other IR courses, I got bored being in an informational feeding environment. In a case course, I have the chance to become an active participant in my own education. I can test theories verbally. I am also challenged by a spontaneous discussion."[14]

Students like the pace of these classes, the interaction, the pressure, the relevance of the case stories, and the skill practice in good case discussion. A case class is a clear break from the passive lecture, and students seem to like taking some responsibility for their learning. They accept the fact that these classes are more demanding, and they seem to appreciate the fact that professors also have to devote more time and energy to case preparation. One student described a case course as one with a final exam every week. The student found the class challenging but stated that the frequency of cases provided an opportunity to improve each week and get almost immediate feedback from the professor.[15]

Not all faculty are comfortable with this approach to teaching and learning. Some colleagues claim that it is too time consuming, taking away from valuable lecturing. Another frequently heard objection is that it can result in a shallow discussion of important issues. In an effort to cover the case and maintain a certain discussion pace, some issues may indeed be covered inadequately. Also, to encourage participation and promote the process of interactive discussion, some claim, case instructors tread too lightly on students who may be misinformed or trying to promote some ideology. Many of these points have merit, and all case instructors should consider them. No one is ever finished learning how to teach.

A good case teacher is a discussion facilitator with a clear plan of action and questions aimed at eliciting productive interaction. Some ask if this is simply a process in which the instructor manipulates the students and directs the discussion toward his or her image of the correct analysis. The conversation can, in fact, become artificial if the instructor discourages students from taking it in a fruitful direction that he or she may not have anticipated. As the prime minister, not the authoritarian leader, the instructor must manage the conversation and maintain an environment that is conducive to learning, one in which everyone's ideas are respected.

Students are capable of seeing things that we do not, and we should encourage them to share their insights. This is not to say that the instructor surrenders the class to the students. Students simply have more control of the learning process and more influence over the outcomes of the discussion. Thus, the students and the faculty member are all accountable for the quality of the class. Case classes work because responsibility for learning is distributed. This is not a place for the sharing of ignorance but an open environment for the exchange of opinions, ideas, and simple facts about important issues.

> I have learned many valuable skills through case teaching specifically, and studying IR generally. Most importantly, I have learned to be a critical thinker. I am able to look at a puzzle, see its complexities, and analyze it from many different perspectives. I have learned that some ambiguity is okay. The analyzing process is as important as the answers that are found.[16]

Notes

1. Joan Konner (1998), "Fred Friendly 1915–1998," *Columbia Journalism Review* (May/June), pp. 1–6.
2. Page Smith (1991), *Killing the Spirit. Higher Education in America* (New York: Penguin), p. 215.
3. The Pew Initiative in Diplomatic Training, 1986–1992, was an initiative of The Pew Charitable Trusts. The University of Southern California

was one of five institutions selected to develop teaching cases focusing primarily on negotiations involving the United States. In a later phase, the goal became the integration of cases into graduate and undergraduate courses across several areas of international relations. Case teaching workshops accompanied case development efforts, and the initiative ultimately evolved into the Pew Faculty Fellowship in International Affairs, 1990–1995.

4. See Steven Lamy (1995), *Worldviews and International Relations Theory* (Dubuque, IA: Kendall/Hunt).

5. Jennifer Olsen and Thomas Princen (1994), "Hazardous Waste Trade, North and South: The Case of Italy and Koko, Nigeria," Pew Case Studies in International Affairs, no. 161, Washington, D.C.: Institute for the Study of Diplomacy.

6. See Steven Lamy (1995), *Worldviews and International Relations Theory*.

7. USC student in International Relations 210, Fall 1997.

8. Mark Boyer (1993), "The G-7 Negotiates Soviet Aid: From Enemies to Benefactors and the 1991 Summit Aid Package," Pew Case Studies in International Affairs, no. 155, Washington, D.C.: Institute for the Study of Diplomacy.

9. Rhoda Howard and Jack Donnelly (1990), "Confronting Revolution in Nicaragua: U.S. and Canadian Responses," Pew Case Studies in International Affairs, no. 507, Washington, D.C.: Institute for the Study of Diplomacy.

10. The Kennedy School case catalog is available online at http://www.ksgcase.harvard.edu/.

11. Gregory Treverton and Pamela Varley (1992), "The U.S. and South Africa: The 1985 Sanctions Debate," Pew Case Studies in International Affairs, no. 443, Washington, D.C.: Institute for the Study of Diplomacy.

12. USC student in International Relations 341, Foreign Policy Analysis, Spring 1996.

13. Richard Neustadt and Ernest May (1986), *Thinking in Time: The Uses of History for Decision Makers* (New York: The Free Press), pp. 75–85.

14. USC student in International Relations 210, Fall 1996.

15. USC student in International Relations 341, Foreign Policy Analysis, Fall 1996.

16. Comment by a USC student in International Relations 210, Fall 1997.

3 | Teaching International Relations Theory Through Foreign Policy Cases

Joe D. Hagan

For many theoretically oriented teachers of international relations, this chapter's title might appear to be an exercise in wishful thinking or an outright contradiction. At the heart of this skepticism are suspicions that case studies are simply descriptive narratives about decisionmakers, their perceptions, and how they arrived at decisions; that cases are essentially atheoretical and, at best, provide anecdotal illustrations to supplement lectures on various international relations theories. Furthermore, cases can be dismissed because much of what they describe about leaders and decisionmaking is not crucial to understanding the fundamental dynamics underlying world politics. These skeptics would note that reigning perspectives such as neorealism and neoliberalism persuasively treat government decisions as dictated by deeper systemic forces[1] and that even state-level theories such as the democratic peace see leaders as driven by domestic structures. Many international relations scholars likely view cases as a supplement to researching and teaching theories of international relations.

My argument in this chapter is that traditional case studies, that is, detailed narratives, are actually an excellent means of enhancing the theoretical content of both foreign policy and international relations courses.[2] I argue that this is true in at least four ways: that cases specifically (1) cover historical events and trends efficiently and thereby create class time for theoretical discussion, (2) illustrate core concepts in foreign policy decisionmaking theories, (3) suggest the deeper domestic sources of foreign policy, and (4) ultimately provide the empirical basis for rejecting the state-level logic of foreign policy explanations in favor of systemic theories such as neorealism. Taken together, descriptive cases provide highly focused factual materials that enable students not only to discuss the theories themselves but also to illustrate, explore, and evaluate competing theories on the merits of case facts.

In presenting these four arguments, I draw upon my course, Politics of War and Peace. Typical of an upper-level, undergraduate international relations course, its objectives are both substantive and analytic. The more basic substantive concern is to survey Great Power diplomacy since the beginnings of the nation-state system in the 1490s by identifying the distinct periods of Great Power relations, the issues that dominated international politics in each period, and the wars and peace settlements that marked the passage from one period to another. The other substantive concern is to explore the logic of Great Power foreign policies as they relate to the initiation of war and the maintenance of peace, that is, policies ranging from the extremes of appeasement and isolationism to those of militant confrontation and revolutionary expansionism, as well as more restrained policies in between such as pragmatic diplomacy and cooperative moderation with a Great Power concert. The course's theoretical objectives, which are also twofold, center on the explanation of why Great Power wars break out or, alternatively, why they do not and why, instead, stability persists for an extended period. The more immediate explanations concern how leaders have handled international crises, focusing not only on international pressures but also on how leaders perceived those pressures and the extent to which domestic politics affected their management of these crises. These decisionmaking explanations are, however, placed into a broader context, embedding leader perceptions and decisionmaking processes into the deeper roots of each power's history, culture, economy, and regime structure as well as the structure of the international system.

Cases Make Efficient Use
of Substantive Historical Materials

The first advantage of case-based teaching is that it avoids the major problem with a political science course such as Politics of War and Peace: namely, that its broad historical substance leads to a continuous survey of Great Power relations for the past five hundred years. The value of cases begins with their focusing attention on the pivotal events in the ebb and flow of Great Power relations, that is, the outbreak of wars and the peace settlements afterwards, and providing concise material to understand those events. At the core of any foreign policy case are three sets of details key to explaining the outbreak of war. The first is the situation that triggered the decisionmaking: information on the issue(s) provoking conflict, the involvement and influence of various foreign powers, and the immediate events that provoked the crisis.[3] The second detail set concerns aspects of the decisionmaking process itself: the specific personalities involved in the decision, alternative policy options articulated in the decisionmaking, and the process by which decisionmakers selected among those options. Finally, with careful class analysis of the case details, it is possible to isolate the government action (the dependent variable) precisely and cast it as part of a broader class of foreign policy outcomes or even portray it as a theoretical puzzle that one might not originally expect from standard theories. In short, good cases provide focused and concise treatment of the critical ingredients of a theoretical exercise.

Of course, courses include multiple cases, usually organized into a sequence that links them theoretically and/or historically. Thus, in my course on Great Power conflicts, I use cases on the outbreak and settlement of the following wars: (1) the Thirty Years' War and the Westphalia settlements, (2) the French Revolutionary and Napoleonic Wars and the Congress of Vienna, (3) World War I and Versailles as well as World War II and Yalta, and (4) the Cold War (Cuban missile crisis) and the Gorbachev-Bush Malta meetings.[4]

This sequence serves several conceptual and theoretical purposes. One is to use great power wars and settlements to define basic periods of Great Power relations. These conflicts mark four basic periods in Great Power diplomacy, consistent with prominent historical surveys of European diplomacy:[5] the Habsburg quest for mastery of Europe (1495–1648), the traditional European balance of power of the ancien régime (1648–1789), the modern European balance of power marked by nationalism and industrialization (1789–1940), and the rise of a global balance of power (1945–present).

Another valuable use of these cases is to connect different types of conflicts with research into their causes, conduct, and settlement. Thus, the Thirty Years' War arguably reflects the severity of what Holsti called "wars of third kind," whereas the French Revolutionary and Napoleonic Wars reflect Walt's arguments linking wars with con-

vulsions resulting from domestic political revolutions.[6] And, following Kagan's pairing of World War I and World War II, the earlier
wars illustrate Jervis's key distinction of conflicts resulting from a
conflict "spiral" and those resulting from the failure to deter an
aggressive state.[7]

The value of these cases to enhancing the theoretical contents of
the course goes far beyond the substance of the narratives themselves. In fact, the cases shift the entire class's structure away from a
lecture format covering the Great Power diplomacy across decades,
if not centuries, since 1500. Instead, with the focus on pivotal cases,
there is no attempt to cover entire periods or issues comprehensively.
Class time now belongs to the examination and analysis of the outbreak of wars, in terms of both the immediate crises as well as the
longer-term dynamics characteristic of the preceding era of Great
Power diplomacy.[8] This is not to say, however, that class is only
about these episodes: crucial to teaching cases is ensuring that students have the background to the making of these decisions as well
as an understanding of their impact. Much of that background,
though, can come from required reading in supplementary historical
surveys on, for example, the rise and fall of Great Powers, issues that
generated wars, domestic political development, and peace settlements.[9]

Cases Illustrate
Competing Decisionmaking Theories

Many, although not all, cases focus on decisionmaking. Such cases
can offer a basis for exploring decisionmaking theory by providing
crucial facts about the decision process, that is, who was involved,
what policy positions were taken, and how the political basis to
authorize government action was achieved. If cases are used comparatively, their descriptions of the decision process expand this discussion by allowing consideration of alternative decisionmaking models
across different situations, problem areas, and national political systems.[10] In this way, cases form the basis for not only examining certain processes but also understanding the "contingencies" in which
one dynamic comes into play as opposed to the other. This is the ultimate value of the three primary questions I use to initiate analysis of
any decision episode: who? what? and how?

Who made the decision? This question moves the discussion of the case problem to the decisionmaking arena and elicits certain basic facts, for instance, which government officials participated in the decision that authorized the government to act. But the question can quickly extend to the more general structure of the "decision unit" that has ultimate authority to commit the resources of the state in international affairs. The following three types of decision units follow Hermann, Hermann, and Hagan:[11]

- *Predominant leader.* A predominant leader is a single individual who has the ability to stifle all opposition and dissent, with the power to make the decision choice alone, if necessary. Examples include not only such war-prone leaders as Philip II, Napoleon, and Hitler but also Chamberlain at Munich and Roosevelt at Yalta.
- *Single group.* A single group is a set of individuals, all of whom are members of a single body, who collectively select a course of action in consultation with each other and reach a collective decision. Examples are Kennedy's Executive Committee in the Cuban missile crisis, the Brezhnev Politburo, and—in the July 1914 crisis—Britain's divided Liberal Party cabinet and Russia's Council of Ministers.
- *Coalition of autonomous actors.* A coalition of autonomous actors consists of separate individuals or groups that, if some or all concur, can act for the government where no overarching authoritative body combining all necessary actors exists, but no one of which can decide and force compliance on the others by itself. Examples of such coalitions include both military and democratic governments in interwar Japan, the Austro-Hungarian Crown Council in July 1914, and the isolationist Congress and internationalist Roosevelt administration in the United States before World War II.

The chief value of the notion of alternative decision units is that different "processes" characterize them. Those processes, in turn, lead to a discussion of alternative theories of foreign policy decisionmaking. Getting to that point requires exploration of the next two questions about the case.

What was (were) the policy position(s) taken by the members of the decision unit? Of concern here are the precise arguments advocated by the participants in the decisionmaking process. Although this question provides further factual details, its main value is to shift the discussion from matters of decision "structure" to ones of the "processes" that underlie various models of foreign policy making. At this more theoretical level, the question then becomes, what "types" of positions were argued and, in turn, what was the range of debate? For example, in the Cuban missile crisis, it is possible to identify arguments ranging from the use of military force (e.g., air strikes) to nonmilitary confrontations (e.g., blockade and diplomatic bargaining). In even more extreme cases, such as Third Republic France before World War II, debates were polarized even to the point of arguing who was France's primary enemy: Nazi Germany or Soviet Russia? There is the possibility of the opposite extreme, however, in which there is the absence of any real debate in the policy process. At this extreme, decisionmakers not only agree on what is the threat or problem but, indeed, concur on the precise strategies by which to respond to it. An example is the Cold War consensus in the United States on the military intervention in Vietnam by 1965.

How did members of the decision unit arrive at a common position to authorize government action? This question gets at the heart of different decision processes, each of which is associated with an alternative decisionmaking theory. First, where disagreement exists with a single group or coalition, the decisionmaking process becomes inherently political as some agreement is reached among adversaries, which thus points to theories of bureaucratic politics or coalition formation. Even with simple case information on contending positions, students can flesh out the bargains, compromises, side payments, or influence strategies that were executed to gain majority support for a particular position and, ultimately, can judge whether this outcome was a rational choice along the lines of "multiple advocacy," a suboptimal political resultant ranging from bargaining to logrolling, or even a complete deadlock preventing any meaningful action.[12]

Second, in cases where there is strong consensus, the dynamics of another prominent theory of decisionmaking may be at play: "groupthink."[13] The opposite of bureaucratic politics,[14] the occurrence of close agreement on all aspects of an issue invites class discussion of decisionmaking dynamics that would suppress disagreements and alternative opinions, for example, the role of a key decisionmaker or the pressures for loyalty among members of the decision unit.

Finally, in the cases of decisionmaking by a single predominant leader, the issue is the sort of influences driving the leader's choice.[15] Was he or she open to the alternative opinions of advisers, or was the leader mentally closed off from outside influences? In cases of the latter, theories of personality are important, whereas in the former, explanations have to do with influence attempts on the leader and his or her calculations in responding to them.

Cases Suggest Deeper Domestic Sources of Foreign Policy

Many theories of foreign policy embed the preceding decisionmaking structures and processes within deeper forces reflective of domestic structures and political culture. Cases, even ones that focus exclusively on the decisionmaking, can easily invoke such deeper explanations, simply in response to questions about the sources, or origins, of leader perceptions and the decision structures and processes. And, in comparison, cases can tap into the different contingencies associated with varying perceptions and decision dynamics across nations with different historical experiences, political cultures, and political regimes. The character of decisionmaking processes, the nature of leader perceptions, and, ultimately, the theoretical connection between those perceptual and political influences raise the following questions.

Why were decisionmaking structures fragmented and polarized (or, alternatively, highly centralized with little debate)? This question seeks explanations of the decision processes noted earlier, that is, why was decisionmaking authority highly dispersed or, alternatively, highly concentrated, and why was there sharp debate or, alternatively, minimal debate? Some answers to these questions might be found within the decisionmaking setting, for example, the personalities of presidents, the decision situation, or the character of an issue area. It is possible to push the discussion further by directing it toward aspects of the nation's political structure and political realities. Thus, one might ask students to consider how, or whether, the institutional arrangements of the decisionmaking process resulted in the representation of diverse interests. One way to begin is to place the discussion in the context of the prominent "democratic peace theory."[16] Namely, to what extent did the concentration of authority and range of debate conform to the images of democratic and authoritarian regimes, for example, that the former would have broader debates while the latter would have minimal debates given a single ideological mind-set or a single predominant leader? Note, also, that a discussion of British, French, and U.S. responses to the Nazi threat clearly gets at the differences in decisionmaking across parliamentary and presidential regimes.

Both democratic and authoritarian systems, however, present interesting and instructive *exceptions*, ones ranging from the pluralistic decisionmaking in the post-Stalinist Politburo or in Czarist Russia under Nicholas II to the extreme cohesion in the democracies of the United States at the height of the Cold War and of Britain under Chamberlain before World War II. These examples not only point to the limits of democratic peace theory but also can expand class discussion to other sources of decisionmaking structures and processes. One argument relates leadership politics to the political system's pattern of economic development, noting, in particular, the "anocratic" relationships and concentrated economic interests often found in political systems undergoing dramatic political restructuring and rapid economic transformation, including not only Revolutionary France and several pre–World War I powers but also post–Cold War China and Russia.[17]

Alternatively, the pattern of decisionmaking might simply reflect certain political realities underlying a regime's survival, for example, the fear that overruling certain interests would lead to their intolerable defection (e.g., the pivotal role of the Hungarian prime minister in Austria-Hungary) or to the collapse of the regime (e.g., the power of army and navy factions in militarist Japan). Similarly, the level of debate might reflect certain norms or fears of the domestic political consequences of going to war or not going to war.[18] Recall, for example, not only the fears of domestic revolution in pre–World War I Germany and Russia but also how the Cold War doctrines of successive U.S. administrations were rooted in the memories of domestic political backlash against the Truman administration in the "who lost China?" debate of the late 1940s. Although other theories could also apply here (most notably, those of political culture), these influences suggest some of the directions class discussion can take in considering the deeper sources of foreign policy decision structures and processes.

Why did leaders (either hard-liners or moderates) perceive the situation the way they did? Not all foreign policy is embedded in the political process, and recognizing this enables students to appreciate the broader perceptual logic underlying foreign policies across different historical episodes and political systems. Even when leaders have disagreements about specific policy issues and how to respond to them, major theories of foreign policy draw attention to the explanatory power of the *shared* beliefs of leaders.[19]

For teaching purposes, a wide variety of theoretical and historical sources suggests it is useful to begin with the simple distinction
between "moderate" and "hard-line" belief systems, which differ on
the fundamental question of how threatening is an adversary and,
more generally, how dangerous are world affairs. Hard-liners are
likely to see relations with adversaries as an inherently zero-sum
game, in which a threat can be dealt with only through militant confrontation, whereas moderates are likely to see common interests
that permit, indeed require, diplomacy that often involves pragmatic
compromises and restraint. And, following Vasquez, the rise of
hard-liners in the governments of opposing nations is likely to be a
critical step on the road to war.[20] Note, for example, the rise of hard-
line leaders in all of the European powers (except Britain) before
World War I as well as the rise of extremely hard-line governments
in the fascist nations confronted by extremely moderate democracies.

With leaders classified as hard-line or moderate, the key questions for class discussion then become why these leaders held hard-
line (or moderate) beliefs, and why these hard-liners (or moderates)
came to prevail over groups with the opposing beliefs. One important
perspective concerns historical influences, for example, the "lessons
of history" from past experiences in international politics, particularly policy failures.[21] The rise of hard-liners in both the United States
and the Soviet Union, for instance, had a great deal to do with not
just strategic issues but also the lessons and policy failures of the
1930s in failing to stop the aggression of Nazi Germany and militarist Japan.

Another key factor accounting for hard-line strategies is economic. Along with the balance between protectionist and free trade
interests, economic factors come into play with respect to leader perceptions of the viability of international markets, and often recession
and the collapse of markets are key to shifting to a unilateral (or
autarkic) strategy of accessing foreign resources.[22] Thus, for example, the collapse of U.S. markets in the 1930s played into the hands
of Japanese militants and undercut moderates favoring international
cooperation, and the worldwide recession of the 1890s provoked
hard-line demands to stimulate the economy by building larger naval
forces in Germany and the United States.

Finally, the class can consider the impact of political culture, or
what Dallek called "cultural politics."[23] Conflicts ranging from the
Thirty Years' War to World War II and the Cold War were sharply
intensified because they involved adversaries with opposing political

ideologies, with each side seeing the other system as evil and thus inherently aggressive and threatening.

To what extent did domestic political processes drive leader beliefs? At one level, this question is simply an extension of the previous question, in that it explores the role of leaders' shared beliefs by suggesting that their implementation may be conditioned (either amplified or constrained) by domestic political pressures. Thus, for example, the political deadlock in the United States and in France in the late 1930s undercut the ability of either government to respond to international threats. Just the reverse occurred in the Cold War and in World War I, as hard-line beliefs were sharply amplified because most governments had long used nationalism to shore up their legitimacy and ultimately could not appear to be backing down in a major crisis.

At another level, though, this question invites a juxtaposition of perceptual and political explanations by pushing the class to consider which explanation really matters more. Cognitive arguments would suggest that political processes account only for relatively narrow aspects of policy, for example, the choice of instruments of diplomacy, whereas overarching shared beliefs get at the fundamental sources of foreign policy that influence the identification of threats and the long-term strategy of confrontation or cooperation. Political explanations argue just the reverse. These hold that leaders are motivated by the desire to retain power and pursue parochial interests. Thus any shared beliefs are really myths manipulated to legitimize agreements among parochial interests or to keep the leadership in power. Either way, an interesting final exercise is to have students consider the relative importance of the two conceptions of foreign policy making. How that question is answered has clear implications for the debate between constructivist versus rational choice approaches to incorporating state-level phenomena into international relations theory.

Cases Can Favor Systemic Theory over Foreign Policy Explanations

It is important to recognize another key question that lurks throughout the discussion of any foreign policy case. This ultimate question raises the possibility that all of the preceding perceptual and political phenomena do not matter and that, instead, leaders in the case largely responded *directly* to more or less obvious and compelling pressures of international structures. This logic is, of course, central to the reigning neorealist and neoliberal theories of international politics.[24] The point here is that decisionmaking cases also provide students with the key ingredients for upholding systemic logic, because they provide details on the international (and domestic) context in which decisionmakers operated. Thus, any decisionmaking case also provides the information necessary to test whether a systemic explanation also holds, that is, that leaders rationally chose the best course of action given their state's place in the international system.

The juxtaposition of decisionmaking and systemic approaches is not necessarily an "either/or" choice, and recognizing this lets the class explore how the two levels of analysis can complement each other. As argued in several major critiques of realist theory, foreign policy decisionmaking explanations are best viewed as supplements to systemic explanations of war.[25] Depending on the case, this line of argument can be pursued in one of two ways. One argument is that, although systemic theory might explain the overall rivalries between adversaries, it cannot account for puzzling state behavior leading to the actual outbreak of war.[26] Thus, how decisionmaking phenomena are embedded domestically accounts for the flawed behavior of states that either overreacted to systemic threats or underreacted to them in the crises leading to war.

The other argument is that decisionmaking theory supplements systemic theory by uncovering the crisis conditions in which the systemic logic actually did work, such that adversaries effectively balanced each other and avoided the trap of war as, say, in the Cuban missile crisis. In short, in even the most systemically oriented international relations theory course, decisionmaking cases are interesting because they can get the class to explore the conditions necessary to enable leaders to respond effectively to systemic phenomena as well as those situations in which government overreaction and underreaction to adversaries become problematic.

This final point illustrates the ultimate value of case teaching in theoretically oriented courses on foreign policy and international relations—that although cases are built around materials that illustrate decisionmaking processes, they also provide the contextual material for constructing tests of alternative theories, ones embedded either in domestic structures or international system dynamics. This possibility highlights the irony raised in the opening of this chapter. Cases, although they are merely descriptive narratives of situations, processes, and outcomes of foreign policy decisions, are actually theoretically very potent. As I have sought to argue, a series of questions can be raised that bring out core concepts of foreign policy making, make the connection to their deeper historical and domestic roots, and even force students to see them within the context of the international system.

Cases, however, are more than just devices for getting students to explore theoretical ideas in the standard literatures. Additionally, because they provide the ingredients for constructing a theoretical argument, cases enable students to juxtapose alternative theories. Alternative decisionmaking structures and processes can be considered in discussion, and the same can be said of the alternative roots, domestic and international, of those perceptual and political dynamics. In short, cases not only illustrate certain concepts and theories, they also provide students with the materials to assess the importance of one theory or another in a theoretically neutral manner. In other words, cases do much more than simply illustrate the substance and logic of theories; they can get students to be creative in judging and modifying theories in a creative and open manner. In doing so, students learn not only theories but also the art of theorizing.

Notes

1. For neorealism, see Kenneth Waltz (1979), *Theory of International Relations* (Boston: Addison-Wesley); for neoliberalism, see Robert Keohane (1984), *After Hegemony* (Princeton, NJ: Princeton University Press).

2. I am quite sympathetic to arguments that case study research is, itself, theoretically rigorous, but the use of such cases is not the basis of my argument here. In fact, for purposes of case teaching, it is the richly detailed narrative that is most important for class discussion. More theoretically focused cases are actually *less* useful for purposes of classroom discussion, because they provide too many answers and likely assert a particular theoretical argument.

3. It is important to note that cases can range from a simple statement of the events immediate to a decision to an extensive historical overview of prior decisions and episodes leading up to a crisis. At least when initiating discussion of the case, I believe that care must be taken in assigning precisely that material dealing with the crisis, even if doing so means having students skip over extensive preceding material. This approach enables the class to cut directly to the decision to be explained. The contextual material should be brought into the discussion in later stages, that is, at the point when the class moves to the explanation of longer-term sources of the state crisis behavior.

4. The primary source of assigned case materials is Donald Kagan (1995), *On the Origins of War and the Preservation of Peace* (New York:

Doubleday). This historical work concisely narrates the long-term and immediate events associated with the outbreak of World War I, World War II, and the Cold War. As noted earlier, it is critical to isolate the key chapters on the July 1914 crisis (pp. 183–205), the Munich crisis (pp. 388–413), and the Cuban missile crisis (pp. 493–548) and then only assign the excellent background material for the subsequent class in which longer-term causes of the crisis are considered. For the other two wars, the chapter in Stephen Walt (1996), *Revolution and War* (Ithaca, NY: Cornell University Press) is excellent (and has additional cases for comparison). For a more purely historical narrative, use the appropriate chapters in T.C.W. Blanning (1986), *The Origins of the French Revolutionary Wars* (New York: Longman). A valuable analytic overview is in Myron Gutmann (1989), "The Origins of the Thirty Years' War," in *The Origin and Prevention of Major Wars,* ed. Robert Rotberg and Theodore Rabb (Cambridge: Cambridge University Press). This overview can be supplemented with narrative sections from the standard work on that war: Geoffrey Parker (1984), *The Thirty Years' War* (London: Routledge).

5. Ludwig Dehio (1962), *The Precarious Balance* (New York: Alfred K. Knopf); Paul Kennedy (1987), *The Rise and Fall of Great Powers* (Boston: Random House); David Kaiser (1990), *Politics and War: European Conflict from Philip II to Hitler* (Cambridge: Harvard University Press).

6. Kalevi Holsti (1996), *The State, War, and the State of War* (New York: Cambridge University Press); Stephen Walt (1996), *Revolution and War.*

7. Kagan, *On the Origins of War;* Robert Jervis (1976), *Perception and Misperception in International Politics* (Princeton, NJ: Princeton University Press).

8. Note that the chronological sequence of cases illustrates how prior wars and their settlements shape the subsequent period of international relations and ultimately contribute to the next war. Thus, the class's examination of the origins, conduct, and settlement of World War I provides the background to understanding Nazi aggression and British appeasement leading to World War II. Similarly, the "nightmare years" of the 1930s provide insights to understanding U.S. policy in the Cuban missile crisis and the Vietnam War. As discussed below, the sequence of cases provides key material for the class's theoretical discussions of why wars occurred.

9. For Great Powers, see Paul Kennedy, *The Rise and Fall of Great Powers* (1987); for issues that generated wars, see Kalevi Holsti (1991), *Peace and War: Armed Conflicts and International Order, 1648–1989* (Cambridge, MA: Cambridge University Press); for domestic political development, see David Kaiser, *Politics and War* (1990); for peace settlements, see Charles W. Kegley Jr. and Gregory A. Raymond (1995), *How Nations Make Peace* (New York: St. Martin's).

10. One of the values of looking at international phenomena such as the outbreak of wars is that the cases involve the interaction of multiple states. Kagan's analysis of World Wars I and II is excellent, because he considers decisionmaking perceptions and processes in each of the major powers—Britain, France, Germany, Austria-Hungary, and Russia in the July 1914 crisis and Britain and Germany at the Munich crisis.

11. Margaret Hermann, Charles Hermann, and Joe Hagan (1987),

"How Decision Units Shape Foreign Policy," in *New Directions in the Study of Foreign Policy,* ed. C. Hermann, C. Kegley, and J. Rosenau (Boston: Allen Unwin), pp. 311–312.

12. For "multiple advocacy," see Alexander George (1980), *Presidential Decision Making in Foreign Policy: The Effective Use of Information and Advice* (Boulder, CO: Westview Press); for suboptimal political resultant, see Graham Allison (1969), *Essence of Decision* (Boston: Little, Brown) and Jack Snyder (1991), *Myths of Empire: Domestic Politics and International Ambition* (Ithaca, NY: Cornell University Press); for deadlock, see Joe Hagan (1993), *Political Opposition and Foreign Policy in Comparative Perspective* (Boulder: Lynne Rienner).

13. Irving Janis (1972), *Victims of Groupthink* (Boston: Houghton Mifflin).

14. See Charles Hermann (1993), "Avoiding Pathologies in Foreign Policy Decision Groups," in *Diplomacy, Force, and Leadership,* ed. Dan Caldwell and Timothy McKeown (Boulder, CO: Westview Press).

15. Margaret Hermann (1993), "Leadership and Foreign Policy," in *Diplomacy, Force, and Leadership,* ed. Dan Caldwell and Timothy McKeown (Boulder, CO: Westview Press).

16. For example, Bruce Russett (1993), *Grasping the Democratic Peace* (Princeton, NJ: Princeton University Press); John Owen IV (1997), *Liberal Peace, Liberal War* (Ithaca, NY: Cornell University Press).

17. See Jack Snyder (1991), *Myths of Empire*; Stephen Walt (1996), *Revolution and War.*

18. Jack Jevy (1989), "Domestic Politics and War," in *The Origin and Prevention of Major Wars,* ed. Robert Rotberg and Theodore Rabb (Cambridge, MA: Cambridge University Press); Charles Kupchan (1994), *The Vulnerability of Empire* (Ithaca, NY: Cornell University Press).

19. Robert Jervis (1976), *Perception and Misperception*; Ole R. Holsti (1976), "Foreign Policy Decision Makers Viewed Psychologically: 'Cognitive Process' Approaches," in *In Search of Global Patterns,* ed. James N. Rosenau (New York: Random House).

20. John Vasquez (1993), *The War Puzzle* (Cambridge, MA: Cambridge University Press).

21. Ernest May (1976), *"Lessons" of the Past* (New York: Oxford University Press).

22. Etel Solingen (1998), *Regional Orders at Century's Dawn: Global and Domestic Influences on Grand Strategy* (Princeton, NJ: Princeton University Press).

23. Robert Dallek (1983), *The American Style of Foreign Policy* (New York: Alfred A. Knopf).

24. For example, Kenneth Waltz (1979), *Theory of International Relations*; Robert Keohane (1984), *After Hegemony.*

25. Jack Snyder (1991), *Myths of Empire*; Charles Kupchan (1994), *The Vulnerability of Empire*; Richard Rosecrance and Arthur Stein (1993), *The Domestic Bases of Grand Strategy* (Ithaca, NY: Cornell University Press).

26. Richard Ned Lebow (1981), *Between Peace and War* (Baltimore: Johns Hopkins University Press)

4 | Teaching About the Third World with Cases

Jeanne A. K. Hey

Teachers of international relations and foreign policy meet special challenges when addressing the Third World in their courses.[1] The case method is effective in meeting many of these challenges. Most students have no firsthand experience with the Third World, so their understanding of its regions is not only limited but often characterized by stereotypical images and overgeneralizations. Similarly, given that much of the scholarship in social science is a product of the United States and Europe, the Third World has often been overlooked in our major theoretical conversations, perhaps especially in international relations. In this chapter I detail the way in which case teaching addresses two key problems—the academic problem and the humanizing problem—in the teaching of international relations and foreign policy in North America.

The academic problem refers to the poverty of understanding by many North American students about the Third World's history, politics, social structures, and modern-day realities. Also included here is a theoretical and conceptual weakness characterizing much of international relations education. That is, many models and explanatory theories exclude Third World experience, and students are often not asked to apply theories to the Third World. The humanizing problem refers to students' difficulty in perceiving, and therefore treating, Third World peoples as real and fully human.

In this chapter I discuss these two problems, recommending a specific case for each problem and discussing ways of teaching the case that will alleviate the problem. A section on the pitfalls of case teaching about the Third World also includes suggestions for how these pitfalls can be avoided.

The Academic Problem

The academic problem encompasses those concrete aspects of international relations and foreign policy that educators demand their students know and understand. Although no one suggests that these fields are simply about "the facts," few will dispute that a grasp of factual material is crucial to a critical understanding of the political world. Sadly but not unexpectedly, many North American students lack concrete information about Third World countries, especially their international behavior. I perform an exercise in my classes that illustrates this point. During pre-case discussions, I ask students about their impressions of Third World states and leaders in foreign policy. Almost without exception, these images include "dictatorships," "few foreign policy skills," "all-powerful leaders," and "puppets of the USA." Note that these perceptions contradict each other. Students believe that Third World despots can do whatever they choose in foreign policy, regardless of domestic or international popular opinion. At the same time, they believe that Third World foreign policy makers are severely restricted, implementing essentially what their respective regional hegemons dictate. Students' images of foreign policy making in the Third World are simplistic and reflect little appreciation for the domestic and international political realities that Third World foreign policy makers face or for their skill in the policy arena.

These impressions change after the students have engaged in case discussions about concrete events in Third World politics and foreign policy. Armed with knowledge and awareness about real leaders managing real problems at the domestic, regional, and global levels, students begin to see the process with greater complexity. The simple experience with real-life examples that cases provide goes a long way in breaking down misperceptions developed through ignorance about and distance from Third World realities. Post-case discussions about Third World impressions reveal a much richer understanding of the regions as well as a new reluctance to see the Third World as a monolithic entity whose leaders all behave in the same manner.

An equally important component of the academic problem is the fact that political science's theoretical and conceptual models are often developed with little regard to the Third World. In international relations we often lament that most of the theoretical work in our field is designed for and applied to First World countries. Although many scholars have argued for greater theoretical attention to the Third World, research in this area remains limited and undervalued. Cases provide teachers with a unique way to circumvent this problem in the current literature. After introducing theoretical paradigms, students can examine their applicability and propriety for the Third World through cases. Even if a particular theory has not been written with the Third World in mind, an appropriate case sets the stage for an engaging student discussion about the strengths and weaknesses of that theory as applied to a specific example of Third World international politics or foreign policy. Thus, even though students restricted to the published literature often find an absence of theoretical analysis of the Third World, cases fill this gap by providing students with an empirical referent from the Third World.

Example Case: "Operation Blazing Trails"

I am the author of a case that is effective in meeting the challenges of the "academic problem" in both international relations and foreign policy classrooms.[2] "Ecuador Confronts U.S. Military Intervention: Operation Blazing Trails" recounts Ecuador's 1985 decision to bring in a host of U.S. Army reserve troops to construct a road in the country's eastern provinces as well as the government's management of the political crisis that the U.S. military's arrival induced. Part A, the bulk of the case, presents readers with the factual material needed to understand the Ecuadorian president's decision to invite U.S. troops and the political backlash occasioned by that decision. Part A ends by asking students to predict what action President León Febres Cordero will take in the face of congressional and judicial action against his decision to permit the U.S. troops in Ecuador. Part B recounts the outcome of the case, in this instance President Febres Cordero's decision. The narrative includes details about the president himself, his advisers, the Congress, interest groups, public opinion, and components of Ecuadoran history crucial to this case. This level of detail, although not overwhelming to students, immediately undermines any notion of Ecuador as a monolithic policymaking body that acts in accordance with the demands either of some all-powerful leader or of the United States. Reading and discussing the case require students to accept and analyze the complexity that characterizes policy-making in Ecuador as well as in any other country.

The "Operation Blazing Trails" case directly addresses the two aspects of the academic problem. First, the case presents factual information about Ecuador—its historical, political, and economic situation and its relationship to the United States—that most students would otherwise never learn. The case also details the country's political structure, debt, and trading profiles and geography. Furthermore, the case aids teachers in addressing the theoretical component of the academic problem. The case is designed in part to encourage students to examine the case from a levels-of-analysis approach. It reveals that the state, bureaucratic, individual, and system levels of analysis all play a potential part in explaining Ecuador's foreign policy behavior. In predicting what action President Febres Cordero will take, students tap into a series of theories about the foreign policy behavior of Third World countries. In case discussion, the teacher and students make explicit these theories and levels of analyses as well as the behavioral expectations associated with each. The case provides the empirical material with which to evaluate and compare these theories.

This case lends itself to a standard case discussion format that consists of three stages. First, students read the case and answer a set of study questions before coming to class. In the second stage, the teacher poses discussion questions aimed at fostering an analytical discussion. Third, a debriefing session concretizes the lessons learned in the discussion.

Study questions for this case include the following: (1) What motivates Febres Cordero's critics in this case? (2) Are Ecuadorians' fear of U.S. imperialism well founded? (3) What do you think Febres Cordero will decide about Operation Blazing Trails? Is this the choice you would recommend? (4) Which level of analysis (individual, bureaucratic, state, or system) best accounts for Ecuador's foreign policy behavior in this case? Answering these questions requires students to both read the case carefully and think about it before case discussion. I collect their answers at the beginning of class and immediately distribute each student's answers to another student. I then give students five minutes to read and write comments on a peer's answers. These two exercises, answering study questions and reflecting on another's answers, contribute to the richness of the ensuing case discussion. The process demands that students analyze the issues for themselves and consider others' points of view. It is by no means necessary that the teacher repeat all the study questions during discussion. Indeed, study questions often work best as launch-pads to related and deeper issues. Students do the preliminary work before reaching class and can engage in the more intricate matters in case discussion.

I begin in-class time by asking students if they have factual questions about the case. I ask other students to answer any questions that emerge. I address those questions only if other students are unable to. This exercise allows students to clarify their understanding of any issues in the case, a particularly important procedure when beginning case discussions about the Third World. With little or no background knowledge about the issues at hand, students often feel overwhelmed and intimidated about the case material. Providing them with a chance to clear up any confusion eases students' anxiety and allows them to proceed with more confidence in the case discussion.

Discussion questions relate to both the empirical and the theoretical. Empirical questions include the following: (1) Why is there such resistance to the U.S. troops? (2) What issues divide the different political factions on the Operation Blazing Trails issue? (3) Is congress's opposition to the troops motivated by political, ideological, or other concerns? (4) What alternatives does President Febres Cordero have at the end of this case? These are but a few of the myriad empirical questions aimed at deepening students' understanding of the sensitive political situation described in the case. The discussion frequently evolves into a rich exchange about U.S. imperialism in Latin America as well as about the politics of foreign policy in Ecuador and elsewhere.

Theoretical questions such as the following are posed both during the initial case discussion and in the debriefing after Part B is read. (1) Which level of analysis is best suited to explaining this case's outcome? (2) If Ecuador had had a president with different ideological leanings, would the case be explained by a different theory? (3) What evidence do you find of either the "all-powerful dictator" or the "puppet of the United States"? To the extent possible, I allow the discussion to flow in the directions that the students will take it. If it veers substantially off course, I redirect the conversation to the analytical issues at hand. As often as not, the students engage in a conversation that I had not foreseen but that is analytically powerful and engaging.

I typically hold the debriefing session during the following class period. Time away from a discussion allows students to reflect on the case and change or deepen their views. For the "Operation Blazing Trails" case, debriefing questions include (1) What did you learn about Third World foreign policy? (2) In what way does this case represent Third World foreign policy and in what way is it unique? (3) What do you know/think/believe now that you did not before this discussion? (4) Which level of analysis best explains this case? (5) How well does traditional foreign policy theory account for Ecuador's behavior? The debriefing discussion generally begins slowly, as students work out the "lessons" of the case in their heads. It remains a critical part of case discussion, however, and students usually suggest "lessons" that I had not thought of myself. At the end of the entire process, then, students have received a large dose of Ecuadoran politics and U.S.-Ecuadorian relations as well as of foreign policy theory as applied to a Third World context. As such, this case is very useful in ameliorating both components of the "academic problem" described here.

The Humanizing Problem

The humanizing problem is more difficult to describe than the academic problem, though it is certainly no less real. Put simply, students often fail to demonstrate that they consider Third World people to be as real or as human as themselves. Instead, students feel that Third World people, when compared with themselves and their peers, are less important, more expendable, and less worthy of concern. Indeed, there is a sense in my North American classrooms that Third World people are somehow suited to the kind of hardship that most students in these classrooms would find intolerable for a single day, much less a lifetime. For example, when I speak about poverty in the Third World, some students say, "Well, they're used to it." When I speak about war in Rwanda, some respond, "They're uncivilized. They've been fighting for centuries." Such statements are not only untrue but represent a mind-set that sees African people as less human. Perhaps the most illustrative example of the humanizing problem is that students easily sit through a lecture about hundreds of thousands of Ethiopians dying from starvation or the same number of Rwandan Tutsis killed during the genocide. These lectures rarely produce more than a few questions or other indicators of special interest. But as soon as I show a video documentary that produces photos of people or recounts individual stories of suffering and horror, more students are incensed, upset, and keenly interested. This reaction tells me that it is relatively simple for students to remain remote from Third World experiences, as long as they have no connection with individual Third World people.

This attitude is understandable. The Third World is remote, both geographically and in experience. This distance combines with a superiority complex nourished in most North Americans and enhanced by a media industry that heavily favors North American and Western European topics. Yet although comprehensible, the dehumanization of Third World people is a crucial factor undermining students' ability and willingness to study the Third World. The key to treating the Third World as equal, both in academic discussions and in human interaction, is to see Third World people as as human and deserving of attention as we.

Perspective taking is perhaps the single most useful device to advance the humanizing task. When a student enters the experience and mind-set of another, he or she is able to empathize in a way that detached observation does not encourage. Cases that lend themselves to role-play exercises are especially effective in encouraging students to assume a Third World person's perspective.

Example Case: "Brazilian Foreign Debt"

"From Miracle to Crisis: Brazilian Foreign Debt and the Limits of Obligations" is a case that allows students to assume the roles of Third World peoples and to imagine the impact a country's debt crisis can have on individual lives.[3] Interestingly, the case does not focus on any poor Brazilians or even spend much time on the common person's plight. Instead, it details the Brazilian government's different approaches to managing its burgeoning debt. The case provides ample information on the perspectives of different members of the Brazilian government, international creditor banks, and U.S. wheat farmers (who risk losing exports to Brazil). The case nonetheless allows one to discern debt's effects on middle-class and poor Brazilians.

I assign roles to some six or seven students before class begins. The case certainly allows for more or fewer roles to be played. These roles include some real people found in the case: the Brazilian president and finance minister, a member of the International Monetary Fund or World Bank, an executive from Chase Manhattan, and a U.S.

wheat farmer. But I also add the roles of Brazilian peasants, factory workers, and middle-class citizens. I even give them names, such as Fernando Da Costa or Luisa Braganca, and refer to those names during case discussion. The discussion then evolves as a debate as to which path Brazil should take in managing its debt crisis. Each actor defends the policy that meets his/her own financial interests. The discussion is without fail lively and intense. The case arms students with the factual information required for the policy discussion, and the role-play exercise demands that they see the issue from a perspective other than their own.

Quite often, those who played the roles of regular Brazilians are the most affected. Students frequently remark that the role-play exercises are among the most enduring and profound experiences in the course. Even if only for one hour, students experience the frustration of a marginalized person whose life is profoundly affected by decisions made by those in power. It is important not to exaggerate here. There is only so much a role-play exercise can achieve. Students rarely have more than one class period in which to play the role, and they do so in the comfort of their classroom and university. They certainly never truly achieve the full experience of a Third World person. They do, however, come closer to it than through objective analysis. Role-playing remains a very useful tool to create the perspective taking that is so necessary to the humanization task.

There are a number of ways to extend the role-playing, making it a lasting experience for the students. Assigning the roles ahead of time is a good idea, because students spend time preparing the role. Doing so lengthens the time they spend in the role as well as the amount of thought devoted to it. Debriefing the role-playing in a written essay, or class discussion, also deepens and lengthens the experience. Similarly, an instructor can choose a series of cases that lend themselves to role-playing and have students play the same role (a Third World person) throughout the semester. That said, there is sometimes value in students' assuming different roles within the same case discussion. This change allows students to experience the conflict among multiple perspectives.

In effect, cases are discussed in character. Imagine the discussion of a case on the Gulf War by a group of North American students. Now imagine that same discussion but with all the students playing the role of Iraqi, Kuwaiti, or Jordanian people. The result is profoundly different and instructive because one's feelings about the issue are at least in part determined by one's position within the conflict. Those feelings often determine one's policy position as well.

The role-play exercise therefore helps students not only to realize the perspective of other actors but also to question the motivation behind and validity of their own opinions and policy prescriptions.

The Pitfalls of Teaching the Third World with Cases

Case teaching's drawbacks are in many instances the negative side of its benefits. In other words, the pitfalls and advantages derive from the same sources. For instance, the lack of research in Third World studies, which makes cases an attractive supplement to currently available texts and other materials, is also a drawback. Relatively few cases have been published on the Third World, especially in the area of foreign policy. There are abundant cases about U.S. foreign policy toward the Third World but few about foreign policy processes in Third World regions themselves. Similarly, in the broader field of international relations, Third World case material is sparse.

A second pitfall is that First World authors write the majority of available cases that treat the Third World. Political science and international relations are disciplines dominated by North Americans and Europeans. The same is true of the institutions that publish cases, such as the Institute for the Study of Diplomacy and Harvard's Kennedy School of Government. This means that most cases are written, at least to some degree, from a First World perspective (as is this chapter). Many cases contain some of the same problems already attributed to students with little exposure to the Third World. The cases employ stereotypes and simplistic assumptions about political behavior in the Third World and provide too little information about the policy process. This approach stems from the fact that most case writers rely on First World sources. Few authors conduct the in-depth fieldwork that would give their cases authenticity and local perspectives. This is not to say that case writers are not careful in their analysis and fact reporting or that case publishers do not scrutinize case material. It only suggests that distance, both geographical and cultural, makes distortions in reporting about Third World political events more likely than in reporting First World issues.

This problem interfaces with the reality that few students are knowledgeable beforehand about the cases. This means that both teacher and student are more limited to the author's interpretation than they are with cases on U.S. foreign policy, European politics, or other well-known topics. For instance, imagine a case about the 1989

U.S. intervention in Panama. It is likely that students and teacher will be somewhat familiar with this historical event. They can draw on their memories, readings, and discussions from other classes and conversations with family and friends about the case. Although their information will be heavily biased by the North American perspective on the invasion, at least the participants will have some outside information about the case. Such familiarity is unlikely in a discussion of Jordanian foreign policy toward Iran. This simply means that case discussions about Third World events are very reliant on the interpretation of the author, which is a problem, but certainly not an insurmountable one.

A final disadvantage of the case method when teaching about the Third World concerns the method itself: it is by definition a student-centered activity. When the instructor puts learning in the hands of the students, the group is to a certain extent prisoner to its members' peculiar views and understanding. Hence, the stereotypes and misconceptions discussed above often enter the discussion in a way the instructor wishes to avoid. If these misconceptions go unchecked, students run the risk of leaving the case discussion with their stereotypes fortified, rather than diluted, as these stereotypes will have gained voice and legitimacy during the case discussion. Such a result is true of any case discussion, but its likelihood increases when discussing a Third World topic about which students are little educated. It is compounded, of course, if the case itself fails to give enough or appropriate information on the Third World perspective.

Suggestions for Managing Problems

The pitfalls outlined in the previous section are real but manageable. They certainly do not overwhelm the benefits of case teaching about the Third World. The key to alleviating these problems is to encourage critical thinking during case reading and especially during case discussion. The instructor should cultivate an environment in which students know, expect, and feel safe about the fact that their views and assertions will be challenged and reworked through the discussion. Once critical challenges become second nature to the participants, students feel less threatened by requests to consider the veracity and implications of their statements. Indeed, the students themselves should urge each other to engage in critical thinking, by questioning and disagreeing with assertions aired during class discussion. It is my experience that when a student makes a claim based on a stereotype or misconception, another student in the class will challenge it. If I keep my mouth shut, one or more students will address my concerns.

The teacher creates such an environment by making clear at the beginning of the class that he/she will challenge students in a respectful manner and then doing so. It is important, of course, to treat students fairly and equally so that no one feels singled out. Simply telling students that they should expect challenging interactions with the instructor and other students goes a long way toward creating the atmosphere in which this occurs. During case discussions, teachers should provide affirming comments as frequently as critical or challenging ones. Written evaluations of students' in-class performance can also commend students for their participation.

As stated above, role-play exercises are an excellent means to address students' difficulties in taking a Third World perspective. Student' critical thinking reinforces and enhances role-playing. Students do not merely play a role as they see fit but instead are assigned the task of investigating their characters' history, perspective, and other features pertinent to understanding their position. Students should prepare their roles in advance and research them in sources other than the case. These demands broaden students' understanding of the people they play and minimize the chance that they will represent them as unidimensional or stereotypical characters. The process further brings more material, facts, and perspective to the case discussion than would exist if role-players relied solely on the case itself.

Noncase cases help to alleviate the problems associated with a lack of Third World cases. Historical narratives, eye-witness accounts, autobiographies, newspaper clippings, Third World films, and a whole host of other sources can be treated as cases. Third World sources supplement much of the case material written by First Worlders. For example, chapters from *I, Rigoberta Menchú: An Indian Woman in Guatemala* written by the 1992 Nobel Peace Prize winner, are gripping accounts of political events in Guatemala written not only from a Third World perspective but from an indigenous one as well.[4] Readers of Rigoberta Menchú's story will find it difficult to stay detached from her experience or to maintain stereotypes of Guatemalan indigenous peoples as ignorant.

Teachers can use such noncase cases as the sole item of discussion or as a point of comparison for other accounts of the experience or event under study. A case discussion might, for example, compare

I, Rigoberta Menchú with *The CIA in Guatemala* by Richard Immerman.[5] The discussion could begin by outlining the goals of the Central Intelligence Agency (CIA) intervention in Guatemala in 1954. What U.S. national interests were at stake, and how were they protected? Detailing the effects of the intervention and its aftermath on Rigoberta Menchú's community could follow this. Comparison of the two lists would reveal a striking disconnect between what the CIA had presumably hoped for Guatemala and what the Guatemalan *campesinos* experienced. A second suggestion would be to create a role-play exercise in which students playing Rigoberta Menchú and her family debated the effects of U.S. military assistance to Guatemala with those playing CIA representatives. A third discussion might ask students to contrast the perspective, information, facts, and knowledge gained from the firsthand account in *I, Rigoberta Menchú* with Immerman's academic chronicle. Such a case discussion would not only be informed by a Third World perspective but would also allow an examination of how First World authorship influences students' understanding of the Third World.

It is important to remember that students often feel uncomfortable when approaching case discussions about the Third World. Both place-names and people's names may be unfamiliar and difficult to pronounce. Students are usually unfamiliar with even the most basic elements of Third World states' political systems, constitutional norms, and colonial histories. This lack of knowledge often makes students at first hesitant to discuss the case, fearing they may embarrass themselves with gross errors in fact or pronunciation. Teachers should proceed with care and encouragement and acknowledge up front that these issues are new and perhaps difficult for students. For example, when I teach the case on Ecuadoran foreign policy, I write on the board the name of the president under study, León Febres Cordero. I pronounce his name carefully and explain that he has two last names, Febres and Cordero, and that students must say both of them when referring to him. This brief exercise releases some of the anxiety for students who simply did not understand which of the man's three names should be used to refer to the Ecuadoran president. As is mentioned above, it is also useful to ask students at the beginning of the case discussion if they have any factual questions about the case. Answering such questions not only makes students clearer in their understanding of the case but improves the quality of the discussion that ensues. These initial exercises put students at ease and inform them that they are not alone in their ignorance of the topic at hand.

Conclusion

Case teaching is based on the idea that learning is enhanced in an environment in which students experience the intrigue, complexity, and difficulties of international affairs as opposed to being lectured about them from a teacher. Heretofore, discussions of the benefits of case teaching in international relations and foreign policy have centered on putting students in the shoes of decisionmakers, usually in powerful countries. This chapter broadens that view and emphasizes the utility of cases in helping students appreciate the situation of people in the Third World, be they foreign policy decisionmakers or ordinary citizens.

Third World studies have been growing since the fall of the Soviet Union and the end of the Cold War. The relaxation of East-West tensions permits us to give the Third World the scholarly attention it is due. At the same time that social scientists focus renewed research efforts on Africa, Asia, Latin America, and the Middle East, the pedagogical value of case teaching is spreading across universities in North America and beyond. The confluence of these events creates an exciting moment for those of us who teach about the Third World. Cases provide us both new material and a new method to convey information and perspectives about the Third World.

It is crucial to address both the academic (information) problem and the humanizing (perspective) problem related to teaching about the Third World in North American classrooms. Giving students all the data available about a Third World region or country will not alone open their eyes to the humanity of Third World people. Similarly, the ability to assume a Third World perspective is next to impossible if students are not armed with factual information about the regions that they purport to understand. Case studies, combined with case discussions, address both of these problems in a very effective way. The case method gives reason for optimism that our teaching about the Third World in North America will improve.

Notes

1. The term *Third World* is here used to refer to most countries in Latin America, the Caribbean, Asia, Africa, the Middle East, and Pacific islands. I understand that the term is laden with problems, not the least among them that it suggests a normative hierarchy of countries and peoples that I firmly

reject. Nonetheless, the term remains useful simply because readers understand the regions to which it refers. Alternative phrases (e.g., "the South," "developing world," "less developed countries") carry their own semantic baggage and conceptual inaccuracies. I therefore employ the term *Third World* in this chapter, recognizing its deficiencies and hoping that case teaching about these regions will help to develop improved terminology.

2. Jeanne A. K. Hey (1995), "Ecuador Confronts U.S. Military Intervention: Operation Blazing Trails," Pew Case Studies in International Affairs, no. 362, Institute for the Study of Diplomacy.

3. Thomas Landy (1990), "From Miracle to Crisis: Brazilian Foreign Debt and the Limits of Obligations," Pew Case Studies in International Affairs, no. 509. Institute for the Study of Diplomacy.

4. Rigoberta Menchú (1984), *I, Rigoberta Menchú: An Indian Woman in Guatemala* (London: Verso).

5. Richard Immerman (1982), *The CIA in Guatemala* (Austin: University of Texas Press).

5 | Using Cases to Teach Analytical Skills

David Schodt

Students taking courses in international development not only face the normal academic challenge of learning new methods of analysis; they must also learn to apply these methods to situations that are truly foreign to their experiences. Few of my students bring any knowledge of theories of international development to the classroom, and even fewer bring the concrete knowledge of Brazil or Zambia that would provide a context for their learning. Furthermore, in the courses that I teach, an important objective is that the student's application of theory to practice involve the use of quantitative data.

I have found that teaching cases are powerful vehicles for helping students to meet these challenges. As Lee Shulman has written, "what is so alluring about a case is that it resides in that never-never land between theory and practice, between ideas and experience, between the normative ideal and the achievable real."[1] Cases bring reality to the classroom, providing context for theory. For courses in international development, cases allow students who have little experience with other countries to work with information that, although complex, is contained by the boundaries of the narratives. At the same time, students with experience in other countries, whose "expert" comments might otherwise stifle participation by less knowledgeable students, are restrained by the use of a common text. Cases also allow students to work with data: to make judgments about which data to use, to undertake calculations in a messy but real context, and to present their results in tables or charts.

Teaching with cases in the classroom involves three elements:

the written case, the discussion of the case in class, and student preparation of the case prior to its discussion. Cases are narratives that provide information and, frequently, pose problems to be solved. They do not supply analysis or answers. For example, an interesting case on land reform in a country just after a successful revolution puts students in the role of a foreign consultant who has been asked to contribute to designing a land reform program. The case contains substantial detail about the country's economy and its political system. The class discussion engages the students in drawing on their knowledge of theories of revolution and land reform to analyze the case and provide a solution—in this instance a feasible plan for land reform. There is, of course, more than one solution, and part of the power of using cases for learning derives from the students' ownership of their solution. Students prepare for class discussion by reading the case carefully and, frequently, discussing it in small groups. Some instructors may choose to provide students with discussion questions to which they can be asked to provide written responses. Others may ask their students to submit a written analysis following the class discussion of the case.

Teaching analytical, or technical, skills in a case discussion class poses particular challenges that have their origins both in the nature of the material and in students' attitudes toward learning this material. "Technical" courses do tend to contain a larger proportion of questions to which there are "right" or "wrong" answers. In analyzing capital flows to less developed countries, students need to learn that a positive inflow of capital must be accompanied by an outflow on the current account. Although important, this relationship does not generally lend itself to productive and engaged discussion. Other questions about capital flows do provide material for excellent discussion. To what extent should countries rely on external capital to finance development? What kinds of capital are most conducive to sustainable development?

Students are likely to have difficulty distinguishing between these two kinds of questions. Their prior experiences in learning technical material are likely to have taught them that most questions have one answer. Furthermore, many students believe, with some reason, that if there is a single "right" answer, the instructor must know it, and that, if their response to any question is a sufficiently long period of silence, the instructor will inevitably tell them that answer. The net effect on class discussion can be quite chilling.

Students come to technical material convinced "that there is a logical progression to the subject matter, and that technical content comes in neat, complete packages."[2] Nor are they necessarily wrong in this assumption. Even simple models of something like exchange rate determination are constructed through a series of logical steps. Case discussion, however, is not a linear process. Learning with a series of cases is much more spiral in nature. What cases offer for learning technical, or analytical, material is a context for the theory and a problem to which the theory can be applied. Models of exchange rate determination cease to be abstract constructions and become the tools for understanding economic crises in Mexico. In addition, the data supplied in cases are never as neatly packaged as that which students have encountered in traditional problem sets. In a manner that mirrors the reality facing decisionmakers, the data are typically not easily accessible, and often incomplete. Students need to wrestle with using a neat, theoretical package to make sense out of a messy world. This is an important skill, but it is not necessarily consistent with the ways our students expect to learn technical material.

Students' anxieties about learning technical material, their belief that all questions in a course they perceive as technical have "right" answers, and their understanding that knowledge is acquired only through a series of logical, linear steps must be recognized and addressed if discussion-based learning in technical courses is to be successful.[3] The instructor needs to be clear with students about when there are "right" answers but equally clear about when there are not. Similarly, material that is logically constructed, such as economic models, is probably best presented to students in that manner. The problem, of course, is that neither of these activities necessarily generates the kind of animated discussion normally associated with case teaching, where the class engages in lively debate and takes ownership of the solution to a problem.

My experience teaching case-based courses in international development has convinced me that student learning of technical, or analytical, material is enhanced by mixing lectures and case discussion, sequencing cases, structuring case discussion, and using written case preparation exercises. Courses need not be thought of as either discussion or lecture. The lecture may be the most effective way of communicating to students the logical structure of a model or theory, and its use toward this end may help alleviate student anxieties about learning this material. To be sure, students may not really learn the theory without having a meaningful context and opportunities to practice its application. But the cases provide those things. I recall my dismay, after I had begun to use case discussion and was congratulating myself on not lecturing, when some of my students comment-ed to me how much they appreciated my lectures. It took a while before I understood that what they were telling me was that I was now lecturing only when it was most useful to them.

The richness and complexity of cases allow them to be used as more than just examples to illustrate theory. As Velenchik has noted, most undergraduate courses in economics teach theory first and then present examples of the application of the theory.[4] This is counter to what most learning theories tell us about the contextual nature of knowledge acquisition. Cases allow this sequence to be reversed, by presenting the application first as the reason for learning the theory. Properly chosen cases that are sequenced effectively can provide illustrations of theory that has been introduced earlier as well as gen-erate questions to motivate theory that will be presented later.

Case discussions with technical material may require more forceful direction from the instructor. The role of the instructor in case discussions is often likened to that of a referee. The instructor starts the conversation with a set of carefully chosen questions, man-ages participation so as to involve as many students as possible and to draw on a broad range of opinions, and steers the class back when it wanders outside the boundaries established by the case. In general, however, the instructor seeks to stay out of the way of the students. Although this analogy is a useful one, instructors leading case dis-cussions involving technical material may find the analogy of traffic cop even more appropriate. Students often need to be directed to considering relevant theories or to important data. They may need to be shown through the instructor's questions that a particular avenue of inquiry is a dead end before they spend most of the period driving down that road. Since most cases used in courses in international development involve policy questions, students can be directed toward theory and data while they still retain responsibility for, and ownership of, the solution. Although imposing this structure may run the risk of a less animated discussion, I find that it works well with complex and data-rich cases where students need more guidance.

Although successful case discussions always depend on serious preparation by students, this is particularly true for those that will involve technical material. Students need to read the case carefully. Asking students to write case briefs prior to the class discussion is a valuable way to ensure a thorough reading. I have found that a writ-ten case brief also provides an excellent opportunity for me to ask students to apply theory and to work with data. It is rarely useful to ask students to undertake calculations in the midst of a case discussion, but the results of these calculations may be essential to that discussion. For example, a case that asks students to consider macroeconomic policy in Indonesia may require that they determine whether the exchange rate was overvalued. If the data in the case allow the calculation of real exchange rates, student can be asked to do this as part of their case brief assignment. In this way, students gain experience working with data, they draw on theory, and they do so in a context that helps them learn both skills.

Example

One of the courses that I teach with cases is an undergraduate course in economic development. Students who take this course are expected to have completed a course in principles of economics, but otherwise their backgrounds vary widely. Some are economics majors with substantial work in the discipline, whereas others are typically political science, Asian studies, or Latin American studies majors with only the prerequisite course in economics. My goal for the course is to have students learn relevant economic models and concepts and learn to apply these models to analyze policies and performance in the developing countries, using both qualitative and quantitative data. To this end, I have structured the course around a sequence of six cases, each of which describes the political economy of a different country.[5] I selected each case to allow me to teach one or two theoretical issues and to allow students the opportunity to work with economic data.

I will illustrate my use of cases by focusing on the sequence of the first three cases students discuss in this course. My objectives for the first part of the course are to work with the concepts of economic growth and economic development. The first case, one on poverty in Panama, allows students to become familiar with case discussion.[6] In addition, the focus on poverty in this case highlights for students the importance of economic growth for reducing poverty. There is little empirical data in this case, and it can be discussed without knowledge of economic development. It signals to the economics majors that the course is not just about technical economic models, and it reassures the noneconomics majors that the course is not just about those models. Discussion of this case also demonstrates to students the importance of careful preparation. When I survey students about what they have learned from this first exercise, they consistently mention the importance of reading the case thoroughly.

After we have spent some time learning about simple growth models and discussing early models of development that stressed reliance on foreign capital, state direction of the economy, and industry as the leading sector of the economy, I introduce a second case—this one on Brazil.[7] This case, which describes the Brazilian "economic miracle" during the period 1960–1973, is complex and introduces students to a substantial amount of economic data. I ask students to prepare for our case discussion by responding to the set of questions shown below. The first of these questions asks students to use data as a way to understand the economic policies that were being followed in Brazil. The second question has students combine the Harrod-Domar growth model with data from the case to make predictions about economic growth in Brazil. They need to make decisions about what data to use. Should they use figures for savings rates or investment rates? Should they use figures reported in nominal values, or are inflation adjusted (real) figures better? Explaining why their predictions are, or are not, consistent with actual growth rates encourages them to think about how well the theoretical model describes growth. The last question invites students to think about the nature of economic growth in Brazil. Most stay close to fairly technical questions about the sustainability of growth, but others begin to raise questions about Brazil's increasing reliance on foreign debt during these years and to address the growing inequalities in the country.

Brazil: Financing the Miracle

Please answer the following questions in approximately three pages. The assignment is due in class on the date scheduled for discussion of this case. Your task is to analyze what happened, and to assess whether the policies that were followed were appropriate for the circumstances. We will do this in class, but I would like you to prepare for our discussion by considering these criteria.

1. The traditional model of economic development stresses the key roles played by foreign capital, state direction of the economy, and industrialization. Making explicit reference to the quantitative data supplied in the case, indicate how well Brazilian economic strategy from 1968 to 1972 fits this model.
2. Find the incremental capital-output ratio reported in Gillis et al. (Table 3-4, p. 45) for Brazil for the period 1970–81.[8] Use this figure and the Harrod-Domar relationship to predict the growth rate

that would be expected in Brazil in 1970 and 1971. Compare your predictions with the actual rates of growth of GDP and interpret your findings.

3. The Gillis text indicates that ICOR in Table 3-4 was calculated by dividing the average share of gross domestic investment by the rate of growth of GDP. Why does this give you an estimate for ICOR? Based on the data in the case, use this method to calculate an ICOR for Brazil for 1970.

4. As shown in Table 3-4, the ICOR for Brazil increases from 1970–1981 to 1978–1987. Use the information in the case to explain why you think this may have occurred.

5. During the period 1968–1972, the Brazilian economy experienced a remarkably rapid rate of growth. How was this growth financed? Are there any clear trends in the method of financing growth over the period? Be sure to use the data supplied in the case to answer this question.

6. Suppose that you were hired in 1973 by the World Bank as an economic consultant to conduct an analysis of the "Brazilian economic miracle." In brief, what are the major issues that you would want to address in your analysis?

I generally try to structure discussion of the Brazil case so that we spend most of our time in three areas. First, we begin by identifying those "facts" that are useful to understanding economic growth in this country. Although this runs the risk of turning into a fairly boring listing of information, I find the exercise helps students to sort important from less important information. Writing this information on the board also provides a visible record to which we can refer as the discussion moves on. In addition, students may raise questions about unfamiliar terms and concepts that are not essential to our use of the case but that are valuable to highlight because we will return to them in more detail later in the course. For example, the Brazil case discusses concepts such as "overvalued exchange rates" and "import substituting industrialization." When we return to these concepts, students have a context for what might otherwise appear to be abstract theories. At this point in the course, exchange rate models are important because they help answer questions about Brazil.

Second, we move to a discussion of those policies that appear to have been responsible for the "Brazilian economic miracle." After their readings and discussions of simple growth models, my students are generally quick to point to investment rates and the role of foreign capital. They have to be nudged to consider, for example, how Brazil's authoritarian politics also contributed to economic performance. This type of prompting clearly illustrates one of the advantages of using cases in a course with technical material. Students quickly gain an appreciation for the limitations of theory and for when other disciplinary perspectives may offer important insights. Where appropriate, this discussion can draw explicitly on the empirical work the students did to prepare for the case.

Third, I ask students to assess the Brazilian economic miracle. Most agree that performance has been very good as measured by growth in gross domestic product per capita, although some argue about the sustainability of the Brazilian model. However, with further discussion students begin to raise questions about increasing income inequality, poor agricultural performance, or growing regional disparities.

At this point, the class is ready to explore the differences between economic growth and economic development. Students begin to understand the importance of economic growth for reducing poverty but also realize that growth alone will not necessarily lead to economic development. We can then talk about the dual economy models that seek to describe the balance between agricultural and industrial sectors as an economy grows, and we can begin to identify the factors that are most conducive to growth with equity. Students can return to the income distribution data provided in the Brazil case to practice computing empirical measures of income distribution, such as the Lorenz curve and the Gini ratio.

Taiwan, 1961

For this briefing paper I would like you to explore some questions about economic growth in Taiwan. Please answer the following in approximately 3–4 pages. The assignment is due in class on the date scheduled for our discussion of this case.

1. Calculate the terms of trade between agriculture and industry for the years 1951 to 1961. Report your results numerically and graphically (plot terms of trade against years), and explain the significance of the series that you have calculated. Remember that what is important is not the absolute value of the terms of trade in any one year, but rather the trend in this index over time. Do the terms of trade increase or decrease, and what does this mean?

2. The Fei-Ranis dual economy model describes the relationship between the agricultural and industrial sectors during the process of economic growth. Briefly describe the key features of the model and its implications for development policy.

3. Does the Fei-Ranis model help us understand the process of economic growth (policies and outcomes) in Taiwan between 1952 and 1960? (Make explicit use of the data in the case for your answer.)

4. Use the date on income distribution that accompanies the Taiwan case to plot Lorenz curves for 1953, 1959, and 1965 (you can do

this easily on a spreadsheet). Based on your Lorenz curves, what happened to the distribution of income over this period?

5. Calculate GINI coefficients for 1953, 1959, and 1965. A formula for computing the GINI is given by:

$$G = 1 - \sum_{i=0}^{n-1} \frac{(F_{i+1} - F_i)}{100} \frac{(Y_{i+1} + Y_i)}{100}$$

F is the cumulative population share, Y is the cumulative income share, with $F_0 = Y_0 = 0$. The number of categories (quintiles or deciles) into which population and income are grouped is given by n.

6. What do you find to have been the most important factors contributing to the changes you observe in the distribution of income in Taiwan between 1954 and 1964? What seems to have happened in Taiwan that did not happen in Brazil?

The third case, which focuses on Taiwan in 1961, offers rich ground for students to explore the set of circumstances that led to that country's ability to achieve equitable growth.[9] The case as published, however, does not provide information on changes in the distribution of income. To remedy this, I added one table with data on the size distribution of income in 1953, 1959, and 1964. As the preparation questions illustrate, students can now be asked to explore the applicability of the dual economy model to Taiwan, to compute estimates for changes in the distribution of income that accompanied growth, and to examine policies that contributed to these outcomes. Class discussion of this case proceeds with the same structure used in the Brazil case. We can look back to that case to ask comparative questions, such as: "What accounts for the different outcomes in these two countries?" "How much of Taiwan's superior performance is explained by unique historical circumstances?" "How much is explained by policies pursued by the Taiwanese government?" In this case, the results of the empirical work done by students to prepare for the case are critical to our discussion. We can also use the considerable information in the Taiwan case about agricultural policies (such as land reform and price policies) to look forward to material we will spiral back through when we take up a case on Zambia.

Assessment

This model for teaching a discussion-based course in international development that involves some amount of technical material has worked well for me. My students seem to agree. For a number of years, I have surveyed them at the end of the course for their assessment of how well the course has worked for them. I have included here responses from a total of forty-five students from three different semesters during 1995 and 1996. As the data shown below indicate, students felt strongly that cases contributed to their learning in all of the areas indicated. Students felt that cases were most valuable for "learning how to use economics to solve real problems." This was the most visible use for cases in the course, and it is not surprising that students rated it highly. Their choice of F ("learning economic theory") and B ("learning how to use an economic argument") as the second and third most valuable contributions of cases is evidence of the value of this model of case-based teaching for motivating these objectives. Qualitative responses from students are consistent with these findings. A partial sample includes comments such as the following:

Student Summary of the Nature of Contributions of Cases to Learning

Question: Relative to readings and lectures, please assess the contribution of the use of cases in this course to the following: Use 1 for "more useful"; 2 for "equally useful"; and 3 for "not as useful." Indicate which two of these you feel to be the most important contributions of cases.

A. Learning how to use economics to solve real problems
B. Learning how to use an economic argument
C. Learning how to write research papers in economics
D. Learning about Third World countries
E. Learning how to organize an argument
F. Learning economic theory related to economic development

Student Assessment of the Nature of Contributions of Cases to Learning

Choice	Rating			Most Important
	1	2	3	
A	39	4	1	31
B	34	10	2	17
C	25	14	6	1
D	28	14	2	7
E	28	10	6	8
F	28	12	4	18

- I learned how to actually pull the information out and how to analyze. Much more effective than just taking notes.
- It promotes learning that shows how to use economic concepts to solve real-world problems.
- Instead of simply memorizing theories and never seeing what exactly happens in the world, using cases shows how the theories are applicable.
- I learned information about individual countries . . . details from the cases are things I can remember more than X and Y examples.
- The use of cases promotes analytical thinking, which is different.
- Cases provided options for all types of learning—we would read the case alone, work on the problems, discuss them in a group, write the answers, rediscuss in class, and so by the end of each case, we had conquered a lot of information.

Conclusion

Case teaching can be a powerful vehicle for promoting student learning in courses in international development. Although instructors who wish to teach analytical or technical material may initially approach class discussion, which forms the basis of case teaching, with some skepticism, it deserves reconsideration. By acknowledging student attitudes about learning technical material and by paying attention to structures that facilitate the integration of technical material with the use of cases, student learning can be deepened and enriched.

Notes

1. Lee Shulman (1997), "Professing the Liberal Arts," in *Education and Democracy: Re-imagining Liberal Learning in America,* ed. Robert Orrill (New York: College Entrance Examination Board), pp. 151–173.

2. Bruce Greenwald (1991), "Teaching Technical Material," in *Education for Judgement: The Artistry of Discussion Leadership*, ed. C. Roland Christensen, David A. Garvin, and Ann Sweet (Boston: Harvard Business School Press), p. 195.

3. See ibid. for interesting comment on these issues.

4. Anne Velenchik (1995), "The Case Method as a Strategy for Teaching Policy Analysis to Undergraduates," *Journal of Economic Literature* 26(1): 30.

5. Most of the cases I use in this course are from the Harvard Business School's case catalog at the Web site http://www.hbsp.harvard.edu. Cases suitable for a course in international development are found in the "Business and Government" section of that catalog. Other case sources are the Kennedy School of Government Case Program at http://www.ksg.harvard.edu/caseweb/ and the Pew Case Studies in International Affairs, Institute for the Study of Diplomacy, Georgetown University at http://sfswww.georgetown.edu/sfs/programs/isd/files/pub.htm#pew.

6. George C. Lodge, "Veraguas Section A: System of Poverty," Harvard Business School Case 9-797-005.

7. Helen Shapiro, "Brazil: Financing the Miracle," Harvard Business School Case 381-140.

8. Malcolm Gillis, Dwight H. Perkings, Michael Roemer, and Michael R. Snodgrass (1996), *Economics of Development,* 4th ed. (New York: Norton).

9. Marc Lindenberg and Noel Ramírez (1989), *Managing Adjustment in Developing Countries: Economic and Political Perspectives* (San Francisco: ICS Press), pp. 107–121.

6 | Case Teaching Without Cases

Maryann Cusimano

Case teaching is a marriage of a particular kind of text—a carefully crafted narrative—with a particular classroom approach, active questioning techniques that encourage students to inhabit the story. Case teachers have found these techniques to be so effective that they can use them with other materials that, on the surface, bear little resemblance to the brief, descriptive accounts in traditional cases. The assignments and procedures that case teachers apply to these materials mirror those they practice with traditional cases. As students and teachers gain proficiency with cases, this strengthens and makes easier the caselike use of other materials, and vice versa.

Case teachers have also found that students extrapolate their case learning experience to other texts, even if the teachers have not planned or encouraged this. This chapter, then, is offered as a guide both to the application of case teaching techniques to other kinds of material and to a process that will probably occur, whether or not you consciously will it, once you start teaching with cases.

What Are Noncase Cases?

Within case teaching circles, a variety of materials utilized as cases have come to be known as *noncase cases* or *nontraditional cases.* These terms, like the equally inelegant phrase *nongovernmental organization,* identify such materials in the negative, because the huge variety of forms they can take overwhelms any positive description of what they are.

Noncase cases include everything from newspaper and magazine articles to book chapters, films, and video clips. Such cases can tell a complete story, as a retrospective case does, or they can present a cliffhanger, that is, one similar to a decision-forcing case that does not reveal the ending, except, perhaps, in a sequel. As with traditional cases, teachers invite students to inhabit the story, through explicit role-playing, group exercises, or debate or through a line of questioning that asks the students to analyze and consider various options and to determine what they would do if they were the decisionmaker.

Noncase cases, however, include more than just the obvious substitutes. Some case teachers use historical or archival materials, other empirical data, or edited volumes to put students into the roles of actors in the story or of social scientists theorizing about the data. Thus, noncase cases can either tell a story directly or allow students to construct the narrative from primary materials.

Why Use Nontraditional Cases?

One of the problems with case teaching is that the demand for cases on various topics outstrips the supply. At some point, as you design your course syllabi to include cases, you will muse, "I wish there were a case on topic X." Applying case teaching techniques to other materials can allow you to fill in the holes among available cases and fit your case exercises to your syllabus. This gap is the primary reason most faculty use noncase cases. Many, for example, use noncase materials to expand the range of cases written from a non-U.S. perspective. But there are other reasons to teach with nontraditional case materials: to keep pace with fast-breaking current events, to teach theory, to increase student skill and experience in analyzing primary data, to deal with specific classroom teaching challenges, or to vary students' learning options. Examples of teaching with noncase cases for all these reasons are given in the next section.

Two further, more general reasons to employ noncase materials as cases are to leverage what we know about how people learn and to capitalize on the extent to which students tend to respond to traditional cases.

Teaching even abstract materials as cases works better than

teaching these same materials via lecture, for the reasons Steven Lamy elaborates in Chapter 2. Learning based on discovery, inquiry, and participation is preferable to passive, lecture-based learning. My students also report that, although they prefer an interactive exercise to a lecture on democratic peace theory, for example, these exercises are not as satisfying as "real" case discussions. This should not be surprising, given what we know about how people process information and learn.

Cognitive psychology suggests that all information is not created equal: people tend to acquire concrete, vivid, specific, image-inclusive, personal and/or emotionally stimulating information more easily than what is more abstract. Information encoded on several sensory dimensions is more accessible than information presented on fewer. Good case, and some noncase, materials often display all of these features. Like analogies and metaphors, these more concrete and accessible materials enable students to connect new information and ideas with those they already know and understand, in ways that make the unfamiliar engaging and comprehensible.

If for no other reason, faculty who teach with cases are well advised to treat noncase materials similarly, because students begin to do this on their own, whether or not faculty invite them to. The active learning process is powerful and contagious, and once you unleash it, it is likely that your students will turn the same critical eye to all the materials you use in your classroom, so you may as well prepare yourself and take advantage of such an approach.

Nontraditional Cases in Use

Nontraditional case materials, like formal cases, can work at any point in the course. For interactive exercises to be effective, however, they should come early and often, to establish and maintain a classroom norm of participation. Students need to get comfortable with active learning, to be socialized in what to expect for the coming semester, and to engage in regular participation to increase their confidence and skill. I try to teach a case, traditional or not, each week of the semester, since it is only through practice that students can improve their analytic and communication skills. Other teachers report that they select about five main themes from the course and use an interactive exercise to emphasize each. Teaching noncase

materials as cases makes either strategy far more feasible than relying solely on traditional cases, and doing so enables you to fulfill the
variety of purposes they can serve.

Supplementing existing cases is, again, the most prominent of
these purposes. As an example, I use John K. Cooley's chapter "The
War over Water" in Richard Betts's edited volume *Conflict After the
Cold War: Arguments on the Causes of War and Peace* in my
Security After the Cold War course.[1] I teach this noncase case to
explore the resource roots of conflict and how resource scarcity and
mismanagement can be considered security problems. It works very
well, because most U.S. students have a predisposition to think of
conflict in the Middle East as stemming from intractable religious
differences and historic disputes over borders. Most are unaware of
the resource and environmental roots of Middle East conflict.

The students role-play the different countries in the region,
describing how the problem looks from their national perspectives,
in a manner that mirrors Lamy's *DEPPP*: after *describing* and
explaining the problem, the history, the interests, and concerns from
their actors' perspectives, students *predict* and *prescribe* by propos-
ing potential policy options. They *participate* directly in the issue by
preparing questions and challenges for the other actors. This ensures
that the exercise will be interactive, rather than just a series of mono-
logues in which students would each present a policy briefing from
their state's perspective without engaging with and reacting to the
other participants' perspectives and proposals. As case facilitator, I
also ensure interaction by asking bridging and follow-up questions,
such as "Lebanon, do you agree with Israel's representation of the
problem?" As a noncase case, "The War over Water" enables me to
run an interactive exercise engaging several non-U.S. perspectives
on a topic that is not covered by current Pew or Kennedy School case
offerings.[2]

Similarly, I and many other faculty use Barbara Tuchman's *The
Guns of August* as a noncase case in our undergraduate Introduction
to International Relations courses.[3] These courses include such major
themes as the balance of power, arms races, and the security dilemma
as well as a recap of major events in diplomatic history in the twentieth century. We assign students to teams to role-play European states
in the months and days before the outbreak of World War I. (This
corresponds neatly to the organization of the book, each chapter
being written from a different state's perspective.) Students engage
in the DEPPP process and debate each other about the origins of
World War I and different nations' culpability for it. Tuchman's book

is a natural jumping-off point for students to consider the unintended international consequences of individual state policies.

The second common reason for using nontraditional case materials is to keep up with breaking international affairs. When current events illustrate a key theoretical or thematic strand of the course, it is fruitful to seize the teaching moment and reap the harvest of increased student awareness or interest that media coverage creates. Integrating news stories into the international relations syllabus helps solve students' "Who cares?" and "What does this matter to us today?" questions. More abstract theoretical discussions can be grounded in current stories and fueled by student interest in them, though newspaper articles only provide raw materials for professors' use in building interactive classroom exercises.

For example, even though the Monica Lewinsky scandal and the threatened bombing of Iraq were bad news for President Clinton, they produced good teaching moments in my class, The Media and Foreign Policy. One of the principal themes of the course is the government-media dynamic in the coverage of foreign policy. After the movie *Wag the Dog* was released, a spate of news articles appeared, questioning whether President Clinton was cynically manipulating foreign policy in order to divert attention from his domestic political troubles. These articles also questioned the motives of the press in their "feeding frenzy" coverage of both the scandal and the proposed air strikes on Iraq: Was the CNN effect dictating foreign policy, that is, was high-profile media coverage forcing the president to take a more aggressive foreign policy stance?

Most international affairs professors probably hand out news articles on breaking events that dovetail with their syllabi. The difference in active learning classrooms is that the instructors do not merely distribute these pieces as additional reading material; they base interactive exercises on them. My students wrote answers to a set of study questions on the Lewinsky and Iraq bombing articles to prepare for our class discussion. In class, I split the students into four groups, representing print and broadcast media and the president's foreign policy and political advisers. Students then engaged in role-playing and debate and responded to DEPPP questioning tactics to explore the media-government dynamics and to articulate and analyze options for press and government behavior. Treating these materials as cases allowed us to tap into a mother lode of stories whose content was both custom made for the course and extremely current. They were also useful because there are only a few cases available on the topic of the media and foreign policy.[4]

Teachers of some courses in particularly fluid issue areas of international affairs, such as Russian foreign policy, report routine use of news articles as cases. Anne Henderson, then a professor at the College of William and Mary, wrote

> I did of lot of that in my class . . . In a couple of instances, I put together a portfolio of chronologically arranged newspaper clippings on a relevant issue and distributed the portfolios to students. This was very successful in generating discussion about policies and alternatives, although I had to supplement the clippings with more scholarly articles in order to give the students some theoretical background on issues of ethnic conflict . . . It worked quite well (better than some of the actual cases, in fact).[5]

The third key reason for noncase case teaching is to address quite abstract theoretical topics with texts that do not look at all like traditional cases involving actors with differing interests confronting a policy problem or decision. Edited volumes of theoretical essays, for example, often work well as cases. In my graduate International Relations Theory course, I use Richard Ned Lebow and Thomas Risse-Kappen's edited volume *International Relations and the End of the Cold War*[6] as a case. I assign the students one chapter each, and they come to class prepared to present their authors' arguments and debate the other "authors" present on whether the dominant theoretical approaches in international relations could adequately explain, predict, or describe the end of the Cold War and the demise of the Soviet Union. Again, the book is raw material out of which the faculty member creates an interactive exercise.

Although far from leading concrete discussions of traditional cases, teaching theory in this manner is much more effective than lecturing about it. The authors emerge as actors with particular points of view, operating in historical contexts and responding to contextual stimuli while making their arguments. Students engage and recall the material better than when they encounter theory as abstract, disembodied concepts delivered from on high. Treating collections of tightly paired essays as if they were cases literally puts flesh on the dry bones of abstract arguments. Concepts are rejoined to the bodies of their authors, and students can inhabit the case as an argument between real people.

For theoretical essays to work as an interactive caselike exercise, however, the materials chosen must be tightly enough organized so that the arguments do, in fact, speak to one another. For example, Denis Sullivan of Northeastern University reports success using *The*

Clash of Civilizations reader published by Foreign Affairs, which outlines both Samuel Huntington's argument and critical responses to it.[7] Similarly, I have used an article version of Francis Fukuyama's "The End of History" argument[8] paired with responses and critiques by Samuel Huntington and others. Analytically loosely organized theoretical volumes or article pairings will not work as well. For the students to step into the authors' shoes; experience, present, and debate the arguments; and react to, analyze, and critique the opposing arguments, the essays have to be speaking to, and not past, one another.

Mary Ellen Fischer of Skidmore College reports success in her Russian Foreign Policy classes with Stephen Sestanovich's edited volume *Rethinking Russia's National Interests*, which provides chapters by Russians and non-Russians on competing conceptions of Russian interests today.[9] To focus the debate, she pairs this volume with newspaper articles about a specific, current situation confronting Russian foreign policy. Students then role-play the authors and analyze what Russia should do about the current issue, using the competing conceptions of Russia's interests outlined in the edited volume.

Faculty can teach theoretical essays as cases successfully in introductory undergraduate courses as well as in upper class or graduate courses. In such courses as Global Issues or Introduction to International Relations, for example, I assign students brief excerpts from such major thinkers in international relations as Woodrow Wilson, Hans Morganthau, and Karl Marx. We then discuss the text as case, exploring such questions as: Who was this person? What historical context influenced him? Who was he responding to? Who was he trying to persuade and why? What are the pros and cons, the implications and ramifications of his argument, the alternatives to his argument? Humanizing the arguments in this way helps make the abstractions more concrete and makes room for real people in the study of states.

The fourth major reason to teach nontraditional cases is to increase student skill and experience in analyzing primary data, such as historical or archival data. Although cases often thrust students into the role of policymakers struggling with particular decisions, primary sources, when used as the basis of interactive classroom exercises, can place students in the role of political scientists, historians, sociologists, or economists struggling to make sense out of some empirical data.

Such classes as U.S. Foreign Policy or Foreign Policy Decisionmaking often use the plethora of now-declassified documents on the Cuban missile crisis. I have assigned students the transcripts of the Executive Committee meetings of President Kennedy's advisers.[10] Students can role-play the participants in the debate, guided by faculty questions on particular points the group considered: What were Khrushchev's motivations? What options were there for a U.S. response, and what were the pros and cons of those options? Students can also use the documents to role-play international relations theorists, looking for evidence supporting or undermining various theories of group dynamics or foreign policy decisionmaking behavior, such as Irving Janis's "groupthink" or Graham Allison's "bureaucratic politics" approaches.[11]

Fifth, faculty can teach nontraditional cases in order to respond to specific classroom challenges. You might wonder what interactive exercises you could run to set a participatory tone during the first day and week of class, when students will not have had time to prepare a case or may not have even purchased the course materials yet. Nontraditional cases are ideal for this purpose. After distributing the syllabus and introducing the course, you can hand out a brief article and then discuss it as a case. Actions speak louder than words: resisting the temptation to lecture students about participation, and running an interactive exercise instead, conveys the message. I do nontraditional cases each class meeting for the first week or two. This allows students who add the class after the first meeting to participate fully.

My favorite new noncase case is an article from the January 2, 1999, *Washington Post,* "How Wealth Divides the World." I use it in a course I am currently teaching, Rethinking U.S. Foreign Policy Institutions. The article lays out statistics from the latest United Nations *Development Report* in a sobering comparison of what it would cost to provide basic health care worldwide, to eliminate global hunger, and so on, compared with what Americans and Europeans spend on cosmetics, ice cream, and, of course, the military. It is a great consciousness raiser and a good opener for discussion classes. I note that realists would look at these statistics a certain way, interdependence theorists another, and ask, "Does this division of wealth seem strange to you?" After discussing this question, I announce that, throughout the semester, we will learn more about how and why the division has evolved this way.

What about other problematic dates on the university calendar when professors have good reason to believe students will not come to class prepared, such as the day after the "big game" or the day the term paper is due? Faculty can earmark such dates on the syllabus for teaching nontraditional cases that students can discuss without advance preparation. The case material can be videotape shown during the class time or brief newspaper or magazine articles distributed and read at the start of the class. This use of nontraditional cases allows you to make sure that all students are doing the assignment and to turn what otherwise might be an unproductive class into a stimulating interactive exercise.

Some faculty use nontraditional cases to solve other classroom challenges. Al Pierce of the National Defense University reports that professional military and foreign service students or more senior adult students in his classes are often reluctant to enter the story of a recent case because of a professional ethic that keeps them from second-guessing their peers. Students at any type of institution may feel so bound by historical events as they actually occurred that they have difficulty identifying or analyzing alternatives. Using fictional cases can overcome these difficulties. Pierce uses excerpts from fiction to fuel group discussions on the ethics of different international relations dilemmas. Doing so allows him to sidestep the twin constraints of students' reluctance to critique peer handling of real-life situations and to think outside the box of what did happen in some historical situation.

Finally, teaching nontraditional cases allows you to expand the menu of learning options in your classroom. Since different people learn in different ways, it is important to use a variety of teaching techniques and materials. Basing interactive exercises on films can enable you to reach students who respond better to visual information. Fiction or magazine articles may help you interest students who otherwise might not respond to political science texts. After you have hooked these students on alternative materials, it is easier to reel them into the more theoretical texts, because *they will want to know* those concepts so they can make better sense of the stories that hooked them.

Films can either tell stories directly or provide students with materials to access the story. The challenge in using films for active learning exercises is that the culture of film and television viewing is inherently passive: shut off the lights, turn on the projector, and students can immediately turn into couch potatoes. Press the stop-play button frequently when teaching with film, so you can create the thinking and participation space for active learning and so your students realize that the film or video clip is an alternate vehicle for analysis of class themes and theories, not an occasion to be passive or ill prepared.

We routinely use film clips as cases in my Media and Foreign Policy course. For example, we run a clip on Edward R. Murrow's treatment of the Korean War, from the History Channel series *From Newsreels to Nightly News,* and discuss questions drawn from our readings on the media and foreign policy. We explore how place is being used or portrayed and whether the broadcast reflects or manipulates public sentiment favoring the war, the journalist's role as both observer and participant in the conflict, the origins of the media's self-censorship, and so on. Students also respond to questions about specific shots: If you were Edward R. Murrow, would you have aired this shot? Why? We then look at Mike Wallace's coverage of the burning of a village during the Vietnam War and President Lyndon Johnson's reaction to the news broadcast, stop the video, and discuss the same questions. This leads inevitably to comparative questions: What changed? Was media coverage different because the war, public support, or technology was different? Or did media coverage change the war and public support?

These clips are very effective at putting students into the roles both of journalists deciding what to air on a particular day in a particular war and of policymakers responding to a particular item on the evening news. This discussion allows us to connect easily with arguments in the readings about the interaction between the news media and foreign policy. My jobs as faculty are to choose the video clips that best fit the course syllabus; to generate a questioning strategy that engages students in the case; to facilitate the discussion, focusing it enough that students can connect theory with historical fact; and to open up thinking and participation space.

Questioning Techniques

Case teachers take similar approaches to both cases and noncase materials, but since the latter obviously do not come with teaching notes and suggestions, here are some standard questioning techniques that prove useful in creating interactive exercises. In Chapter 2, Steven Lamy catalogs six types of discussion questions and encourages liberal use of all six in order to encourage participation from students with divergent learning styles (see "Instructor Preparation" in Chapter 2). Some of these types, however, may be more appropriate at different times in the semester or in the class session.

Think of the semester, and each classroom session, as a learning curve. At the beginning of the semester, and perhaps at the beginning of each class, ask more "softball," descriptive questions. For example: Why were people starving in Somalia in the spring of 1992? This procedure allows the students to get warmed up and to gain proficiency and confidence in participation; it also allows you to lay the facts of the case on the table before wielding the knife of more analytic questions. As each class session (the semester) progresses, raise the level of difficulty to ask more analytical, prescriptive, and evaluative questions. For example: Is it the responsibility of the United States to respond to starvation in Somalia? Why or why not? If you were President Bush, what would you have done? It is imperative that you continue to raise the bar for participation so that student skill levels continue to rise.

A number of other questioning techniques can help you devise interactive exercises. One standard technique is the actors-interests-options questioning rubric. Ask students to identify the actors in the case and their interests, then the options for dealing with the problem, and perhaps catalog the pros and cons of the various options as well. It is useful, both then and later in the discussion, to list students' responses on the blackboard. Depending on which theoretical issue is on the table that day, you can then parse this information appropriately. For example, if you are studying decisionmaking processes, you can explore whether policymakers adequately considered all the possible options and whether they correctly identified the costs and risks of the options they considered, or whether their search was truncated for some reason. In a U.S. Foreign Policy course, the class might examine which actors' interests seem to prevail in the policy selection process and why. The actors-interests-options method is especially good earlier in the semester when students are just gaining proficiency in active learning.

The buddy system is also a good device earlier in the semester, because there is strength in numbers. Pair students, or place them in small groups, either to role-play some individual or group or to represent some policy option or theory. Students feel emboldened when they are not left on their own to represent some position, and the feedback from other students can help to weed out weak or incorrect responses.

Debates work well early in the semester for the same reasons; they also work later in the semester if the questions you pose for debating are more challengingly analytic or prescriptive. An effective wrinkle in the debate format is "the switch." After students have been debating a question, you can interrupt the session and have them switch sides. Although this change is usually met with a great deal of groaning, it is a good method to ensure that students learn to look at both sides of an issue and learn to think on their feet.

Another questioning technique is the "whipsaw" or "puzzler." List all the reasons against a particular course of action or turn of events on the board. For example: Why did the Bush administration opt not to intervene in Somalia in the spring of 1992, when the death rate was highest? Then ask the class to consider why the seemingly impossible eventually occurred: Given all these excellent reasons against intervention, why did President Bush order U.S. troops into Somalia in November 1992? Again, this is an effective way to get students to look at alternative sides of an issue, and it is a particularly good method for examining change.

The "big bang" questioning technique is appropriate later in the semester, when students have gained more proficiency and confidence. With this technique, you can dispense entirely with the descriptive, warm-up questions and proceed immediately to some high-voltage, emotional, or controversial issue. For example, was the Bush administration's policy of repatriating Haitian refugees racist? When students are ready to take on such a challenge, your discussion can begin at a deep level and a high pitch.

Selecting Good
Nontraditional Cases and Using Them Well

Most faculty report that the noncase materials they find best are those that most closely resemble traditional cases: brief, specific narratives with sharply cast problems; credible actors constrained by limited time, information, and resources; and a range of plausible options. Such materials work very well as cases—as vehicles for discussion of concrete problems in international affairs that students can experience, analyze, and work to resolve. The more specific and well focused the materials, the more they engage students, and the more readily students learn from them. Newspaper and magazine articles are the most common source of noncase cases, because these accounts often fit that description.

Good cases tend to be good stories. In addition to context, character, and conflict, they have enough detail and drama to be real and compelling, and they invite the reader to connect the specifics of the story to larger general lessons or their own lives. The conflict, puzzle, or dramatic tension at the center of the story is key. People, including students, are naturally curious: the story has to provide them some object of curiosity and something to wrestle with. Case and noncase materials can be stories about cooperation and peace; they do not have to be about violence and war. But the issues cannot be easy. The characters have to be challenged for the students to care, and the challenge has to be specific and complex enough for reasonable people to disagree about the best response to it.

The story also has to withhold judgment and leave the students free to analyze it. They present the story, not what people should think about it. The entire point of introducing active learning materials is to open up, not close off, the thinking space.

In selecting materials, the fit with course themes is the primary consideration. Even a well-told story will fail as a case if the exercise does not fulfill the teaching objectives of key points on the syllabus. If students cannot connect the case with the course, their evaluations will say, "I liked the [book, article, film], but I didn't really get the point. I didn't see how it fit in with what we were studying." Conversely, a story with less specific characters, a longer format, or a more abstract tone can succeed if it fits the syllabus well, so students can readily connect the case or noncase material and the rest of the course. This "plug-in point" is critical: the case has to provide a hook for theoretical constructs as well as student interest.

Although even an abstract, theoretical text can serve as a nontraditional case, its utility depends on good design and execution of the interactive exercise the teacher builds on it. In effect, the exercise supplies some of the elements already provided by a traditional case: context, perspective, conflict, issues, and, if the text is paired with a news story, for example, grounding in specific events. Materials that include these elements tend to work well as nontraditional cases, but their successful use still entails faculty effort, whether it is selecting and assembling the materials or generating the questions that stimulate active learning.

How well noncase cases succeed depends on how much legwork faculty do to cut, paste, and parse the material and on how well they construct the interactive classroom exercise that they base on that material. Faculty can supplement existing cases with nontraditional materials and customize them to fit course topics and teaching goals, but these materials' biggest draw thereby becomes the chief obstacle to their use: teaching with noncase cases is largely a do-it-yourself enterprise. It requires locating such items as articles, essays, or film clips; matching plug-in points to the syllabus; assembling the materials; and developing assignments and discussion plans.

Faculty must judge whether nontraditional materials contain the elements of a good case, whereas traditional cases are already prepared as such, and they pass through an editorial screening process before being published. They often come with teaching notes that propose various discussion question plans, interactive exercises, and related assignments, so they can be easier to teach. In using nontraditional cases, you generally have no feedback from other faculty, as in discussions of widely used cases on the CaseNet listserv. Thus, with noncase cases, although you gain in specialization to your own course needs, you lose in institutional memory or group feedback.

Similarly, what you gain in currency with breaking news stories you may lose in reusability. The time and effort you invest when you first teach a case presumably pays off when you can teach it again. But a news story may have a shorter shelf life, although it is certainly possible you can reuse the overall framework of the related exercise you create with an updated news article on the issue.

Finally, once all the legwork is done, nontraditional cases may succeed as well as or better than some traditional ones but also become subject to the same caveats: cases are only as good as their fit with the syllabus as well as the teacher's willingness and ability to run the case in a truly participatory way.

A Generative Learning Process

One of the reasons the editors of this book on active learning in international studies included a chapter on case teaching without cases is that case learning is a generative process. Experienced case teachers found that once they had uncorked the genie of case techniques in the classroom, there was no going back. Cases did not just occupy certain dates on the syllabus, with other classes reverting to traditional form. Students began treating other materials as if they were cases, even abstract theoretical articles that looked nothing like short, descriptive, journalistic case accounts. That is, students were asking questions and participating in the story.

If we read an abstruse article by Hans Morgenthau on the balance of power, my students would ask, "Who is this guy?" "What is he trying to prove, and why?" "What in his life experience or in his historical context led him to make the argument he is putting forth?" "Who is he trying to convince, how and why?" "What are the alternatives to his viewpoint?" In a sense, nothing was taken as a given, as a text that ought to be accepted uncritically. Everything became a text that the students were gaining the tools not only to access but also to question.

The process of case teaching showed the professors' respect for the students' dignity and thoughts, and as the students gained experience, they were gaining confidence in their own abilities to think. The students were seeing the connections among the materials and between the materials and their own lives. Those connections were more powerful because the professors were not serving them up cold; the students were actively creating them. The learning process had a life of its own that transcended cases.

The process works very well in studying international affairs, because it makes room for real people in the study of states, in two ways. First, the case method works the way people learn, favoring concrete, vivid information and connecting new ideas to existing knowledge. Second, the process humanizes the study of international affairs by putting a face on global dynamics. Not only does the face make the material less foreign and more compelling, it also renders the material in a scale in which students can approach it. Once students begin asking questions and taking ownership of the learning process, they acquire skills that go beyond cases and beyond the classroom. Spillover is one means to measure the success of the method. The learning process not only spills over beyond case materials, but classes often spill over beyond the time period. No one watches the clock, and no longer do students ask whether this will be on the test, because they are invested in the process.

A master teacher once said that too often we teachers give students the answers to questions they have not asked yet.[12] In essence, we give away the story without ever getting the students involved in it. With or without cases, case techniques impart something more valuable than answers. With these techniques, students are learning not just the content of a bounded and discrete subject matter but ways to be lifelong learners and critical thinkers across a spectrum of subjects, most of which are yet to be encountered. Students become expert in the art of asking questions, a skill that lasts longer than the next global economic downturn or the result of the next Russian election.

Notes

1. John K. Cooley (1994), "The War over Water," in *Conflict After the Cold War: Arguments on Causes of War and Peace,* ed. Richard K. Betts (New York: MacMillan), pp. 413–424.

2. See the Pew Case Studies in International Affairs online catalog at http://fswww.georgetown.edu/sfs/programs/isd/files/pub.htm#pew and the Kennedy School of Government Case Program's catalog at http://www.csgcase.harvard.edu/caseweb/.

3. Barbara Tuchman (1962), *The Guns of August* (New York: Macmillan).

4. These cases are all available from the Kennedy School of Government Case Program: "Siege Mentality: ABC, the White House, and the Iran Hostage Crisis," "John Lehman and the Press," "Breaking the Bad News: Divad," and "The High Price of Free Speech: Story of a Guatemalan Journalist."

5. E-mail correspondence on the CaseNet listserv casenet@csf.colorado.edu.

6. Richard Ned Lebow and Thomas Risse-Kappen (1995), *International Relations and the End of the Cold War* (New York: Columbia University Press).

7. Samuel P. Huntington with responses by Fouad Ajami, Robert L. Bartley, Liu Binyan, et al. (1993), *The Clash of Civilizations: The Debate* (New York: Foreign Affairs).

8. Francis Fukuyama (1989), "The End of History?" *The National Interest* 16: 3–26.

9. Stephen Sestanovich, ed. (1994), *Rethinking Russia's National Interests* (Washington, DC: C.S.I.S).

10. Ernest R. May and Philip D. Zelikow, eds. (1997), *The Kennedy Tapes: Inside the White House During the Cuban Missile Crisis* (Cambridge: Harvard University Press).

11. For "groupthink," see Irving L. Janis (1982), *Groupthink: Psychological Studies of Policy Decisions and Fiascoes* (Boston: Houghton Mifflin); for "bureaucratic politics," see Graham T. Allison (1971), *Essence of Decision: Explaining the Cuban Missile Crisis* (Boston: Little, Brown).

12. John Boehrer, in discussions with Pew Faculty Fellows in International Affairs, June 1994. Boehrer attributes the observation to his colleague in faculty development, Marilla Svinicki, director of the Center for Teaching Effectiveness at the University of Texas, Austin.

Part 2 | SIMULATIONS AND GAMES

7 | Coalitions, Motives, and Payoffs: A Simulation of Mixed-Motive Negotiations

Mark A. Boyer

Relative gains versus absolute gains; zero-sum versus non-zero-sum games; balance of threat versus bandwagoning in alliance formation; cycling in coalition politics. Any political scientist who has tried to teach these concepts at the undergraduate or graduate level likely recalls the quizzical looks he or she has received from students grappling with these abstractions of international relations. The problem is not only one of introducing students to the technical way these concepts are often presented in the cutting-edge research of our field. It is also one of dealing with a level of abstraction in these concepts that makes it difficult for students to understand the relevance of such ideas in their everyday life.

The simulation laid out in this chapter is designed to provide social science instructors with a method for teaching such abstractions to their students in an active learning environment. It is also a way for students to understand the concepts of mixed-motive negotiations without necessarily having to decipher the often heavily formal theoretical constructs of the field. In terms of the intellectual genesis of this simulation, it was created out of the need to teach some rather technical material on coalition formation found in Chapter 17 of Howard Raiffa's *The Art and Science of Negotiation*.[1] Faced with a group of graduate students who were not enjoying other pieces of formal theory, I found this simulation to provide a useful tool to teach Raiffa's material without directly working through the formal logic. Nonetheless, this simulation produced an understanding of that material that could then be applied by students to international relations cases for analysis.

The following discussion first lays out the basics of the simulation and then moves on to a discussion of how this simulation helps teach the concepts listed at the beginning of this chapter. My primary goal is to make this method of teaching coalition politics available to other teachers and scholars attempting to present such material in understandable and relevant ways.

Educational Objectives

Making abstracts concepts real and applicable to the everyday lives of students is a challenge faced by every teacher. Simulation in its many forms is one tool for coping with this educational challenge. The simulation discussed below falls into the category of a human-machine simulation in which students play the simulation roles and the machine acts as a facilitator for the smooth operation of the educational exercise. Case-method teaching (as discussed in other chapters of this book), task-oriented learning where students are given a specific assignment to perform (such as presenting students with a set of quantitative data and asking them to develop in class a simple research design for analyzing it), and other forms of discussion teaching can often be used as complements to simulation approaches as ways of helping students make the bridge from theory to practice. In fact, I have regularly used this simulation in an undergraduate course on negotiation and bargaining that makes extensive use of cases and also includes participation in the International Communications Negotiation Simulation simulation developed by Jonathan Wilkenfeld at the University of Maryland.[2]

In almost all of my teaching, I stress the need for students to cross the theory-practice bridge, especially given that few will end up pursuing careers as pure theorists of any variant. It is much more likely that they will end up in professions where they are constantly asked to take theoretical or conceptual constructs and implement them in practical and usable ways. Just as a civil engineer must take theoretical physics and apply it accurately in his or her efforts to make sure a suspension bridge can sustain the weight of the thousands of vehicles that will cross the bridge each day, businesspeople and policymakers at all levels take theories of politics and negotiation and apply them in their efforts to achieve the goals of their employers and constituents. And as we all know, all of us have our implicit theories about the way that the political world works, but we rarely identify them as such and even more rarely examine the underlying assumptions of those theories.

Simulations immerse students in a model of reality that makes them experience the political and social interactions that take place to make policy. Simulations can be used as the laboratory for the social sciences in rigorous and ordered ways, but they can also be used more simply as experiential learning about theoretical constructs. As a result, many students experience for the first time what it is like to make decisions for themselves that even in a simulated world have policy implications. They also confront the substantial degree of constraints on decisionmaking and policy effectiveness that exist in any policymaking environment. More often that not, after participating in simulation exercises, students no longer wonder why our governments accomplish so little. Rather, they begin to recognize that what is actually accomplished is dramatic given the extent to which policy constraints ranging from countervailing bureaucratic interests to legislative procedural controls limit the ability of all actors in the political realm to achieve what are perceived as optimal outcomes.

Through these simulated political processes, students become distinctly aware of the disjunctures that occur between political theory and political practice in contemporary world affairs. This understanding then raises issues for the students regarding the development of strategies for coping with uncertainty in decisionmaking, the need for coalition-building throughout the policy process, and the degree to which structure and process condition and determine outcomes no matter how "logical" a particular proposal or policy option at first appears.

Design Parameters

This simulation explicitly integrates both the cooperative and conflictual elements of interpersonal and international relations. Often, the peaceful resolution of conflict depends on the mix of those elements in any given relationship. Cooperative elements are built into this game by providing incentives for coalition formation, and conflictual elements are introduced through bargaining over the distribution of payoffs within a particular coalition.

Students are divided into teams, and each team is assigned a pay-off or value that it possesses in isolation from others in the game. These payoffs and the payoff matrix that shows the payoff impact of coalition formation, discussed in more detail in the next sections, are handed out immediately at the start of the simulation period. Payoff values can be interpreted as power, prosperity, wealth, or whatever other measure of welfare is appropriate in the substantive teaching environment. In the international relations context, I have generally emphasized to students the idea that the payoffs in the game are measures of power, whether defined in a narrow nationalistic sense or in a more broadly cooperative sense relating to longer-term coalition or alliance relationships. Interpretation of the payoffs is variable and dependent upon the substantive setting in which the simulation is used.

Each of the seven times this simulation has been used, students have been divided into eight teams with initial payoffs, as shown in Table 7.1. These payoffs represent not only the initial "welfare" rating for each team but also the payoffs obtained by each team in isolation from all others. In other words, these payoffs are the ones obtained from noncooperation or "go-it-alone" strategies. Students are given instructions and are shown the payoff matrix that lays out in tabular form the benefits obtained through coalition formation.

Table 7.1   Initial (or Isolation) Team Payoffs

Team	Initial Payoff
Team 1	10
Team 2	8
Team 3	7
Team 4	6
Team 5	4
Team 6	2
Team 7	1
Team 8	1

Procedures

The basic materials for the bargaining simulation can be viewed from two perspectives: (1) what the student gets to see and work with and

(2) the facilitator's mechanics of creating the spreadsheet for use throughout the simulation. The creation of the spreadsheet allows a personal computer to be used as a specially designed calculator so that the facilitator can easily input potential coalition payoffs and generate those payoffs for students to use in their negotiations with other groups.

Student Instructions (Including the "Payoff Matrix for the Simulation")

Your goal is to strike the best deal you can for your team. The pay-offs—individual and coalitional—are listed below. You must negotiate over the distribution of the coalitional payoffs among the members of any coalition that you wish to form. In other words, given that there is some synergy in payoff amounts from coalition formation (as laid out in the table below), which members of the coalition obtain those added benefits and in what amounts? As a result, negotiations are two-stage: (1) over formation of a coalition among any interested teams, and (2) over the distribution of payoffs within that prospective coalition. You are free to ask the instructor to generate an exact calculation of coalition payoffs at any time during the simulation.

Initial team payoffs are as follows:
  Team 1 = 10   Team 5 = 4
  Team 2 = 8   Team 6 = 2
  Team 3 = 7   Team 7 = 1
  Team 4 = 6   Team 8 = 1

Coalition Payoffs: The payoff calculations for the various possible coalitions that might form during the negotiation period are listed in Table 7.2. A synergy payoff is associated with each coalition. The larger the coalition, the greater the synergy. In other words, larger coalitions receive greater increments added to their initial payoffs as summed across coalition members. For example, based on Table 7.2, a coalition of three teams receives an additional 15 percent of the total sum of their individual payoffs. A seven-team coalition receives an additional 50 percent of their summed payoffs.

Students are able to see from this matrix the exact amount that is gained through coalition synergy. For instance, if Team 6 (individual payoff of 2) and Team 7 (payoff of 1) decide to form a coalition, they would obtain a total coalition payoff of 3.3 (2 + 1 + [3 x .1]). It is then up to the members of Teams 6 and 7 to decide how to divide up the synergy of .3 among the coalition members. As this illustrates, coalition formation is positive sum in that both parties gain from formation, but the distribution of those gains is zero sum.

Table 7.2 Payoff Matrix for the Simulation

	A	B	C	D	E	F	G	H	I	J	K	L	M
											Payoff Without Synergy	*Payoff with Synergy*	*Synergy*
	2 Teams	T_1	T_2								Sum T_1, T_2	Sum + 10%	10%
	3 Teams	T_1	T_2	T_3							Sum T_1 thru T_3	Sum + 15%	15%
	4 Teams	T_1	T_2	T_3	T_4						Sum T_1 thru T_4	Sum + 20%	20%
	5 Teams	T_1	T_2	T_3	T_4	T_5					Sum T_1 thru T_5	Sum + 30%	30%
	6 Teams	T_1	T_2	T_3	T_4	T_5	T_6				Sum T_1 thru T_6	Sum + 40%	40%
	7 Teams	T_1	T_2	T_3	T_4	T_5	T_6	T_7			Sum T_1 thru T_7	Sum + 50%	50%
	All Teams	T_1	T_2	T_3	T_4	T_5	T_6	T_7	T_8		Sum T_1 thru T_8	Sum + 65%	65%

Note: T_1, T_2, and so on refer to the number of teams in a coalition, not to specific team numbers. The numbers input to this matrix are the payoffs for each coalition member.

The synergy payoffs can thus be interpreted as the positive-sum gains that are achieved through cooperation with other teams. In an international relations context this might mean the augmentation of the political-military power held by two different teams' forming an alliance that would not have been obtained if they simply "added" their power together. For example, during the Cold War, the inclusion of Iceland as a North Atlantic Treaty Organization (NATO) member was often pointed to as something that did not augment NATO military power in a traditional sense (especially as Iceland had no military forces). Rather, it augmented NATO's force projection capabilities and its ability to monitor and potentially choke off Soviet naval access to the Atlantic. In an economic context, one could interpret the synergy payoffs as efficiency gains made by pooling resources and capitalizing on increased economies of scale or comparative advantages possessed by different actors in the production of particular goods.

As discussed in a procedural way in the next section, students are allowed to ask the facilitator (and will do so) continually for calculation of synergy payoffs as they negotiate for the best deal for their team in the simulation. Variations in the team groupings in prospective coalitions and the way synergy payoffs are divided among prospective coalition members cause the students to repeatedly reevaluate their coalition membership options and provide for a fluid set of negotiations among teams.

Creating the Faculty Facilitator Spreadsheet

The computer applications in this exercise are quite simple. The spreadsheet payoff matrix shown in Table 7.2 was generated with Microsoft Excel and is used as a specially designed calculator during the negotiating period. During the exercise, students are continually in need of exact payoff calculations for the various prospective coalitions, and the spreadsheet allows the facilitator to generate these values quickly, minimizing disruption to the flow of the simulation.

The spreadsheet can be created using the following steps:

1. Open a new spreadsheet in any spreadsheet program (e.g., Excel or Lotus). The gray shaded left-hand column and top row in Table 7.2 correspond to the column and row markings in most spreadsheet programs and will be used through this discussion as spreadsheet matrix reference numbers.

2. Type in the pieces of text in the nonshaded areas of the table (i.e., type all text and numbers except those in the shaded left-hand column and shaded top row). Please keep in mind, as is indicated in the note to the table, that the "Ts" with subscript numerals represent the number of coalition members and not a specific numbered team.

3. Next you must input a series of formulas into various spreadsheet cells. They are given in Table 7.3 and are indicated with specific cell reference labels. In most spreadsheet programs, you will need to type an equal sign (=) in the input area of the program before typing the formula in a particular cell to indicate to the program that you are typing a formula that will calculate a value. The formulas have been typed using the standard Microsoft Excel format for such equations. The asterisk (*) is the traditional spreadsheet multiplication symbol; the colon (:) means all cells included between the two cell references. For example, the notation "sum (B8:E8)" for cell K8 means that the values in cells B8, C8, D8, and E8 are added for a K8 cell value that is the sum total of B8 through E8.

These formulas will then generate three numbers that the facilitator can provide to the student. In column K are the basic additive values of prospective coalition members. In column L are the additive values for all coalition members with the payoff for cooperation added into the total value. In column M is the synergy payoff that the coalition receives from cooperation. This allows the students to quickly recognize the effects of cooperation within the simulation. It also clearly identifies the synergy amount, the amount the coalition members must divide in some fashion among themselves before a final coalition agreement can be made. The value in column M is also the focus of the conflictual aspects of this simulation, as division of this additional amount of welfare is zero sum in nature. All three of these formulas will be generated by the spreadsheet formulas when the facilitator enters the individual team payoff values in the B through I cells for the appropriate coalition size.

Table 7.3   Spreadsheet Cell Formulas for Calculating Payoffs

Cell	Formula	Cell	Formula	Cell	Formula
K4	Sum (B4:C4)	L4	Sum (B4:C4)*1.1	M4	Sum (B4:C4)*.1
K6	Sum (B6:D6)	L6	Sum (B6:D6)*1.15	M6	Sum (B6:D6)*.15
K8	Sum (B8:E8)	L8	Sum (B8:E8)*1.2	M8	Sum (B8:E8)*.2
K10	Sum (B10:F10)	L10	Sum (B10:F10)*1.3	M10	Sum (B10:F10)*.3
K12	Sum (B12:G12)	L12	Sum (B12:G12)*1.4	M12	Sum (B12:G12)*.4
K14	Sum (B14:H14)	L14	Sum (B14:H14)*1.5	M14	Sum (B14:H14)*.5
K16	Sum (B16:I16)	L16	Sum (B16:I16)*1.65	M16	Sum (B16:I16)*.65

The computer in this instance, then, is a support tool for the smooth functioning of this simulation. It is not an absolute necessity for the functioning of the game, but without it the instructor would be required to do the math longhand or through repeated calculation with a hand calculator. In either case, significant informational bottlenecks would occur in terms of students' obtaining the payoff information needed during the course of the negotiating period. Given that holding student interest is often the key to success in the pedagogical use of simulation, such time delays could prove costly for the success of this exercise. In addition, throughout the simulation, students will repeatedly ask for different coalition payoff values. Using the spreadsheet matrix, the facilitator only needs to replace the values in the cells for the appropriate size coalition to generate whatever mix of teams is desired by the student negotiators.

The simulation should run a minimum of forty-five minutes and usually runs for about an hour. It can be allowed to run longer, depending on the class setting and teaching goals. There is usually about a ten-minute warm-up time during which the students figure out what they are supposed to do. In my experience with this simulation, students first read the instructions; wonder what the point is of the whole exercise; ask a few questions for clarity; and then ultimately get very wrapped up in the activities of the day. Most of the questions from students at the start of the exercise pertain to definitions of what the team payoffs actually mean. Those definitions are left to the instructor, as they can be adapted to whatever substantive setting is deemed appropriate.

Assessment and Debriefing

Most of the substantive applications of this exercise that I discuss here reflect my scholarly background in the international relations subfield of political science. This is not to say, however, that the simulation's relevance does not go beyond international relations. A number of non–international relations applications immediately come to mind.

1. *The stability of coalitions in legislative bargaining environments.* This simulation relates directly to issues of cycling in coalition formation and stability as such topics are discussed extensively in the public choice literature. In my experience with this exercise, I have witnessed many circumstances where one coalition appears sta-

ble and lasting for a period of time. But often someone within that coalition is made a "better offer" from a noncoalition member, particularly in terms of the distribution of the synergy payoff, and decides to withdraw from coalition membership and negotiate to join another.

2. *Labor negotiations.* This simulation could be used to illustrate the mixed-motive nature of management-labor negotiations, where motives exist that are both cooperative (e.g., not shutting down a business through strike or long-term disagreement) and conflictual (e.g., over the distribution of pay, benefits, and profits between management and labor).

3. *Issues of fairness and justice.* This simulation can be use to help students understand the formation of coalitions and the distribution of coalitional payoffs from the perspective of distributive justice, as discussed by Rawls and by Frohlich and Oppenheimer, among others.[3] Specifically, how does one fairly distribute the synergy payoff among coalition members? What measures of fairness or justice, if any, were used to determine the distribution?

Beyond these possibilities, the following sections provide examples of a number of conceptual issues within international relations that have been developed in actual classroom uses of this exercise.

Application I: The Relative Versus Absolute Gains Debate

One of the higher profile debates in the field of international relations in recent years has centered on the issue of whether nation-states pursue relative gains in power and status in the international system or whether they pursue absolute gains.[4] In other words, are nation-states (or their decisionmakers) concerned more about their power and status relative to their evaluations of the power and status of other actors in the system, or are states more concerned with the provision of some absolute notion of welfare? If the latter case is true, then once that absolute notion of welfare is achieved, decisionmakers will not concern themselves with "keeping up with the Joneses" of the world in international policy decisions. This issue has been part of the grand theoretical debate between realists (emphasizing the national gains *relative* to other potentially competing states) and neoliberals (emphasizing the importance of *absolute* gains that potentially help spread benefits from cooperation across many states).

This simulation provides students with ample illustration of the diversity of perspectives and value structures that actors bring to international negotiations. For example, in a recent running of this exercise, one group of students representing a "strong" team (Team 1 or 2 from Table 7.1) was primarily concerned with trying to help the "weak" states in the game. In terms of its individual gain from cooperation, the team was only concerned with gaining *something* in a coalition, no matter how small that gain proved to be. As a result, "weak" teams gained more relative to the stronger ones. Another "middle-power" group was constantly asking for payoff calculations to make sure they were not getting the bad end of the deal. They were much more concerned with their payoffs relative to their partners and would not join a coalition when they viewed the distribution of synergy payoffs as inequitable or skewed away from augmenting their individual team power. During the debriefing session, these contrasting motivations in negotiation were readily evident, and a useful discussion ensued about the different ways states approach opportunities for international cooperation. In other words, do states cooperate purely out of self-interest, as realists argue, or do they cooperate because of a set of values that defines welfare in broader than national terms?

Application II: Coalition Formation and Stability

Stephen Walt's *The Origins of Alliances* focuses on the forces that cause military alliances to form.[5] He concludes that the need to *balance* against a threatening country by joining together with other countries to obtain stronger collective military forces is the dominant cause of alliance formation. This simulation moves students beyond the narrow applications of military alliance formation and illustrates various motives for coalition formation. In particular, it highlights the following divergent ways of thinking about the need to cooperate with other actors.

• Some teams aim to "win" the game by trying to maximize the payoff they obtain from any potential coalition. Teams of this sort are often the ones that cause coalition instability during the game, as they float from nascent coalition to coalition looking for the best deal. Almost invariably, if other coalitions are looking for members to increase their synergy payoffs, "better deals" can easily be calculated among existing coalition members. As a result, coalitions in this setting are rarely stable for long.

• Some students will simply sit by themselves, because they view their isolation payoff as good enough. One graduate student in an early running of this exercise viewed this approach from the "live simply so that others may simply live" dictum and felt that competition for additional gains only fed the forces for conflict in the simulation.

• In the seven times I have run this exercise, the grand coalition (all teams in one coalition) has never formed. This has not even happened in cases where students have calculated that on average all teams would be better off if the grand coalition were to form. In most cases, it is the better deal that one or two actors can get from refusing to join or by breaking out of the grand coalition that inhibits its formation or duration.

In addition, many of the same dynamics discussed above regarding the absolute versus relative gains debate manifest themselves as forces that promote and inhibit coalition formation.

Application III: Issues of Fairness in International Development Studies

One of the recurrent themes in the international development field focuses on the fairness of the distribution of wealth within and across countries. In particular, given the skewed distribution of isolation payoffs in this exercise, there is ample cause for concern over the resulting distribution or potential redistribution of wealth or power in the game. For instance, in distributing synergy payoffs among members of a coalition, should members receive payoffs in proportion to the amount of wealth or power they bring to the group? Or should the weaker states receive larger shares out of fairness and in line with progressive taxing systems? Or in yet another approach, should stronger states receive more proportionally, because they provided more of the benefits by virtue of their larger size? In other words, students must grapple with issues of fairness in order to distribute the payoffs they obtain from forming coalitions. For many, this is one of the first times they have had to divide up wealth and make decisions that affect not only themselves but also others in a collective arrangement.

Unique Situational Dynamics

As with any simulation exercise, the uncontrollable variable is the human element. Even with the structure of the game well defined, the teacher never quite knows what will happen in the simulated environment. A few examples from this game follow:

• *"Secret" Negotiations.* In one running of the simulation, there were three bilingual students in the class. Just by chance, they were assigned to three different teams. About twenty minutes into the game, these three students began negotiating in "secret" by speaking only Spanish and not informing others of what they were deciding. In about ten minutes they had brokered the formation of a rather large coalition and a distribution of payoffs that was ultimately acceptable to the other participants. This is the only running of the game where coalitions formed and remained stable until the end of forty-five minutes.

• *"Coercive" Benevolence.* In another recent running of the game, a member of one of the powerful teams became very aggressive in her efforts to persuade other teams to join her large coalition. She was offering them what seemed to be very favorable payoffs and was in fact willing to give up some of her team's original payoff amount to entice prospective members to join. What she quickly discovered, though, was that these prospective members did not like being told what was best for them, even if she was right. Near the end of the game, she began apologizing for her "imperialistic" behavior in an effort to achieve her goals of widespread coalition membership. No coalitions formed by the end of the time period.

• *Double-Dealing.* In another exercise, two teams wanted to know if they could join multiple coalitions and obtain synergy payoffs from all of those coalitions. This type of student query demands a discretionary decision by the instructor. Are teams allowed to join multiple groups? Must they split their original individual payoff across the coalitions? Must they tell the different coalitions that they are in fact members of multiple coalitions? Will that lead to their ejection from one or all coalitions? The answers to these questions depend largely on the substantive setting. I made the decision in this instance to allow them to double deal but required that they split their original payoff across groups. This allowed them the flexibility to do what they perceived as useful from the standpoint of negotiating their best deal but also forced them to think about the implications of their actions over the long term. Such a decision is similar to the decisions that many states face in the contemporary international system when deciding about joining one international organization or another.

Suggestions for Debriefing

This simulation provides a powerful tool for teachers to use in making negotiation theory understandable and relevant to everyday life. In order to integrate theory with practice effectively in the classroom, however, the teacher must be able to take the simulated world and place it back within the context of the course material. As a result, the most important component of any successful simulation is the debriefing period after the exercise. The debriefing puts the exercise into the theoretical context of the course and ensures that the students realize that the past hour of "fun" has educational relevance.

In general, the use of open-ended questions allows students to provide their impressions of what occurred during the game and usually generates lively reactions from others in the class. Some examples of debriefing questions that I have used with this exercise—and the types of answers I hoped to obtain from them—are as follows:

- *Why did you join the coalition that you joined?* This is often where issues of relative versus absolute gains come out. More generally, this question has helped students reveal their motivations for action during the simulation.
- *What incentives or payoffs did other coalition members offer to you?* This question helps get at the specific details of the bargains struck between students. Student creativity has been remarkable at creating unique sets of incentives for coalition formation.
- *Why did you choose not to stay a member of that coalition?* Coalitions often cycle (i.e., are unstable for a period of time) in this simulation, and this question helps identify why cycling occurred.
- *What were your goals? What were you trying to achieve as a team?* This is another variant of the first question about exploring motivations.
- *How did the goals of strong teams differ from weak teams? Why did they differ?* Students in the United States frequently (and not surprisingly) view the world through very ethnocen-

tric eyes regarding the power of the United States in the world. This question helps them focus on the power dynamics explicit and implicit in the simulation and gives them a feel for what it is like to be without preponderant international power.

- *Do you feel that the payoffs you obtained were fair? Why?* The question of what is fair in international relations is a difficult one for students to grapple with, at least partly because of the privileged position the United States plays on the world stage. This simulation confronts the students with power relationships and the impact they have on what is defined as fair and who determines what is fair in international relations. It also helps them focus on what strategies are available to weaker actors who are attempting to change existing relationships toward what might be interpreted as more equitable outcomes.

A more extensive discussion of debriefing and questioning techniques can be found in Smith and Boyer and in Christensen, Garvin, and Sweet.[6] Both of these sources provide a more extensive and generic treatment of how to debrief classroom simulations.

Generally, debriefing provides the instructor with an ad hoc way of assessing what students have learned during the simulation. In many ways, the debriefing is often the only way that students make the connection between the simulation and the concepts of the class. Debriefing also serves the purpose of explicitly making the bridge between theory and practice, identified as one of the primary goals of this simulation. At times, students cross the bridge implicitly, but the debriefing makes the connections more explicit and in a form that the instructor views appropriate to the goals of the course.[7]

Notes

Mark Boyer wishes to thank Carmen Cirincione and Jeff Lantis for valuable comments on earlier drafts of this chapter and the many graduate and undergraduate students who endured this simulation during its evolution, all the while providing him with insights into the human element of cooperation and conflict and also into the effectiveness of simulation as a teaching tool.

1. Howard Raiffa (1982), *The Art and Science of Negotiation.* (Cambridge: Harvard University Press).

2. The syllabus for this course is available online at http://www.lib.uconn.edu/~mboyer/facboyer.html/.

3. John Rawls (1971), *A Theory of Justice* (Cambridge: Belknap Press of Harvard University Press); Norman Frohlich and Joe A. Oppenheimer (1992), *Choosing Justice* (Berkeley: University of California Press).

4. For example, see Duncan Snidal (1991), "Relative Gains and the Pattern of International Cooperation," *American Political Science Review* 85(3):701–726; Robert Powell (1991), "Absolute and Relative Gains in International Relations Theory," *American Political Science Review* 85(4):1303–1320; Joseph M. Grieco (1990), *Cooperation Among Nations: Europe, America and Non-Tariff Barriers to Trade* (Ithaca, NY: Cornell University Press).

5. Stephen Walt (1987), *The Origins of Alliances* (Ithaca: Cornell University Press).

6. Elizabeth T. Smith and Mark A. Boyer (1996), "Designing Your Own In-Class Simulations," *PS: Political Science and Politics* 29(4):690–694; C. Roland Christensen, David A. Garvin, and Ann Sweet (1991), *Education for Judgement: The Artistry of Discussion Leadership* (Cambridge: Harvard Business School Press).

7. Assessment at a more systematic level can also be performed but also requires significant time and monetary resources to perform effectively. The use of Web-based evaluation surveys to assess student learning and faculty experience now allows educational psychologists to analyze data on the impact of simulation approaches in international studies. Such surveys allow for ease of administration and data collection but are costly to produce. At a simpler level, faculty members can administer their own surveys with simple questions to gain a sense of what effect the simulation experience has had on the achievement of teaching objectives. Anyone interested in samples of either of these types of surveys may contact the author at boyer@uconnvm.uconn.edu.

8 Securing Tomorrow: A Simulation of the National Security Policy Process

Thomas Preston

"Securing Tomorrow" is a policymaking simulation designed to complement upper-division undergraduate courses on U.S. national security policy. Intended for use in standard, lecture-based courses, the policy exercise provides students with hands-on experience in dealing with the substance of difficult and complicated issues of foreign and defense policy making. Book or lecture learning is complemented and reinforced by engaging students in *active learning exercises* designed to bring security-relevant concepts and problems to life in as realistic a manner as possible. Assigned roles as White House staffers within a new presidential administration, students are divided into task groups that focus on issues relevant to the Department of State (DoS) and the Department of Defense (DoD) as well as to the National Security Council (NSC).[1]

From the beginning of the semester, students are aware that, as a group, they must perform the same tasks as real-life White House staffing groups—that is, they must

1. decide as a group which foreign and defense policy issues or problems (out of the myriad of potential candidates) require presidential attention
2. assign staffers to research and develop specific, detailed policy recommendations to address these problems
3. produce concise, ten-page policy memorandums outlining each of the identified policy issues and their proposed solutions

4. compile all the individual staff reports into an overall, comprehensive task group report
5. formulate and deliver a class-length briefing of the task group's policy recommendations to an actual president (played by an outside policy-area specialist acting as president) during mock NSC meetings held the final two weeks of class.

Within the limitations imposed by the classroom context, the simulation attempts to provide students with as realistic a policy staffing experience as possible.[2] Throughout the semester, students receive communications from senior administration officials and other materials (based upon actual policy documents retrieved from presidential archives) to which their groups must respond in their policy deliberations. Since my undergraduate course also routinely includes a large number of cadets in the Reserve Officers' Training Corps (ROTC) who are training to become military officers, as well as graduate students specializing in the security field, my goal is to provide a simulation experience that will help to make them not only better officers or analysts but also more educated consumers of security information as they move into their careers.

Although this simulation is a challenging one for students and demands a great deal of creativity and thought, it has consistently been evaluated positively by participants as "fun" and "incredibly useful" in helping them to understand the complexities and substance of security problems—and what it is like for the real-life policymakers who have to deal with these issues.[3] Indeed, this simulation is an excellent tool not only for creating empathy among students for the plight of policymakers but also for communicating to students (through their own active involvement in substantive policymaking) the fact that real-world policy problems often lack simple answers. The lessons learned by students are, by their own accounts, "vivid ones" that profoundly influence how they view foreign and defense policy, international relations, and other political science courses. In fact, students who have subsequently taken other international relations courses after experiencing this simulation tend to demonstrate far more awareness and understanding than their peers of political issues and of how the policy process works and are much more realistic as policy analysts in their assessments of events. They have also repeatedly expressed to me how much more confident they are in their understanding of politics and material in other political science courses taken elsewhere in the department. By taking an *active learning* approach, I have made the subject matter of the course not only interesting and fun for students but *relevant* to them—a necessary first step toward effective teaching.[4]

Educational Objectives

Among the educational objectives emphasized during the development of "Securing Tomorrow" was the need to provide students with the following: (1) a better understanding of the complexity of security issues through the creation of realistic policy staffing experiences requiring "hands-on" study of substantive topics; (2) a politically "neutral" context through which to study security policy, thereby facilitating development of a less-biased learning environment; (3) increased empathy for the tasks faced by real-life policymakers; and, finally, (4) experiences geared toward improving students' critical thinking, writing, and communications skills.

The primary goal of this simulation is to provide students with a realistic policy staffing experience designed to illustrate the complexity of post–Cold War security issues through hands-on study of substantive topics. The tasks of designing policy memorandums and preparing a presidential briefing requires students to delve deeply into the real substance of foreign and security policy problems. Superficial, purely political treatments of topics are usually avoided by students, who recognize that an outside policy specialist in the area of their research will be portraying the president during their NSC briefing and will be contributing an evaluation of their report that will affect their final course grades. As a result, students are forced to avoid making ideologically driven (and justified) proposals in their memos and to instead focus upon in-depth analysis of the substantive elements of their policy issues. Students will usually have also heard through the grapevine from previous participants in the course about presenters being "grilled" or "taken to task" by presidents who were not convinced by either their arguments or the supporting evidence given to them during their NSC briefings. Obviously, I am more than happy to repeat and expand upon these horror stories (with much exaggeration) at every opportunity for the class! As a result, students within the task groups tend to take their presentations—and the supporting memos and documentation of their evidence—very seriously indeed! These efforts to adequately prepare memos, and to address the substantive nature of their policy problems sufficiently to meet the critical gaze of the president, lead students to study their issues in far greater depth (and learn far more about the topic) than would be the case in normal term papers.

Another major design consideration for this simulation was the creation of a more politically "neutral" context in which to study security policy. As is usually the case with political issues, students typically arrive in political science courses with a significant amount of baggage, or preexisting beliefs and biases, regarding the subject matter. This is especially problematic for courses dealing with topics in which the ideological divisions between students themselves (or society at large) are sizable. For example, U.S. public policy courses dealing with the merits of social programs, gun control, welfare reform, or tax cuts pose the serious problem for instructors of getting students to see past their ideological biases in order to pursue a more objective discussion of the issues. Too easily, substantive discussions of the problems themselves become lost in an ideological haze.

A similar challenge faces instructors of national security courses, who must cover controversial topics such as what the appropriate role is of the United States in the post–Cold War world, which potential problems or countries constitute legitimate security threats to our national interests and which do not, and what the appropriate uses are of military force and who must examine in a critical fashion the present nature of U.S. defense spending (is it too much or too little?). As one would expect, students arrive fully equipped with ideological blinders that invariably pose a challenge for instructors seeking to foster critical thinking and open-minded debate of these issues. For some students, no amount of defense spending or use of force is sufficient, whereas for others, there is a perceived aura of illegitimacy to both. At best, these preexisting views regarding security policy are based upon erroneous, distorted information accumulated over a lifetime of listening to the simplistic treatments of the subject found in election campaigns or the news media. At worst, the beliefs are completely detached from reality. This represents a critical problem for instructors, who must find a way to reach through these biases and encourage students to consider material objectively.

Thus, one of the main educational objectives for the "Securing Tomorrow" simulation is to engage students in critical thinking regarding security issues in as neutral a political context as possible. In this way, students reflect upon and reconsider their own beliefs over the course of the exercise—a technique far more likely to bring about true change in belief systems than are teaching styles that depend solely upon lectures by professors, which are more easily discounted by unreflective students.[5] Further, given the intense individual involvement the simulation requires of staffers, a keen awareness and empathy rapidly develop among students for the challenges and problems faced by real-life policymakers. Although many students originally approached politics as if they were the ultimate Monday morning quarterbacks, a common remark on student evaluations after the simulation is the observation that they just had not realized how difficult and complicated policymaking really was! As a result, I believe this makes students more realistic about politics and far better future consumers of security information.

Unlike the Hobbs and Moreno simulation presented in Chapter 10, which presents a crisis decisionmaking scenario that forces bureaucratic bargaining, the "Securing Tomorrow" simulation is much more of a policymaking and analysis exercise highlighting the characteristics of the policy process. The experience of working as staffers within task groups to identify the problems, decide upon an agenda, research and design policy proposals to address the problems, and prepare final policy memorandums to the president brings students across the entire policy process and accomplishes several educational objectives at once. First it builds empathy for real-life policymakers as a result of students' increased awareness of the complexities and difficulties involved in the policy issues themselves as well as of the political obstacles that must be dealt with in formulating policy proposals. Second, the scenario forces students to work together as a team to help the president develop good policies that are politically defensible against potential critics of the administration. As social psychologists have long observed regarding group formation, the best way to bring individuals of differing beliefs and backgrounds together into a positive, cohesive group is to assign the group tasks that require the individuals to work together toward a common goal.[6] In the classroom context, students of diverse political backgrounds and beliefs are placed in a scenario that puts them all on the same team, and the requirements of developing policy proposals within the task groups over the course of a semester result in students' having a substantial personal investment in the product. Essentially, given the nontraditional political positions taken by the president, students of all ideological stripes end up counterarguing their own beliefs and attempting to reformulate policies so that they can withstand criticisms by either Democrats or Republicans. This constitutes a political education for students that greatly increases their empathy (or pity) for actual policymakers.

Finally, the simulation provides experiences geared toward

improving the critical thinking, writing, and communications skills of participants. As students quickly discover, writing a "short" ten-page policy memorandum requires as much research as, and is in many ways more demanding than, writing the more traditional twenty- to thirty-page term paper. The emphasis within the policy memorandum is upon writing a concise, tightly argued piece absent the normal fluff common in longer papers. All points and statements must be thoroughly documented and footnoted in the memo. Since the president expects his or her advisers to be sensitive to both security and political issues in making their policy recommendations, students are forced not only to back their arguments up with solid data but also to persuasively argue in their favor as advocates. Given the complexity of the issues and the need to provide a detailed set of recommendations regarding them, students soon discover that condensing their arguments down to "only" ten pages represents a real challenge. Students routinely observe that their experiences in writing short memos, although more difficult, were more likely to be useful to them in their future careers than writing long research papers. Like the president in this simulation, most bosses (whether in business or government) will expect brief, concise, and well-written reports from their subordinates, not dense tomes. Again, because the assignment is relevant to students' professional development, they tend to place greater effort into the exercise and get more out of it.

Good-natured competition among the task groups for "bragging rights" to the best group presentation often take place during the final two weeks of NSC meetings, with groups routinely meeting outside of class to practice and hone their presidential briefings. Since the groups are given complete freedom to set up their presidential briefings in any way they see fit and to use any presentational style they desire, tremendous thought goes into how they can make the best impression on the president and "waste" the other groups. From an educational standpoint, this provides students with valuable experience in public speaking and in developing and giving concise presentations (a useful communications skill in academia or business) and engages them in a creative, enjoyable learning experience.

Design Parameters

"Securing Tomorrow" begins with the following scenario, which outlines both the general political context and the nature of the role to be played by the student within the simulation.

After a surprising political upset in the November 2000 presidential elections, General Winston C. Marshall, running as a New Independent, has been elected president of the United States. Reacting to dirty campaigning, political scandals, and a general climate of dissatisfaction with politicians promising easy answers to the nation's problems, the public turned away from more traditional Republican, Democratic, and Reform party candidates to stage a write-in campaign for Marshall's New Independent Party across the nation. Winning the White House with 63 percent of the popular vote, President Marshall seized upon the results as a "mandate from the people" for major changes in existing policies. Immediately, using a coalition of newly elected Independents, along with splinter groups of Democrats and Republicans, Marshall succeeded in gaining enough votes in the Congress to enact two very popular measures: (1) Campaign Finance Reform (i.e., ending all financial contributions to political parties by PACs/interest groups, limiting total expenses allowable during all political campaigns, and severely limiting lobbying on Capitol Hill) and (2) A Major Initiative to End the Annual Budget Deficit Within Four Years (i.e., by eliminating all politically motivated tax cuts that would increase the deficit; by putting all federal programs under review for deficit reducing cuts, including defense and other previously untouched areas; and by limiting government spending on all domestic programs to 1998 levels). As a result, by the end of February 2001, the president's public approval ratings were at 69 percent favorable, and sizable numbers of congressmen from both parties were defecting to the New Independent banner, creating for the White House a majority in both houses of Congress.

President Marshall has emphasized the need to avoid partisanship and to reach across party lines to staff the administration with "the best and the brightest" advisers possible. Thus, advisers and staff from both Republican and Democratic administrations have taken up positions within the Marshall administration alongside staffers from the New Independent Party. As a result of your previous policy experience and expertise in the field of foreign and defense policy, you were approached by the administration after the election and subsequently recruited into the government. Upon accepting your post, it was emphasized to you personally by the president that you had been brought into the administration with the clear understanding that you would put aside your own political leanings and work with others on the White House staff to make "good policy for the country" in the areas of foreign and defense policy. You quickly discover, upon starting your new White House job, that the staffs within the administration are indeed (as advertised) composed of a mix of Republicans, Democrats, and New Independents. Despite your individual differences, all members of the White House staff recognize that their main goal must be to make the Marshall administration as successful as possible and thereby help to ensure President Marshall's reelection in 2004.

Your primary policymaking task is to develop creative, innovative policy approaches in the areas of foreign and defense policy, while at the same time protecting the president politically from any negative political ramifications of the policies you propose. In other words, you need to think about BOTH the substance of policy and the potential

> political problems that could arise from the solutions you propose. You should also study carefully the letter from President Marshall and take the president's wishes into account during your policymaking, since staffers would be expected to be loyal to Marshall's general policy goals and objectives.

The scenario seeks to create a more neutral political climate for the simulation by characterizing President Marshall as an independent (outside of the traditional parties) who not only seeks a staff of all political persuasions but also actively desires revolutionary thinking with regard to policy. This serves to avoid activating the existing political biases of students, opens up policy debates within the task groups, and encourages critical thinking by students beyond familiar party-line approaches. Marshall's platform of policy change also encourages critical thinking by students, since the president's message discourages staffers from settling for the existing policy status quo. This platform of change is a critical feature educationally, because it forces students to think beyond merely ratifying existing policies to really reconsidering the premises and goals behind these policies.

For example, prior to the insistence within the simulation for the DoD group to reduce the defense budget by at least $100 billion from current spending, the DoD task groups tended to submit policy proposals that simply continued (with only minor adjustments) existing defense spending levels and programs. This represented the "easy" solution and did not require students to challenge their own assumptions (or those of existing policies). Further, since DoD groups tend to be represented predominantly by ROTC cadets in this course, these individuals arrived with strong preconceptions regarding defense issues and the need to avoid weakness. As a result, the simulation materials were changed to force critical thinking and a reevaluation of core beliefs in these participants. President Marshall was given a strong military background (à la Eisenhower), and the DoD staffers were required to reduce defense spending in line with post–Cold War realities *without* undermining U.S. national security. With this rubric, these students soon began producing quite creative and thoughtful reassessments of U.S. defense policy and easily found the required budget reductions while maintaining realistic security requirements. Students have often remarked at the end of the course that they could not believe how much their own views on the subject had changed after having dealt in such detail with the problem in their task groups. This example illustrates how important the underlying scenario in the simulation is to sparking the desired response in students.[7]

After reading the basic scenario, a letter from President Marshall is given to the students, which further underscores their roles:

THE WHITE HOUSE
Washington

August 24, 2001

Dear Colleagues and Staff,
    The election has provided us with a unique opportunity to meaningfully address many of our country's most pressing national security and foreign policy problems! However, the tremendous complexity of these problems has led me to recognize that one individual alone cannot possibly come to grips with these problems sufficiently to set the administration's policy during the next four years. Further, although we have presented our positions on these issues during the election, this presentation was, of necessity, quite simplistic and skeletal in form. It is our task to now develop the specifics of our policy positions, to reassess our positions where necessary, and to adopt the best policy positions both for the nation and for our administration. Therefore, I have decided to establish three departmental task groups, composed of experts from the Department of Defense, the Department of State, and the National Security Council, to further develop well thought out policy papers on several critical areas of U.S. foreign and defense policy.
    Again, *I emphasize the need for creative and revolutionary thinking in these areas.* As you know, during the campaign, I promised to reduce government spending and deficits by taking a realistic look at our policies—including those areas previously untouched in any meaningful way by the Democrats and Republicans. Obviously, we no longer have unlimited funds to engage in a "go it alone" foreign and security policy—with the Cold War over it is an untenable position to take. Therefore, I am relying upon those of you in the Defense Department to put together a strong national defense for the post–Cold War era for at least $100 billion less than it costs in present defense budgets! The State Department and NSC need to take into account the changing world, and likely defense budget cuts, in reformulating a dynamic foreign policy approach for the United States that DOES NOT abdicate our leadership role or compromise our national interests. I recognize that these are tall orders and difficult policy problems to deal with—but that's why we get paid "the big bucks"! *In approximately 12 weeks, we will gather together in the White House for National Security Council meetings to finalize these proposals.* I greatly look forward to reading and hearing the finished proposals that will come from all of you—"the best and brightest" on my staff.
    This is a critical time for us and it is essential that we arrive at the best possible policy options so that our administration can be identi-

fied as both innovative and responsible. Further, we need to be politically realistic and move away from stale conventional thinking if we are to pass what I am sure will be an ambitious and dynamic policy agenda.

Yours faithfully,
President Winston C. Marshall

Having completed a survey indicating their preferences regarding task groups and issue areas, students are then assigned to task groups. This self-selection of roles allows students to focus upon areas of potential interest for their careers (i.e., ROTC cadets tend to select the Defense Department task group; graduate students interested in the Foreign Service select the State Department group, and so on). Although the task groups themselves make the final decisions regarding what specific issues to focus on in their reports to the president, they also receive guidance in the form of memos from the White House chief of staff, Robert Eastwood (portrayed by the instructor). I also provide a sounding board for the task groups and individual students regarding the likely reactions of the president to policy ideas they might have. In a series of memos, I provide the three task groups (DoD, DoS, NSC) with general instructions from President Marshall regarding their policy areas and his expectations for the final group reports.

The DoD group is instructed to focus upon restructuring U.S. defense policy and budgets to better fit the post–Cold War world and an era of budgetary constraints. Among the specific instructions given to the group:

1. Develop an assessment of legitimate U.S. security requirements by identifying the most serious (and realistic) threats to U.S. interests.

2. Given these threats, outline what security goals should form the basis of U.S. defense policy.

3. Provide a plan for reducing the existing defense budget (assume present spending levels) by $100 billion per year (more if possible) while at the same time maintaining a strong defense capable of protecting our nation's security against all realistic threats (i.e., are there areas of wasteful spending, redundant or unnecessary programs, and so forth that can be targeted by DoD in order to reduce its budget requests?).

4. Outline how the U.S. military force structure should be restructured to meet our security needs while still allowing for significant downsizing of existing forces and missions (i.e., what are the

most critical things that should be preserved in U.S. defense planning re capabilities, goals, missions, strategies?).

5. Provide a new set of goals and missions to be performed by this downsized force structure, and recommend for adoption any new military strategies required as a result (i.e., what kind of strategies should be employed by this downsized force structure that emphasizes force-projection capabilities, elite forces, use of reserves, and advanced technology?).

The DoS is assigned the task of restructuring U.S. foreign policy to better fit the post–Cold War context and an era of budgetary constraints. Among the specific instructions given to the group:

1. Identify U.S. foreign policy requirements in the post–Cold War era (i.e., what are the *most* critical things that should be preserved in U.S. foreign policy planning re what we try to do, how we go about it, our goals and missions, and so on?).

2. What is the nature of existing foreign policy threats or problems that should be addressed by the administration and how should our policy be restructured? (I.e., try to realistically assess these issues and how we should deal with them given the existing international situation, the limitations of U.S. power, and budget constraints.)

The DoS group decides for itself what foreign policy issues should be addressed, but the memo provides some general guidance by giving examples of specific policy areas of importance, such as Russia policy (i.e., support for reformers, North Atlantic Treaty Organization expansion, arms control, aid), Middle East policy (i.e., Arab/Israeli dispute, Iran/Iraq, Islamic fundamentalism), United Nations policy (i.e., how can the United States most profitably utilize this institution to advance our policy/security/national goals?), U.S. trade/financial policy (i.e., support for International Monetary Fund/World Bank, trade deficits with Japan, European Union, aid), Asia policy (i.e., North Korea, China, human rights, and so on), and Cuba policy (i.e., sanctions, refugees, and so on).

The NSC task group is assigned the role of identifying other potential security threats facing the United States and developing policies to address them. In particular, the NSC is asked to focus upon threats posed by nuclear proliferation and terrorism. Among the specific instructions given to the group:

1. Review and propose changes in U.S. nuclear nonproliferation policy (i.e., how to prevent or stop proliferation [if possible], how to deal with states already possessing nuclear weapons programs, and so on).

2. Address the current nature of the threat to U.S. security caused by nuclear, chemical, biological, and delivery system proliferation.

3. Address the problem posed to U.S. security by the sale of conventional arms to other nations.

4. Review and suggest improvements in U.S. policy dealing with the problem of international terrorism (i.e., how can we prevent it; how should we deal with states sponsoring such acts, and so on?).

5. Review and suggest improvements in U.S. policy dealing with the problem of domestic terrorism.

6. Address the current nature of the threat posed to U.S. security by the international drug trade.

The feedback students receive from these memos not only provides guidance but also allows for considerable freedom of action for groups to decide for themselves what is important, what will be studied, and how it will be reported to the White House. This flexibility encourages creativity and makes the groups themselves *accountable* for the final product.

Procedures

After members are assigned to groups based upon their policy interests, elections are held by secret ballot for the main leadership roles in each group (i.e., secretary of defense, secretary of state, and NSC adviser). With this simulation, the group leaders play an important role, and those wishing to run for the position must give a brief speech to the class explaining why they would be effective. Once elected, these task group leaders have the following duties:

1. Chair all task group meetings.
2. Lead group discussions.
3. Arrange with other group members (staffers) what specific policy questions they should work on for the final group report.
4. Organize the presidential briefing, compile and write intro-

ductory sections for the overall group report, and make decisions regarding the presentational style to be adopted for the briefing.

It is expected that the task groups will follow reasonable democratic norms and take votes regarding all policy positions recommended by each group. Group leaders should avoid taking on the role of dictator and should work to form a consensus within their groups to obtain the best possible options for the president. The group leader role requires accepting a responsible leadership position, so students who adequately perform this role throughout the semester (based upon instructor and peer evaluation) receive 5 percent extra credit for their final course grade.

The group leaders also appoint, from within their groups, an assistant secretary to help them with their duties during the semester. These assistant secretaries assist the departmental secretaries in conducting group discussions and submit to the professor minutes of each task group meeting, listing attendance, agreed-upon work assignments for group members, and the results of any votes taken within the group on policy matters. This provides the group with a record of what has been decided upon for later meetings. Copies of these minutes are returned to each group by the chief of staff for their own records. The role of assistant secretary requires additional written work by the student and active assistance to the group leader, so students who adequately perform this role throughout the semester (based upon instructor and peer evaluation) receive 2.5 percent extra credit for their final course grade.

After the task group has discussed and debated the general policy positions, staff within the groups should volunteer for the topics they would like to research and be responsible for in the final report. Each individual within the group will then be responsible for producing a ten-page memorandum for the final report. These individual memos are combined to form the task group's report to the president. Each individual policy memorandum must include the following sections:

1. A statement of the general nature of the problem and what existing U.S. policy is regarding it.
2. Assessments as to whether existing U.S. policy is effective or ineffective in dealing with the problem.
3. Detailed proposals for addressing the issue.[8]

A common question arising during the simulation involves the estimation of costs or savings from the adoption of specific programs. Particularly for the Department of Defense, this is a very real problem when trying to trim the defense budget to $200 billion/year or less. The following guidelines are applied:

1. Estimates of program or option costs used by task groups in their recommendations must be obtained from a published figure cited by any of the following sources: actual government officials, congressional sources, academic or research institutes, or newspapers or magazines.

2. A reference for the cost figure must be cited and included as a footnote in the group's policy memorandum.

3. If a lower cost figure for some program is used by the group in their budget—because they have eliminated or omitted an element from the program's cost that was cited by a published source—this lower figure must be approved by the instructor and an explanation/justification of its lower cost stated in the policy memorandum.

The role of President Marshall in this simulation is portrayed by an outside actor who is a specialist in the policy area being discussed by the task group. This person's identity is unknown to the class until the day of the NSC meeting itself. Every effort is made to have this outside individual be as prestigious as possible (for instance, a department chair, commander of the ROTC, or a professor known for his or her expertise in the area in question). This helps to create more realism for the students, who as staffers would tend to be a bit awed by the presence of the president in a meeting. Further, by bringing in an actor from outside of the class, the simulation mimics the normal relationship between lower-level staffers and the president—in which staffers would not necessarily be personally close to or know the president well.

This particular aspect of the simulation is enjoyed by the students, who engage in speculation regarding who the president will be. Outsiders also stimulate greater effort by students in preparing their documents and practicing their briefings. Students are forced to assume a clean slate with each president and recognize that they will have to fully brief and explain their positions to these individuals—a situation that would not exist were the role filled by the instructor. By playing the chief of staff, the instructor is able to provide guidance and advise the groups over the course of the semester while at the same time maintaining the appearance of working with the students rather than against them in preparing for the final NSC meetings. This is a useful tactic in terms of creating greater rapport between the instructor and students and also serves to encourage students' creativity and confidence as they interact on equal terms with their professor.

Assessment/Debriefing

Assessment of this simulation includes evaluations of individual student papers and participation by the instructor, evaluations of task group performance by the instructor, evaluations of each group's briefing by the outside president, evaluations of group leaders by the members of their group, and evaluations by group members of each other and their leaders. As a result, the "free rider" strategy is not a viable option for students, since the evaluation reports by other group members (whose grades are affected by their behavior) are usually brutally honest regarding those who do not carry their own weight. Further, since 50 percent of the course grade is based upon the simulation (30 percent on the individual paper; 20 percent on group performance), students have a self-interest in taking the exercise very seriously indeed. This addresses one of the greatest problems inherent in all simulations—that of getting participants to take their roles and the game seriously.[9]

In addition, I spend time encouraging students to evaluate the simulation itself and to make suggestions regarding ways to improve the game structure to make it run more smoothly and realistically. This stage of the evaluation process is very important in an active learning sense, because it involves students in both reflecting upon their experiences and helping them to connect the dots between the simulation's educational goals and the actual results. Indeed, my experience has been that by explaining the manipulations used in the simulation and what the educational objective of each was, instructors receive truly valuable feedback from the participants for improving both the simulation and how they run it. Such feedback is critical for instructors who intend to design future simulations for other courses, for research, or for training professionals outside of academia.[10]

The final day of the simulation is devoted to a debriefing session during which students are encouraged to reflect upon their experiences as policymakers. Task groups are encouraged to discuss and compare their own policymaking experiences with those of the other groups, especially surrounding their decisionmaking at what they perceived to be critical decision points during the simulation (i.e., from their decisions regarding what topics were and were not important to how these topics were researched, what approach was decided upon for their task group's final presidential memo, and how their briefing strategies for the president were decided upon). Other questions posed to participants include: Was the group's briefing to the president successful? In retrospect, what would they do differently if they could run the simulation again? How did their own individual views regarding security policy in general, or their specific task group policy area in particular, change as a result of the simulation? Were the issues more complicated than they had realized prior to the simulation?

These questions, and the subsequent class discussions, help participants to process and reflect upon their experiences, bringing home to students the educational objectives noted earlier. Based upon feedback from student evaluations over the past three years, it is clear that some of the most vivid lessons learned by the students from this simulation correspond nicely with my educational objectives for the exercise. For example, students often comment upon the fact that the simulation provided a politically neutral environment and stimulated them to reconsider many of their preexisting views on security. The most common comments found on the student evaluations involve the degree to which students felt the simulation was "fun," "useful," "interesting," or "relevant" to the subject matter of the course. Indeed, students often remark that the simulation served to bring the lecture material to life and greatly improved their understanding of it. Evaluations have routinely included statements like these: "This simulation was the best thing I have ever experienced at WSU!" "I wish more courses used simulations like this!" "I was never interested in political science before this course, but now I want to take more classes."

To me, these student evaluations speak for themselves and correspond to comments made by students, often years after taking my course, in which they emphasize how profound they felt the learning experience had been. It is clear that active learning exercises like simulations not only add to the popularity of courses with students but also greatly enhance our ability to teach difficult courses with demanding subject matter effectively by motivating and stimulating our pupils. I am a great believer in using simulations as an active learning strategy in the classroom and have incorporated these exercises into most of the courses that I teach, with similar results. As an instructional technique, they have made my teaching far more effective and pleasurable than before.

Notes

1. Because the students are divided into three separate departmental task groups (State, Defense, and NSC), the "Securing Tomorrow" simulation is capable of accommodating relatively large undergraduate class sizes. Indeed, during the past three years at Washington State University, this simulation has been run successfully with classes as large as sixty students (with twenty students in each of the three policy task groups). This simulation probably works better with between ten and fifteen students per task group, however, since a smaller number simplifies the managerial task of the individual group leaders (undergraduates with no previous leadership experience of this kind).

2. A more detailed discussion of the requirements of designing and running successful classroom simulations can be found in Thomas Preston and Martha Cottam (1997), "Simulating U.S. Foreign Policy Crises: Uses and Limits in Education and Training," in a special issue of *Journal of Contingencies and Crisis Management*, ed. M. Cottam and T. Preston, 5(4):224–230.

3. The national security policy course in which this simulation runs has been consistently ranked through student evaluations as one of the top courses in our department over the past three years! The success of this course is, I believe, in no small measure related to the positive experiences of students who participate in this policymaking simulation.

4. See Thomas Preston and Martha Cottam (1997), "Simulating U.S. Foreign Policy Crises."

5. In the absence of the kind of critical thinking exercises provided by *active learning* approaches, students tend to process all incoming lecture material so that it is consistent with their preexisting beliefs. In the event that material significantly challenges these beliefs (cognitive dissonance), students fall back upon stereotyping the messenger. Dealing with this selective perception of information by students is one of the major challenges for professors. As instructors have long observed upon reading their teaching evaluations, when presented with course material or information that challenges their existing political beliefs, students will often "tag" political science professors as either "liberals" (by conservative students) or as "conservatives" (by liberal students). See S. T Fiske and S. E. Taylor (1991), *Social Cognition,* 2d ed. (New York: McGraw-Hill) or V.Y.I. Vertzberger (1990), *The World in Their Minds: Information Processing, Cognition, and Perception in Foreign Policy Decisionmaking* (Stanford, CA: Stanford University Press) for a more detailed discussion of these information-processing strategies.

6. See S. T. Fiske and S. E. Taylor (1991), *Social Cognition*.

7. See Thomas Preston and Martha Cottam (1997), "Simulating U.S. Foreign Policy Crises" and M. Kleiboer (1997), "Simulation Methodology for Crisis Management Support," a special issue of *Journal of Contingencies and Crisis Management*, ed. M. Cottam and T. Preston, 5(4):198–206.

8. Grades for the individual policy memorandums are based upon (1) the quality and coherence of the substantive policy discussion/proposal in the section and (2) peer and instructor evaluation of students' participation and work within the task group. The overall grade for the DoS, DoD, or NSC working groups is based upon (1) the quality and coherence of the substantive policy proposals in the overall report and (2) the quality and coherence of the briefing the group provides to the president during the NSC meeting.

9. See Thomas Preston and Martha Cottam (1997), "Simulating U.S. Foreign Policy Crises."

10. For detailed discussions of these issues, see ibid. See also P. 't Hart (1997), "Preparing Policy Makers for Crisis Management: The Role of Simulations," a special issue of *Journal of Contingencies and Crisis Management*, ed. M. Cottam and T. Preston, 5(4):207–215; K. Yusko and H. W. Goldstein (1997), "Selecting and Developing Crisis Leaders Using Competency-Based Simulations," a special issue of *Journal of Contingencies and Crisis Management*, ed. M. Cottam and T. Preston, 5(4):216–223; S. Babus, K. Hodges, and E. Kjonnerod (1997), "Simulations and Institutional Change: Training U.S. Government Professionals for Improved Management of Complex Emergencies Abroad," a special issue of *Journal of Contingencies and Crisis Management*, ed. M. Cottam and T. Preston, 5(4):231–240; M. G. Hermann (1997), "In Conclusion: The Multiple Pay-Offs of Crisis Simulations," a special issue of *Journal of Contingencies and Crisis Management*, ed. M. Cottam and T. Preston, 5(4):241–243.

9 | The United Nations Security Council Restructuring Summit

Jeffrey S. Lantis

The "United Nations Security Council Restructuring Summit" is a role-playing simulation designed for an introductory international studies course in which students experience the dynamics of international cooperation and conflict. Student diplomats are faced with the challenge of creating a restructuring plan in order for the United Nations (UN) Security Council—an institution created in 1945 at the dawn of a new postwar era—to better represent the global political climate at the dawn of a new millennium. This is a tall order, but the "Security Council Summit" allows students to confront this challenge in a simplified form that requires only three to six class meetings for application. Students' comments from past runs confirm that the simulation is an interesting and effective way to learn more about international relations.

The literature on the use of simulations in the classroom recommends that simulations include four major components:

1. Educational objectives.
2. Design parameters, such as background information and specific role assignments.
3. Functional procedures, including rules of procedure and protocol.
4. A debriefing period for discussion, assessment, and reflection.

Each of these elements was included in the design of the "Security Council Summit."

Educational Objectives

This simulation was designed to fulfill several educational objectives. Broadly speaking, the "Security Council Summit" illustrates key conditions of international cooperation. The simulation complements a section of my introductory international relations course at The College of Wooster devoted to theories and practices of cooperation. This exercise is juxtaposed against a rational choice game that I typically run during the conflict section of my course. The simulation is thus first a vehicle to move students from theoretical discussions about international organizations such as the United Nations to personal experiences with the structure of the Security Council, contemporary debates on restructuring the institution, and different country perspectives toward global challenges.

Second, the "Security Council Summit" presents students with a unique opportunity to experience the real-world successes and failures of international diplomacy. Students are presented with a central diplomatic objective in the simulation: to develop plans for restructuring the UN Security Council that will receive support from the international community. Students experience the *process* of global problem solving firsthand.

Third, the simulation helps students learn more about negotiation, critical problem solving, and communication skills needed for effective diplomacy. Delegates must negotiate and compromise with one another to develop passable restructuring plans, and they gain important insights about group decision dynamics along the way.

Simulation Design Parameters

Role Assignments

It is important that student role assignments in the "Security Council Summit" represent a balance of responsibilities and perspectives. This manifests itself in two ways. First, a controlled set of countries should be selected in advance to represent a variety of perspectives in the debates on restructuring. Second, student assignments should be balanced to create diplomatic delegations, or teams, to represent key countries. This balance also serves to promote an interesting level of intragroup discourse on restructuring.

I typically assign two to four students to each of eleven delegation groups for this simulation. First, all five permanent members of the Security Council (the United States, France, the United Kingdom, the Russian Federation, and the People's Republic of China) should be represented as veto powers who, of course, have a vested interest in all proposals to restructure the organization. Second, several economically powerful countries that aspire to Security Council membership should be represented, including Germany and Japan. Third, regional powers who do not have permanent seats on the Security Council, such as Brazil, India, and Saudi Arabia, can be represented at the summit. Finally, I have created an artificial delegation, the Independent Committee, which is given "special authority from the UN Secretary General to try to develop an independent, nonaligned plan for restructuring and to mediate Council disputes."

Background Information

I devote several class meetings in advance of the simulation providing background information on the role of international organizations in world politics and specifically the United Nations system. I explain that the Security Council was designed in 1945 to be the central institution in the UN system, with a primary responsibility to monitor and maintain global peace. According to the UN charter, the Security Council coordinates all efforts to settle disputes peacefully (Chapter VI) and, if necessary, to challenge threats to peace through concerted economic or military sanctions (Chapter VII).

Second, I describe the membership structure and voting procedures of the UN Security Council. Fifteen states are seated as voting members of the council at any one time. The charter designates five countries as permanent members—China, France, the United Kingdom, Russia, and the United States. The General Assembly elects ten nonpermanent members for staggered two-year terms (with five elected each year). These nonpermanent members are elected to represent a wide geographical distribution, according to Article 23 of the charter, but they are not immediately eligible for reelection after they have served their terms. Each member of the council has one vote on major resolutions, and resolutions require nine yes votes to pass. If a permanent member on the council votes no on a resolution, however, it automatically fails. Thus, each permanent member of the Security Council has a veto power that can be used to effectively block any major substantive initiative in the body. In practice, a permanent member of the council may abstain, which is not regarded as a veto of the pending resolution.

After a lecture on the structure and processes of the United Nations system, I move to a more focused review of the role of the Security Council in the post–Cold War era. I discuss the fact that criticism of the current organizational structure of the Security Council has grown considerably in this era, for several reasons. First, the UN has become embroiled in a growing number of international and regional disputes in recent years that have increased the risk of failure for the organization. Some recent UN Security Council actions, such as the oversight of the peacekeeping missions in Bosnia and Somalia, have led to tragedy. Second, many criticize the Security Council because it is not an accurate reflection of the current distribution of power and influence in the world. Third, critics charge that Security Council membership does not allow representation of the general membership in the United Nations. In fact, countries that contribute a great deal of money, troops, and logistical support for UN operations (such as Canada and India) have complained of being left out of decisions that can affect their own citizens. Finally, critical pressure for change has grown in the post–Cold War era. Some argue that it is important to seize the opportunity presented by dramatic global changes for restructuring the Security Council to better position the United Nations for the twenty-first century.

Although some political leaders and scholars support restructuring, many others oppose major changes in the Security Council. States that have permanent membership in the council have quietly argued that the composition of the Security Council is, and should continue to be, linked to the ability to exercise international responsibility. They argue that permanent membership of the council has always been predicated on the assumption that the strength of these states both permitted and obliged them to accept special responsibility in ensuring the maintenance of international peace and security. Others challenge the suggestions for restructuring by contending that the UN is now working far more effectively than ever before. Security Council debates are no longer characterized by familiar Cold War polemics, and the council is making decisions that have dramatically expanded the scope and mission of UN operations.

Procedures

The overall goal of the simulation is for students to develop, debate, and critically examine plans for restructuring the Security Council. They must attempt to devise plans that could receive the support of a majority of players and not be vetoed by the permanent members. In order to channel students toward this objective, functional procedures of the simulation include a schedule with project deadlines and basic rules of procedure.

Summit Schedule

This summit is designed to run during three successive class periods. On the first day of the simulation, students can be assigned roles as they enter the classroom and join their fellow diplomats in designated seating areas. I welcome students to the summit and distribute a short "Summit Mission Statement," which reads:

> The Security Council is one of the most important institutions in the United Nations system. It was designed at the end of World War II to reflect the political order of the times. But today, many view the Security Council as a historical anachronism—an outdated and weak institution that does not represent the political reality at the end of the twentieth century.
>
> There is momentum in contemporary world politics for reform of the UN Security Council. In fact, many world leaders have publicly pledged their support for restructuring the Security Council. Political leaders of Great Britain, the United States, Germany, India, Brazil, and Sweden have all offered support for some modifications. Meanwhile, scholars have suggested several different ideas for restructuring, including the complete elimination of the veto power, the introduction of a multiple-tier structure of permanent membership, arrangements that would allow immediate reelection of nonpermanent members, the addition of new permanent members, or even the redistribution of the existing permanent membership seats. However, in spite of rhetorical support from many capitals, no major action has been taken.
>
> World leaders have called this special summit to consider restructuring the Security Council for the twenty-first century. Your mission is twofold: (1) to consider ways to restructure the Council for the future and (2) to play your assigned roles as government representatives in the negotiations on a new Security Council arrangement. The world awaits your recommendation for a restructuring plan that will enhance the legitimacy of the institution and truly empower the United Nations at the dawn of a new millennium. Good luck.

After reviewing the mission statement, delegations are directed to begin discussion of their own plan for restructuring of the UN Security Council based on their national perspectives and interests. This intradelegation discussion takes up most of the remaining class period. Each delegation elects a spokesperson who then presents their group plan to the entire class for changing (or perhaps not changing) the institution to better reflect the politics of the twenty-first century. Each group also turns in a written summary of their restructuring plan at the end of the class meeting.

On the second day of the simulation, students are again seated in delegations around the classroom and given a packet of all written country proposals for restructuring the Security Council. They are asked to devote ten minutes to review the written proposals and reflect on their own plans for the institution. The majority of the second class period is then devoted to intergroup diplomatic negotiations to develop compromise restructuring plans. Students should be reminded that the rules of procedure require a majority vote on their plan, and they should consider ways to build coalitions in support of major substantive plans for restructuring. New *compromise* restructuring proposals are due by the end of the class session.

On the final day of the simulation, students are given one last opportunity for intergroup negotiation before a final roll-call vote on each compromise restructuring plan. After the vote, the results are tallied and announced. The remainder of class time should be devoted to debriefing and reflection on the simulation experience.

Rules of Procedure

The "Security Council Summit" runs on a simple set of rules of procedure. The instructor serves as facilitator for the simulation, presenting general background information to students, providing directives and suggestions for delegation work on restructuring plans, encouraging student interaction, and moderating the formal presentations of those plans on the first day of the simulation. On the second day of the simulation, the facilitator should encourage students to play an active role in diplomatic negotiations between delegations in an effort to secure support for compromise restructuring plans. I regularly remind students that all compromise restructuring plans sponsored by two or more delegations can be accepted for consideration during the final roll-call, voice votes on restructuring.

The actual restructuring proposal form can be simple or elaborate. I typically use a one-page worksheet with five basic questions:

1. Sponsor?
2. Cosponsors?
3. What are your general goals for restructuring the UN Security Council?
4. What are your specific proposed changes for the membership of the Security Council?
5. What are your specific proposed changes in voting procedures for the Security Council?

Students are reminded that in order to pass, restructuring plans require seven yes votes from the countries represented at the summit, including support from all permanent members (no vetoes). As difficult as it is to achieve a majority of seven, I explain in the debriefing that any real-world restructuring plan for the Security Council would require an amendment to the UN charter, a two-thirds majority of support from the General Assembly and the Security Council, and support from all permanent members of the Council.

Debriefing and Evaluation of the Summit Experience

The "Security Council Summit" has proven to be a very valuable and effective learning tool. The simulation clearly achieves the educational objectives described earlier, and student comments on their experiences from the fall semester 1997 run illustrate this quite well.

First, the "Security Council Summit" simulation illustrates key dynamics of cooperation in world politics. Students in the fall 1997 run, for example, approached their assigned tasks with a dedication to find common ground for compromise restructuring plans. On the first day of the simulation, most students seemed to assume that cooperation would indeed be possible. They devised their own country's plan for restructuring largely without consulting other groups, and they presented these plans at the end of the first session. But instead of highlighting common ground as students had hoped, most of the country plans illustrated very different perspectives and expectations from different groups. The general assumption that great powers would naturally cooperate began to give way under the pressure of conflicting opinions and loyalties.

Nevertheless, students worked hard during the second and third sessions of the 1997 summit to build a consensus in favor of a compromise restructuring plan that could receive majority support. They were committed to the goal of international cooperation—if only they could assure that their own national interests were met at the same time. In the end, students generated five compromise restructuring plans for a final vote, but none of the plans received enough support for implementation. In written commentary, one student delegate from Saudi Arabia felt that the simulation demonstrated

> how extremely difficult it is to convince different people from many different global areas to agree on one, or even a few, possible restructuring proposals. Change is always one of the toughest tasks to undertake simply because countries are afraid of what they might lose. Unfortunately, no matter how hard we tried, four of the permanent five countries would not even bother to negotiate with us. Our plan failed due to the lack of compromise from these states since they were fearful of what this change might mean for them.

At the same time, a delegate from the United States said that the exercise "illustrated how fragile the negotiation process is, and drove home the point that the UN really needs to reform its procedures." A student diplomat from India found the effort at international cooperation somewhat more frustrating:

> After spending time formulating our own plan for restructuring the UN Security Council (which we thought was pretty good), it was really frustrating to have other people vehemently disagree with our proposal simply because they wanted their proposal to pass. I was amazed that more discussion seemed to focus on forming coalitions than on discussing the real issues and trying to reach a compromise meant to address the perceived problems as best as possible. If this sort of thing happens in a college classroom over the period of two days, I think it's reasonable to assume that it happens in the real UN as well. . . . Negotiation is a complicated process.

The simulation also provided students with a great deal of insight into the system, history, institutional structure, and decisionmaking processes of the UN. Given the goal to create compromise restructuring plans, students learned about the requirements and parameters of decisionmaking authority in the institution. And in the process, they created some very interesting restructuring proposals.

For example, the delegates of Saudi Arabia, France, Brazil, and India joined together to formulate one compromise plan during the 1997 run with the expressed goal to "increase representation on the Security Council." They proposed a restructuring of the Security Council to elect five new permanent members and developed a new voting plan for the ten nonpermanent members of the council that would allow three nonpermanent votes to equal a veto of proposed resolutions. Another coalition of great powers—Great Britain, the United States, and Germany—joined to develop a proposal to increase fairness in the structure of the Security Council. Their restructuring plan called for an increase in council membership to twenty-one states, the elimination of the veto power, and a rotating membership on the council for all states of four years. In a very different spirit, the Independent Committee, France, and Japan joined together to abolish the veto power in the council and to increase the membership of the organization to thirty states. This group stressed the need for the institution to reflect new global political dynamics and proposed equality and openness in council proceedings.

The "Security Council Summit" clearly presented students with the opportunity to *experience* real-world successes and failures of international diplomacy firsthand. This experience turned out to be very real during the 1997 simulation, when five major compromise restructuring plans failed in rapid succession during the final roll-call vote. During the debriefing, a student representative of Brazil said that she thought that "the mock UN summit was an excellent way to gain some insight on how complex international relations could actually be." Reflecting on a similar experience, a student representing Saudi Arabia said that the summit "provided a very constructive learning experience. . . . It was much more helpful to participate in an exercise such as this one rather than relying on readings." Meanwhile, the delegate from Japan indicated that the summit was a "valuable experience as it demonstrated the jump from theory to application." One delegate from Brazil argued:

> It was quite frustrating but enlightening to understand the finer nuances and the trade-off of international diplomacy, and the difficulty in reaching a consensus on any matter. Every nation that was not represented on the Security Council wanted a "permanent" seat. There were some good proposals for restructuring the Security Council, but there was objection to some clause or the other from one of the permanent members, or not enough majority, or abstinence by a crucial permanent power and hence no resolutions were passed. The whole exercise enabled me to understand

that interactions in international relations are based to a large extent on norms—expectations held by national leaders about international relations. The lack of any success to break down the monopoly of the "big five" clearly showed that international norms and standards of morality do not help when the different (powerful) states or world regions hold different expectations of what is normal.

A third educational objective articulated at the beginning of the Global Problems Summit was to help students develop valuable negotiation, critical thinking, and communication skills. Students are encouraged to present creative suggestions for compromise restructuring, and students in the 1997 run took these goals to heart. The simulation promoted the development of interpersonal communication skills, and I was pleased to see students improve their public speaking and rhetorical skills as the summit progressed. Although many use their country plans for restructuring as outlines for their initial negotiations, students are often forced to adjust their positions quickly and to speak on other subjects. Some students were understandably hesitant about speaking out on their country positions, but others set the tone by presenting interesting and convincing arguments. By the end of the 1997 summit, even the most reserved students had become involved to some degree in the practice of international diplomacy.

There was also a clear learning curve on the use of the rules of procedure for the summit. Students became more comfortable with the parameters of the exercise and voting requirements as time wore on. They accumulated valuable negotiation and problem-solving skills throughout the summit. Students engaged in interesting, and sometimes heated, debates about membership and voting procedure–restructuring initiatives. And, for the most part, they were careful to analyze proposals before offering their (often conditional) support. Student reactions to this dimension of the simulation were quite revealing. A delegate from China reflected that

> I realized from this experience that people are running the world. I always have this mental image of things just happening and of powerful beings determining how the world will run. But people are behind all of it. They have emotions, connections, priorities, and pride that must be considered. Negotiating is talking to these people. . . . International diplomacy is a tricky thing. It is not just coming up with the best plan. It is also selling that plan to the people who can implement it. As much as less powerful countries may resent the five permanent countries on the Security Council, it is

exactly those countries that the small countries need to collaborate with in order to change things.

A delegate from Saudi Arabia was even more introspective: "Through my participation in the Summit, I discovered that, in many cases, superior representation can make up for the relative weakness of a particular country. I believe the summit provided me with invaluable experiences in negotiating with others."

Clearly, this simulation provides students with a unique opportunity to learn more about international cooperation, the United Nations system, diplomacy, and negotiation strategies. Consistent with the principles of active learning, students are confronted with a challenge and must seek solutions through negotiation, critical thinking, and compromise. On the basis of successful runs and positive student evaluations, I believe that the "Security Council Summit" represents an interesting and valuable educational tool for the international studies classroom.

10 | Bureaucratic Bargaining Revisited: A U.S. Foreign Policy Simulation

Heidi Hobbs and Dario Moreno

Simulations have been popular in political science and international relations classes for the last four decades. Role-playing exercises are popular because they are a great way to introduce complex theoretical concepts in an active learning environment. A well-designed simulation requires students to actively engage in group problem solving. These activities force passive students to deal with politics as actors instead of silent observers.

"Bureaucratic Bargaining" simulates the executive branch's decisionmaking process.[1] A crisis scenario is introduced, and students are asked to develop an appropriate response based on their bureaucratic role assignment. By means of a belief system questionnaire administered prior to role assignment, "Bureaucratic Bargaining" also explores the tension that can develop between role and belief system when one is confronted with a crisis decision.

Educational Objectives

Simulations are an excellent tool for the teaching of U.S. foreign policy. Role-playing exercises are ideally suited for demonstrating the complexities of governmental machinery and the function of personal perceptions in the decisionmaking process. This is critical because beginning students often enter the study of international relations with a simplistic view of policymaking. Students tend to reduce the elaborate process involved in the making of U.S. foreign policy to such naive constructs as a group of wise men seated around a conference table. They accept a priori what Graham Allison calls the "rational actor model" in which students "package the activities of various officials of a national government as action chosen by a unified actor, strongly analogous to an individual human being."[2] Students often believe that foreign policy is set by a cohesive group of individuals who share common goals and preferences. Moreover, they have an additional tendency to anthropomorphize the state, which results in undergraduates writing papers in which nation-states are portrayed with such common human qualities as sympathy, cruelty, and aggression.

Role-playing exercises are useful devices to introduce students to competing approaches to the policymaking process. Although some scholars claim that the rational choice model is the dominant approach in the field of international relations and foreign policy decisionmaking, others have pointed to limited rationality in the foreign policy behavior of leaders.[3] The debate concerning rational actor models, bureaucratic models, cognitive models, or a combination of approaches is one of the most important debates in the study of U.S. foreign policy. Given the complicated nature of this debate, a creative way to expose beginning students to the literature on foreign policy decisionmaking is through a simulation. Role-playing exercises are useful for the study of decisionmaking because the standard lecture-discussion format simply cannot capture the complexities of the process and multiple levels of interaction that occur, often simultaneously.

The simulation presented here is designed to introduce students to the debate between bureaucratic and cognitive models of decisionmaking. One of the ongoing debates in international relations centers around what is the most potent variable in explaining U.S. foreign policy. One group of scholars contends that where you sit in the bureaucracy, the role variable, is more potent. Even though agreeing that role is a powerful restriction, particularly at the lower levels of the bureaucracy, other scholars contend that cognitive factors such as the individual perceptions and beliefs of policymakers are more important in the decisionmaking process, particularly in a crisis situation. This role-playing exercise in negotiation and compromise seeks to explore the potency of role in contrast to belief in foreign policy making. For student participants, the simulation brings the complexities of the decisionmaking process to life. For the instructor, it provides a refreshing alternative to class lectures and discussions. It is also an innovative method to introduce students to both the bureaucratic and cognitive literatures on decisionmakers.

Design Parameters

To simulate the decisionmaking process, students are first tested on their foreign policy beliefs. The game uses an updated and simplified version of the Holsti and Rosenau Foreign Policy Leadership Project questionnaire to determine the student's belief system.[4] The administration of the questionnaire provides the instructor with an opportunity to discuss the role of beliefs in the policy process. Students can be introduced to the cognitive models of Alexander George, Robert Jervis, and Irving Janis, to name a few.[5] The results from the questionnaires are used to determine the bureaucratic roles to which the participants are assigned.

The game begins as students are divided into three teams representing bureaucratic entities: the Department of State, the Department of Defense, and the White House. A common problem is introduced through a conflict scenario set in the former Soviet Union. Each governmental entity is charged with developing a policy recommendation consistent with its bureaucratic mission. Students are given a game manual that outlines the organizational goals of each team to guide policy formulation. Student assignment based on the belief system questionnaire may provide tension between the student's personal belief system and the team's bureaucratic mission. For example, a student whose personal belief system puts a high priority on defense preparedness might be assigned a role in the Department of State. The bureaucratic mission for this team is to maintain peaceful relations with all the nations of the former Soviet Union and to avoid a crisis that could result in a return to the Cold War.

The simulation also serves as a device to introduce students to some of the elementary concepts of social science methodology: hypothesis testing and independent and dependent variables. This is achieved by operationalizing the concept of belief systems and role variables for students and offering two hypotheses that contrast the role versus belief system variables in the decisionmaking process:

1. If roles are more potent in the simulation groups, then decisions will be made in accordance with the bureaucratic mission of the participating agency or bureau.

2. If belief systems are more potent in the simulation groups, then decisions will be made in accordance with the individual belief systems of the members of the participating agency or bureau.

The strength of belief systems is tested through the preparation of policy statements and debate within the bureaucracies. Either the belief system or role variable will appear more influential through the policy choices that are made within the context of the game.

Procedures

The utility of this exercise is that the actual play can be completed in one to two class periods. Preparation prior to actual play proceeds as follows. Concurrent with a discussion of the role expectations and belief systems in the foreign policy process, the questionnaire is administered one to two weeks prior to the actual simulation. The information gathered from the responses is then used to assign students to their respective roles. Students are not informed of the way in which the questionnaires are used in making their role assignments.

The questionnaire is based on the Foreign Policy Leadership Project conducted by Ole Holsti and James N. Rosenau since 1976. This project has identified enduring belief systems among foreign policy leaders based on a survey administered every four years. The post–Cold War period has revised those belief systems and split them across what Eugene Wittkopf identified as the two "faces of internationalism." From this perspective, attitudes form across two dimensions—militant internationalism (MI) and cooperative internationalism (CI).[6] Holsti and Rosenau use support for or opposition to these parameters to identify four belief systems: isolationists (oppose MI and CI), hard-liners (support MI, oppose CI), accommodationists (oppose MI, support CI), and internationalists (support MI and CI).[7]

For the purposes of this simulation, a short questionnaire has been developed to characterize students by these four belief systems (see Appendix A).[8] Students are asked questions that confront their beliefs about international relations and foreign policy: What is the greatest threat to world peace? What is the greatest threat to U.S. national security? Should the United States think less in international terms and be more focused on national problems? Assignments to roles can then be based on these classifications, whereby students are either placed in roles that would be consistent with their belief system or where their beliefs would be in conflict with their role.

Upon assignment to a bureaucratic role, students are then presented with a crisis scenario. The scenario is designed to highlight tensions between individual beliefs and role assignments. It can change over time and even involve different countries, depending on the instructor's interests. The original scenario developed for this simulation was based on a crisis in the Philippines. Students are required to write an individual one-page policy statement on how they would respond to the scenario. This compels them to come to the simulation prepared to participate. They are clearly instructed to *not* consult with fellow teammates while preparing their initial statements.

The Scenario

The North Atlantic Treaty Organization (NATO) voted to expand membership in the western alliance to Poland, Hungary, and the Czech Republic after four years of deliberations. The Russian Republic, despite major concessions, announced its opposition to NATO expansion.

Two weeks later, Russia and Belarus announced their unification in a new Russian Union. Russian military units immediately moved into Belarus. Moreover, the Belarusian government declared a state of emergency and began an immediate crackdown on opponents of the unification pact. Opinion polls in Belarus showed that unification with Russia was supported by 72 percent of the people.

The neighbors of the new Russian Union, the Ukraine and Poland, were extremely concerned about what they viewed as a new security threat on their border. These concerns were heightened when over a hundred thousand "ethnic Russians" rallied in Kiev, the Ukrainian capital, demanding that the Ukraine enter the new Russia Union.

Both the Polish and the Ukrainian governments responded to the crisis by requesting new security commitments from the United States. The Ukraine asked to join NATO and requested one billion dollars in U.S. military assistance. Poland asked the United States to station troops on Polish territory, despite earlier U.S. assurances to the Russians that "significant numbers" of NATO troops would not be based in Poland.

At the same time, the new government of the Russian Union requested that the United States increase economic aid to Russia from $95 million a year to $250 million a year. The Russians maintained that their actions in Belarus were legal and did not threaten their neighbors. Moreover, they asked for official diplomatic recognition of the new Russian Union.

The argument for taking firm action is to contain Russia in case it returns to its tradition of expansion. The argument for turning down these requests from Poland and Ukraine is that it will unnecessarily provoke the Russians. After all, the Belarussians willingly joined the Russian Union, and Russia has not threatened any of its neighbors. If the United States overreacts, a new Cold War might result.

Given this scenario of events, students will determine what policies their bureaucratic unit would be most likely to pursue. The most important consideration for all teams is that the present administration remain in control and that their policies be consistent with what is perceived to be its safest course.

Actual play is divided into three half-hour phases:

Phase One: intrabureau negotiation and policy formulation. Students use their policy statement to negotiate a bureau policy. The department head is responsible for arriving at consensus within his/her entity.

Phase Two: intradepartmental negotiations and policy formulation. Each bureaucratic entity is given five minutes to present its policy to the department, and the office of the secretary responds. Debate may ensue between bureaucratic entities within departments, subject to recognition by the secretary's office.

Phase Three: resolution/National Security Council meeting. All participants and teams come together for a National Security Council meeting chaired by the president. The secretaries present their position. The president has the option of calling on bureaus for additional information before deciding on the course of action to follow.

Role Assignments

Depending on the number of students in the class, one or more people may be assigned to each role.

Department of State Team

Secretary of State: The secretary is interested in the whole picture of U.S. foreign policy. In this scenario, that includes maintaining good relations with Eastern European states and in doing everything possible to ensure the security of the Ukraine. At the same time, he or she is concerned about antagonizing Russia and starting a second Cold War. The secretary is also concerned with the reaction of our Western European allies to the crisis.

Undersecretary of State for Security Affairs: The undersecretary is the second in command at the State Department. The primary concern of the undersecretary is the security threat that the Russian Union might pose. He or she will be clearly concerned that Russia might be entering a new period of expansion.

Assistant Secretary of State for Europe: As the title implies, this position is interested in U.S. relations with Europe. One of the primary concerns of this official is our relations with our Western European allies (Great Britain, France, Germany).

United Nations (UN) Ambassador: As the U.S. representative to the world's most important international organization, the UN ambassador is interested in promoting the image of the United States in the world. The UN ambassador will be gravely concerned that the crisis in Eastern Europe could escalate into another Cold War between Russia and the United States, which would in turn paralyze the effectiveness of the UN.

Ambassador to Russia: This ambassador has an overriding interest in promoting close ties between the United States and Russia. He or she will also be concerned with how the current crisis would affect the Russian transition to democracy and capitalism.

Ambassador to Poland: This ambassador's primary interest is in Polish-U.S. ties. His or her objective is to assure that Polish integration into NATO goes smoothly.

Ambassador to Ukraine: This ambassador has a fundamental interest in maintaining U.S.-Ukrainian ties and worries that Ukraine independence is at risk because of the new Russian Union.

Ambassador to NATO: The NATO ambassador is concerned with U.S. relations with our NATO allies and the integrity of the alliance structure. He or she is also anxious about the security threat that the Russian Union might pose and will be clearly concerned that Russia might be entering a new period of expansion.

Department of Defense Team

Secretary of Defense: The secretary's priority is the security of the United States. In the past, he or she has voiced concern about the

U.S. political commitment overextending our armed forces' abilities. How much is enough to protect Poland? the Ukraine? Moreover, the secretary realizes that Congress is in no mood to increase the military budget.

Undersecretary of Defense for Political Affairs: The Eastern Europe crisis raises new concerns about Russia's returning to its tradition of expansion and adventurism. If we are entering a new period of hostile relations between the United States and Russia, what should we do about it?

Chairman of the Joint Chief of Staff: The scenario presents several very important questions for this bureaucratic actor. How many troops will be needed to defend Poland and how will we pay for doing so, given the shrinking defense budget?

Secretary of the Army: This secretary is concerned with the practical aspect of defending Poland with U.S. ground forces. The primary issue will be the safety of any forces the United States sends into the region.

Secretary of the Air Force: The concern here is with the practical aspect of defending U.S. interests in the region with air power. Moreover, the secretary will be very concerned with the cost of the mission during a time of shrinking defense budgets.

Secretary of the Navy: Although not directly involved in the crisis, he or she will be very concerned with the effects of the crisis on the defense budget.

U.S. Commander Europe: The issue here is with the practical problem of defending Europe from forward bases in Poland. This official is critically concerned with the safety of U.S. military personnel in the region. Moreover, he or she must consider how such a defense will affect the U.S. relationship with the European military establishment.

White House Team
President: The crisis presents two major problems for the U.S. president. First, what is best for the security and diplomatic interests of the United States? Second, how is this crisis going to affect his or her public image?

Chief of Staff: The chief of staff is the president's principal adviser. He or she is concerned with the political well-being of the boss and understands that if the president mishandles this crisis, it would not only poison his or her relationship with Congress but destroy him or her politically.

National Security Adviser: The main concern here is doing what is in the best interest of the United States. If the crisis is mishandled, it will lead to a new Cold War. At the same time, the natural security adviser realizes that if the United States reacts weakly, Ukrainian security could be compromised.

Political Adviser: This official is concerned primarily with the political interest of the president. His or her job is to keep the president in office.

Assessment/Debriefing

Following the simulation, a general debriefing is held. Students are asked to prepare an essay for the debriefing that addresses four questions:

1. How did you arrive at your policy position?
2. In the course of the simulation, what happened to your original position?
3. How does your simulation experience relate to the decisionmaking literature in U.S. foreign policy? What is the relationship between role and belief system?
4. What did you learn from the simulation?

In the debriefing discussion led by the instructor, observations are solicited from the students about their experiences. These observations give the instructor an idea of the students' perceptions before the conceptual origins of the simulation are outlined and the belief system classifications are introduced. The hypotheses of the role versus belief are then put forth, and the preliminary results are presented.

The feedback offered during the debriefing and contained within the essays not only illustrates what the students have learned but is educational for the instructor as well. The student essays reveal the simulation's potential as a teaching tool. From an extensive review of student essays, four general themes have emerged. First, students learn to appreciate the complexity of the decisionmaking process. They discard simple metaphors and no longer anthropomorphize the state. Second, there is a growing appreciation that foreign policy formulation involves a large number of actors with diverse interests. The president, the secretary of state, and the national security adviser are all key players, but the decisionmaking process also involves a multiplicity of other actors coming from myriad agencies. Third, students receive an appreciation for the competing interests of bureaucratic entities. They experience firsthand the bureaucratic truism of "where you stand depends on where your sit." Fourth, students also experience firsthand the contrasting nature of role versus belief in their individual decisionmaking.

Some of the brightest students are able to relate the simulation to other classes and life experiences. Students will often find connections with other political science classes, sociology, and psychology. One of the most memorable essays that captures some of the dynamics at work was written by a student from a uniquely California perspective:

> I was sure of disagreement before entering the simulation for the disagreements were rooted in entirely different beliefs. It amazes me that such a similar group of people can be operating individually on such different streams of consciousness. The screaming paranoia of some people was really disturbing. Some people got so into power trips while others sat quietly oblivious to the meaning of it all. It was like a real sociological observation, a real statement about mankind. . . . It seems that man is a basically selfish animal and everyone wants his own way.[9]

The success of "Bureaucratic Bargaining" lies in the relative ease with which it can be used in many classroom contexts and in the enthusiasm with which students participate. It is great fun for both the students and the instructor, as everyone benefits from the increased interaction. Using the simulation can be instrumental in providing a positive active learning environment for all.

Appendix A

The Questionnaire

The questionnaire should be administered prior to role assignment. Numerical values are given for each question response. A score range has been identified for the four belief systems as follows:

Isolationists	10–24
Hard-liners	25–40
Accommodationists	41–55
Internationalists	56–70

Simulation Questionnaire and Key

The following questions explore your views on current issues in American foreign policy. Choose the one answer that best reflects your position on these issues.

1. What is the greatest threat to world peace?
   a. increasing international interdependence (1)
   b. particular leaders (3)
   c. lack of an international body to settle disputes (5)
   d. ideology (7)
2. What is the best way to promote peace?
   a. collective security through alliances (7)
   b. trade, technology cooperation, economic interdependence (5)
   c. military superiority of the U.S. (3)
   d. self-reliance (1)
3. What is the greatest threat to American national security?
   a. economic competition from Japan and Europe (3)
   b. nuclear armaments in the hands of Third World countries (7)
   c. our inability to solve domestic issues (5)
   d. American intervention in conflicts that are none of our business (1)
4. What is your assessment of the Persian Gulf War?
   a. too many Iraqis were killed (5)
   b. it was a great victory for the U.S. (3)
   c. the U.S. spent money abroad that needed to be spent at home (1)
   d. it has given the U.S. leverage in the settlement of other Middle East issues (7)
5. What are the consequences of the post–Cold War era?
   a. greater influence for the UN (5)
   b. the world will become more fragmented and disordered (1)
   c. increasingly countries will have to act together to deter aggression (7)
   d. world affairs have generally remained the same (3)

Identify the extent to which you support the following list of U.S. foreign policy goals. Indicate your level of agreement on the following scale: a. agree strongly; b. agree; c. disagree somewhat; d. disagree strongly.

6. America's conception of its role in international leadership must be scaled down. a. (5), b. (1), c. (7), d. (3)
7. The U.S. should exercise its power internationally to assure stability in world affairs, even at the cost of denying self-determination to some groups. a. (3), b. (7), c. (1), d. (5)
8. The U.S. should think less in international terms and be more focused on national problems. a. (1), b. (3), c. (7), d. (5)
9. Military threats and the use of force are no longer an effective means for coping with international issues. a. (5), b. (1), c. (7), d. (3)

10. Matching Russian military power remains an important foreign policy goal. a. (3), b. (7), c. (1), d. (5)

Notes

1. An earlier version of this simulation appeared in *The Political Science Teacher* (Winter 1988), pp. 6–9, entitled "Bureaucratic Bargaining: An American Foreign Policy Simulation."

2. Graham Allison (1971), *Essence of Decision: Explaining the Cuban Missile Crisis* (Boston: Little, Brown).

3. Alex Mintz (1997), "Foreign Policy Decision Making: Bridging the Gap Between the Cognitive Psychology and Rational Actor Schools," in *Decision Making on War and Peace: The Cognitive-Rational Debate*, ed. Nehemia Geva and Alex Mintz (Boulder: Lynne Rienner), p. 4.

4. Ole R. Holsti and James N. Rosenau (1984), *American Leadership in World Affairs* (London: Allen & Unwin).

5. Alexander George (1980), *Presidential Decisonmaking in Foreign Policy: The Effective Use of Information and Advice* (Boulder, CO: Westview Press); Robert Jervis (1982), *Perception and Misperception in International Politics* (Princeton, NJ: Princeton University Press); Irving L Janis (1982), *Groupthink,* 2d ed. (Boston: Houghton Mifflin).

6. Eugene R. Wittkopf (1990*), Faces of Internationalism: Public Opinion and American Foreign Policy* (Durham, NC: Duke University Press).

7. Ole R. Holsti (1997), "Continuity and Change in the Domestic and Foreign Policy Beliefs of American Opinion Leaders" (prepared for delivery at the annual meeting of the American Political Science Assocation, Washington, DC, August 28–31), p. 15. See also Ole R. Holsti and James N. Rosenau (1993), "The Structure of Foreign Policy Beliefs Among American Opinion Leaders—After the Cold War," *Millennium: Journal of International Studies* 22 (Summer):235–278.

8. It is interesting to note how test runs of the questionnaire at North Carolina State University compared with the 1996 findings of the Foreign Policy Leadership Project. Results from the survey were as follows: isolationist, 10 percent; hard-liners, 13 percent; accommodationists, 48 percent; internationalists, 29 percent (based on Ole Holsti [1997], "Continuity and Change"). In contrast, the findings for thirty-three students in an introductory American government class (Political Science 201, Section 6, North Carolina State University, Fall 1998) were as follows: isolationist, 3 percent; hard-liners, 33 percent; accommodationists, 52 percent; internationalists, 12 percent.

9. Anonymous student, University of Southern California, 1982.

11 | Constructing Effective Systems: Simulating the Paris Peace Conference

Michael McIntyre and Patrick Callahan

If a group of second-year students were given the opportunity to create an international system—a structure for peace, stability, and justice—but to do so while being attentive to the real constraints placed on historical statesmen, what would they produce? Would they do better than the diplomats whose roles they played? What would they learn about the nature of international politics?

In this chapter we describe a role-playing simulation based on the last phase of the Paris Peace Conference, which produced the set of treaties that ended World War I. One group of students represents the German peace delegation; the other plays the Allied and Associated Powers (hereafter, Allies) or, more precisely, the French, British, and United States. The simulation follows the structure of the last phase of the Paris Peace Conference. It begins with the Allies presenting the draft treaty to the Germans. The Germans then are given a fixed time to prepare a written response, to which the Allies will respond in a final offer, a definitive draft of the treaty, presented on a take-it-or-leave-it basis.

Following history, the Allies and the Germans do not have face-to-face negotiations. Instead, they separately prepare formal written communications. In addition to researching the positions taken by the principals in Paris, the students have to assess what relative priority should be assigned to the various interests and principles, which demands are likely to be acceptable to the other side and which ones are nonnegotiable, and what the underlying realities of power and bargaining leverage are.

Educational Objectives

We designed the simulation to attain several ends. First, we wanted the students to become emotionally and intellectually engaged in the subject matter. Engaged students, we reasoned, would goad themselves into making a greater effort than they would otherwise. Indeed, they would work harder than they would have simply under the prod of the grading system. Having decided to use a role-playing simulation as a "hook" to engage student interest, we turned to the task of deciding what to simulate. That decision was also driven by our objectives, of which the second was to draw the students' attention to fundamental characteristics of international systems and world politics. This concern motivated us to abandon the simulations we had previously developed for the course, which tended to emphasize either bargaining techniques or acquisition of substantive expertise about a particular problem (e.g., nuclear proliferation) or group of countries (e.g., India and its neighbors). Rather, we wanted the students to learn about the nature, sources, and uses of power in world politics; about the complexity and interrelatedness of problems; about the constraints under which diplomats and foreign policy makers operate, especially those constraints emanating from domestic politics and from the limits of time, patience, and human endurance; and about the tensions that arise between ethical and emotional impulses and the imperatives of hard political realities. In order to achieve this goal, we decided to simulate the process of constructing an international system after the previously functioning international system had failed and disappeared.

Third, we wanted the simulation to lead to the reading of serious works of political theory. One of our core course objectives was to develop analytical reading skills. We attached ourselves to that purpose because of our dismay at the weak reading skills of students who are comparatively bright and otherwise well prepared. The reading of too many textbooks, we surmised, had stunted their critical reading skills.

Fourth, we wanted the students to work with primary historical documents. We wanted them to learn something about history, always a good thing, but in such a way as to alert them to the possibility of doing original research rather than relying on others' interpretations of what has happened.

Design Parameters

Our educational objectives led us to the Paris Peace Conference of 1919. The decision to simulate the establishment of an international system gave us three options: the Congress of Vienna, the Paris Conference, and the series of conferences that established the political arrangements following World War II. Of the three, Paris seemed to provide the most attractive fit with our objectives. First, it seemed the most likely to engage the students emotionally. The Paris Peace Conference was a mother lode of dilemmas and conflicts over the design of an effective international system. Among the prominent issues were the structure of the League of Nations and, even more important, the extent to which the League would supplant traditional mechanisms for assuring national security; the role of great powers in determining the rules of international affairs; the role of law and morality in world politics; the status of empires; the criteria for determining the territory of new nations; and the principles of international economics. Here was real meat into which the students could sink their teeth! Moreover, because the German delegation in Paris was not treated as an equal power, Paris raises the question of how defeated powers are to be treated. Finally, unlike Vienna and the 1940s conferences, Paris failed, spectacularly. Figuring out why it failed, and whether failure could have been avoided, promised to be an intriguing intellectual puzzle that would engage students' interest.

The Paris Peace Conference also seemed ideal for meeting the second objective, that the simulation address questions of international system structure. Two important questions of system structure arose in Paris. First, would peace be maintained by the balance of power or by the League of Nations? Second, what would be Germany's place in the postwar world? We chose to focus on the latter, for which we see three primary answers. One, a second image interpretation,[1] contends that the guarantee of Germany's peaceful place in the system is the survival of the Weimar Republic. A second answer posits that Germany must be restored to its place as a key player in the European balance of power. The third seeks to permanently remove the German threat by destroying the country as a major power.

The third objective—that the simulation foster the reading of serious works of political theory—also was easily met with the Paris Peace Conference. The dramatic failure of the interwar system called for classic analyses. We were originally drawn to two that offer quite different explanations. Karl Polanyi's *The Great Transformation* locates the cause of the failure in the incompatibility of liberal economic systems, especially the gold standard, with the demands for social protection against the disruption produced by free markets.[2] E. H. Carr's *The Twenty Year's Crisis* attributes the failure to the utopianism of Woodrow Wilson and his acolytes, to their naive dismissal of considerations of power in international politics.[3] In our second iteration of the simulation, we substituted J. M. Keynes's *The Economic Consequences of the Peace* for Polanyi,[4] given Polanyi's inaccessibility to those not acquainted with nineteenth-century economic history.

Likewise, there is a substantial volume of primary documents pertaining to the Paris Peace Conference. These include official documents generated in preparation for or at the conference, the transcriptions of the minutes taken by the official interpreter at the deliberations of the Council of Four, documents produced for an inquiry into the war by two committees of the German National Constituent Assembly, memoirs of participants, and contemporary histories.[5]

Finally, one additional quality made the Paris Peace Conference an attractive event to simulate. Its last phase, which began with formal statements by German foreign minister Brockdorff-Rantzau and French premier Georges Clemenceau and the presentation of the draft treaty to the Germans, took seven weeks, a length fully consistent with the ten-week quarter system used at DePaul University. This offered the opportunity of simulating a negotiation in something like real time, giving the participants a sense of the pressures of time.

Several other factors shaped the design of the simulation. First, we teach concurrent sections of the same course as part of a sophomore-level core sequence in the International Studies program. That provides a convenient way of dividing the students into the two basic sides, facilitates the development of identities, and inhibits spoken communications across delegations. Second, the enrollment is restricted to International Studies majors and minors. That mitigates the problem of motivating the unmotivated student. It also increases the stability of the class roster after the first day or so of class, thereby reducing the difficulty of assigning roles. Third, many DePaul University students must work or commute, making group meetings outside of class difficult. As a result, a substantial portion of group work would have to be done during designated class sessions or by electronic communication.

One final design consideration was the need to reduce the complexity of the historical event to manageable dimensions. This was primarily a matter of number of issues and number of actors. We simplified reality first by restricting the number of issues to four: the League of Nations (Part I of the Versailles Treaty), economics and reparations (Parts VIII–IX), military, naval, and aerial (Parts V, VI, XIV), and boundaries and political questions (Parts II–IV, VII). In the second year we dropped the League of Nations, because it had failed to catalyze negotiations or to affect deliberations on the other issues. In its place, we divided boundary and political questions into those concerning the eastern and western parts of Europe, in order to render that set of issues more manageable. Second, we decided to assign students to expert committees, each committee concentrating on one set of issues. That served to reduce the research demands to a more manageable level. Third, we reduced the number of actors on the Allied side to the three main powers: France, the United Kingdom, and the United States.

Procedures

In preparation for the simulation, we place primary source documents on reserve. We also generate a packet of photocopied materials for all students. The packets include documents that all are to be familiar with: Wilson's "Fourteen Points" speech of January 8, 1918; his subsequent elaborations of February 11, July 4, and September 27; and the parts of the draft treaty under review in the simulation. We finally set up a hypernews (a kind of dedicated listserv) for electronic communication immediately accessible to all members of the class.

Our practice is to ascertain student interest regarding expert committee assignments (and, in the case of the Allies, the country to be represented) and to base role assignments largely but not entirely on those preferences. An intractable problem is the designation of leading negotiators: Clemenceau, Lloyd George, Wilson, and Brockdorff-Rantzau.[6] Our procedure of asking for volunteers in the first week of class has not always placed those roles in the hands of the most able folks.

To provide the students with a sense of the immediate historical context, we begin the course with three days of lectures on the Great War. The first lecture emphasizes the genesis of the war and the alternative interpretations of responsibility that can be derived from the historical record. The second lecture describes the fighting itself—trench warfare, submarine attacks, the naval blockade, and such dubious innovations as gas attacks and aerial bombing of cities—and the material consequences of the war: the stupendous number of casualties, the impoverishment of societies, the toll from hunger and illness. The third lecture reviews the end of the war—Germany's desperate last offensive, the collapse of its army, its isolation as its allies surrendered—and the diplomacy that led to the armistice. This lecture seeks to inform the students of the postarmistice balance of military power and the diplomatic commitments that set the context for the subsequent negotiations.

Early in the second week of class, students submit their first writing assignment, a "projection" paper. In this paper students are asked to state detailed and realistic goals for the simulation, based on their reading of the armistice agreement, the draft treaty, and the relevant portions of the final Treaty of Versailles. In addition to providing an incentive to begin working and a safeguard against free riders, the projection papers are used at the end of the simulation. In their reaction papers the students compare what they actually achieved with what they hoped to achieve and explain the differences.

The schedule of activities is designed to mimic the timing of the actual historical event. In the second week of class (the fifth day of a three-day-per-week, one-hour-per-session schedule), the German delegates discuss the arguments and demands that should be emphasized when addressing the Allies. The student playing Brockdorff-Rantzau works those into an address presented to the Allied representatives at the end of the week. At the next class session, the student playing Clemenceau offers the Allied response, drawing heavily on Clemenceau's address in Paris. Subsequent simulation activities follow according to the schedule in Table 11.1.

Following the modus operandi adopted in Paris, our students are instructed not to negotiate face-to-face. Instead, all communications are to be written and distributed electronically. Expert committees meet during class time to write formal communications. Intercommittee conflicts are reconciled in two ways: the German delegation meets as a whole; the heads of state of the Allies meet as a drafting committee.

We require attendance on days reserved for simulation sessions. On these days, the expert committees meet without either a chair or an established agenda. We circulate among the committees to observe their progress and to intervene if needed to keep the committees from going terribly off track. In general, though, we choose to

Table 11.1   Schedule of Class Activities During Simulation Exercise

Session	German Activities	Allied Activities
1–3	Expert committee deliberations; Clemenceau speech	Discussion of Keynes, Ch. 1–4; Brockdorff-Rantzau speech
4–6	Discussion of Keynes, Ch. 1–2; expert committee deliberations	Discussion of Keynes, Ch. 5
7–9	Discussion of Keynes, Ch. 3–5; expert committee deliberations	Discussion of Keynes, Ch. 6–7
10–12	Discussion of Keynes, Ch. 6–7; deliberation of entire delegation to reconcile contradictions among committee proposals and finalize counterproposals	Discussion of Carr, Ch. 1–6; discussion of communications with German delegation in anticipation of German counterproposal
13–15	Discussion of Carr, Ch. 1–6	Discussion of German counterproposals
16–18	Discussion of Carr, Ch. 7–8; expert committee deliberations	Discussion of Carr, Ch. 7–9; expert committee deliberations
19–21	Discussion of Carr, Ch. 9; expert committee deliberations	Discussion of Carr, Ch. 10–14
22–23	Discussion of Carr, Ch. 10–12; expert committee deliberations	Expert committees finalize and deliver final proposals to drafting committee
24-25	Discussion of Carr, Ch. 13–14; expert committee deliberations	Final proposal approved and sent to Germans
26-27	Discussion of Allies' final proposal and decision about whether to sign; debriefing	Reception and discussion of German response; debriefing

err on the side of granting the students leeway rather than guidance. Each week, a brief report on the previous week's accomplishments is submitted in writing and summarized for the class. A member of the committee writes reports on a rotating basis.

At the conclusion of the simulation, the students submit their reaction papers, which serve as the basis for the subsequent debriefing discussion. That leads to the final and major writing assignment, the evaluation paper. This paper, which also serves as the final examination, requires the students to integrate the experience from the simulation with the interpretations presented by Keynes and Carr in order to display what they have learned about the difficulties in crafting a durable peace. They are to address at least two issues: (1) what portions of the treaty were most responsible for the breakdown of the peace in 1939, and (2) why the authors of the treaty produced such a flawed document. They are instructed to assess at some length the merits of explanations found in the readings, in addition to analyzing the roadblocks in their attempts to improve the treaty and how those roadblocks corresponded to actual historical constraints.

Assessment and Debriefing

We have successfully used this simulation twice, in 1997 and 1998. Certainly it needs improvement, but it seems to merit further development. The evidence of its success is threefold: It is open to diverse outcomes; it engages the students emotionally; and it results in the students' learning quite a bit about the historical event of the Paris negotiations and about the basic nature of international politics.

First, the simulation is open to diverse outcomes. Although the students have the historical outcome at their disposal, they have not felt constrained to seek to reproduce the right result. The two runs of the simulation yielded starkly different outcomes. In 1997, the two sides persisted in bluffing each other until the last minute, neither willing to give way. Finally the Allies accepted a kinder, gentler Treaty of Versailles. Their concessions included immediate German membership in the League of Nations; German and Austrian negotiation of a separate treaty determining their future relationship, subject to approval by the League; a plebiscite by the peoples of the Czecho-Slovak region to determine whether they would opt for independence or union with Germany; establishment of a $50 billion upper limit on reparations that, though quite high, would bound the German liability; establishment of a multiparty committee to set reparations charges, the committee to consist of equal numbers of representatives from the Allies, the Germans, and neutral parties; removal of interest charges on the reparations bill; and crediting losses of colonies against the reparations bill. Moreover, the Allies softened their military strategy to promote diplomatic purposes, spontaneously calling off the naval blockade and trade embargo on Germany, both as a humanitarian deed and to signal their intention to be reasonable. Later, during the endgame, they threatened to reinstate the blockade and to occupy Germany unless the Germans abandoned their foot-dragging on what the Allies considered to be minor points on the issue of reparations.

In 1998, the simulation amended the draft treaty to make it even harsher than was the Treaty of Versailles. The Germans adopted an accommodating strategy off the bat, accepting many of the original elements in the draft treaty: all the provisions regarding boundary and territorial matters in the west, including the transfer of Alsace-Lorraine and loss of control over the Saar Basin and its coal resources; disarmament, with only minor amendments to allow the state sufficient forces to maintain internal order and to cope with potential aggression from the Soviet Union; responsibility for the war; and the loss of prewar territory to Poland in areas where Poles constituted a majority of the population. Their demands for amendments grew from two main concerns: that the territorial modifications comply with the principle of self-determination and that the economic and reparations conditions be reasonable and feasible.

Under the influence of Keynes, the Allies tempered the economic provisions while keeping to Clemenceau's vision of a Carthaginian Peace as the solution to the German threat. To balance the more generous economic and reparations provisions, they demanded increasingly draconian boundary and political adjustments. In addition to gaining Alsace-Lorraine, France gained the Saar Basin and the Rhineland, Poland gained all of Silesia, East Prussia was partitioned from Germany and established as a sovereign state, and a commission of the Allies was to be authorized to censor all German propaganda regarding the war until 1944. The Germans refused to sign a document carrying those provisions. The refusal led the Allies to decide to invade and occupy Germany, partition it into sixteen states whose boundaries would be decided later, and impose democratic governments.

The second basis for a favorable assessment of the simulation is that it evokes a high level of student involvement. Although a few students were too lazy or too cool to engage substantially in the exercise, most got taken up in it. They bought into their roles, did substantial research, and participated actively in the discussions in expert committees and plenary sessions. This comment from one student's reaction paper illustrates the point:

> The most interesting aspect of the structure of negotiations is how, even in a class safe in a university, people can get swept up in a wave of self-righteous indignation. I think that we as a class, as well as the original negotiators, looked at our own losses as well as those of our neighbors, placed the blame on Germany's shoulders, and decided to make them pay for it. We all read Keynes and saw that we could not demand lots of money from Germany. This was

simply changed in the acquisition of land. The basic mood of what existed in the original negotiations was felt in the class as well, an attitude of me first. The idea [was] that our own countries were so devastated and in debt, and the quickest and easiest way out was to take from Germany. We did not think in terms of what would be best for Europe as a whole. We looked at others taking things from Germany and scrambled to get our piece of the pie.

Indeed, in both years, we have had to deal with some psychological and emotional fallout. In 1997, the Germans, perceiving the Allies as having done too little work, became angry when they received brief answers to their proposals. (Interestingly, the Germans had the same impression in 1998. Although we cannot rule out coincidence, we will have to examine whether something in the structure of the simulation induces this perception.) The Allies, in turn, were hurt by what they considered an unfair indictment and placed the blame on chaos in the German delegation that resulted in tardy, contradictory, or vague documents to which they were expected to formulate useful responses. Adding to the distress were perceptions that the students in one section were receiving more faculty guidance than were the students in the other.

An especially important ground for satisfaction with the simulation has been the third indicator of success: the evidence that the students seem to gain an appreciation for several aspects of world politics. They certainly leave the process with an appreciation for the role of power. When explaining the outcome of the simulation, just over half the students explicitly recognized that the result of the negotiation mirrored the power relationships of the parties. One participant commented:

> What I could learn . . . is that the stronger will use their power to take advantage of the weaker and will act on behalf of their vengeful feelings instead of listening to the voice of reason. . . . International order is not fair. Those with power act as if their power will last forever, not taking into consideration how their decisions will affect the world balance.

Another observed:

> That realization [that the Allies were in power] curbed our desires for being able to get all that we wanted. The basic fact that we were in no position to demand, since we were the losers and the Allied Powers were the winners and had the upper hand, was very limiting.

Students commented not only on the crude bargaining leverage between the two sides but also on the impact of power on the dynamics of the simulation. One student commented on "the effect that power played in the communications between the two forces. With such capacities that the Allies maintained, they did not feel it necessary to discuss anything with the Germans. They would present the terms to us, and we had no choice but to accept them." Another student noted the impact that expert knowledge had on deliberations in the military/naval/aerial committee:

> [T]he simulation process taught me something about the distribution of power and how it affects what we proposed. For example, within the military group, it was obvious that some members had more knowledge and experience dealing with military issues. This knowledge gave them an advantage and thus, I feel they had a bit more power.

Students also showed an awareness of the relationship between power and security. This awareness is illustrated most impressively in the ruminations of a student of Polish descent (a most relevant demographic fact, we have discovered), who stated the case with chilling concision:

> As a French delegate, my intentions were to secure Europe from any future German attacks. . . . I found cession of German territories as a perfect resolution to the problem. . . . [I]t would bring world security as Germany would be forced to reduce its power through reduction of its capital. Since Germany's economy would be weakened, that would affect its politics, military forces, and other branches of government. . . . Reducing Germany would be a major step toward a secure future.

We also have seen evidence of learning about the motivations of states. Although many students explained the outcome of the simulation in fairly banal terms (the negotiations failed because the Allies did not enter them with a spirit of compromise but instead were moved by powerful, destructive emotions), others offered strategic reasons why the Allies were not in a compromising mood. One German delegate wrote: "They knew that they were right and that Germany had to pay for their actions and had to be dealt with in a manner to keep this type of aggression from happening in the future." Another commented: "[T]he Allied and Associated powers were set on making sure that Germany would not be a major power in Europe or the world again. They feared Germany. There was so much animosity between Germany and the Allied and Associated powers that a fair treaty would have almost been impossible." Yet another student came up with an interesting interpretation of how the Allies and the Germans were situated so as to lead to different definitions of the situation:

> We, being assigned as Germans, were forced to look at the situation in an entirely different way [than the standard history textbook treatment of blaming the Germans]. It is true that committees in the other class were representative of several different countries, but they were nonetheless at a vantage point which pointed the finger at Germany, rather than taking account that Germany has also suffered and also needs to recover from the devastation of war.

We also found substantial indication of student attention to the complexities and difficulties of international negotiations. One of their primary experiences has been cross-cutting cleavages. There have been clashes between committees, such as those over whether territorial concessions should be traded off for concessions on reparations payments. On the Allied side, there have been splits between the head of state and the rest of the delegation—in 1998, the rest of the U.S. delegation rejected Wilson's last-minute concessions to Clemenceau and Lloyd George, to no avail, and in 1997 the French delegation was stunned by Clemenceau's empathic capacity. There have also been fights among the different Allied powers. Students come to see very clearly the conflicting interests of the French, British, and U.S. sides. Moreover, some have interesting insights about the effects of such cleavages on multilateral diplomacy. One argued that they made diplomacy harsher:

> [The Allies] were out for individual goals and dictated terms that were favorable to them as individual states. This most likely made the treaty more vindictive because, if the groups could not agree on the issues that the Germans submitted for consideration, it would have been easier just to ignore them and come up with issues they could agree on.

Many students showed considerable attention to the structure of the simulation, especially how the lack of face-to-face communication degraded the chances of successful bargaining. One noted that the "lack of physical interaction between the two sides merely encouraged hostilities and presupposed notions of the other's identity and motives," and followed up by saying that "the presupposed notions were translated into our more daring propositions. One member of the Committee was sure that the Allied and Associated Powers would reject everything we were asking and in this light, decided to demand more, as a matter of pride." Another observed that "it is a simple matter to ignore morality if the victim is not seen as having a human face."

One last facet of student awareness of the difficulties of international negotiation is the impact of domestic politics. Students have not commented on the constraining effects of domestic politics as much as we had expected, however. This is probably because domestic considerations can enter into the simulation only implicitly, whereas international considerations are an explicit part of the model.

Summary and Conclusion

For two years we have used a simulation of the last stage of the Paris Peace Conference of 1919 in our core International Studies course. The simulation seems to have been successful in meeting several of our objectives: The students have found it a fascinating, enjoyable, and often frustrating exercise; they have done considerable independent reading and learned a lot about European diplomatic and political history in the first part of this century; and they have been sensitized to a variety of characteristics of world politics.

Not everything, however, has worked out as we had planned. Three deficiencies stand out. First, although students have readily grasped the importance of Keynes's work for the simulation, most have not made similar connections for Carr or Polanyi. Second, student performance is terribly uneven. Although many students learn much and form sharp interpretations, others never move beyond a focus on classroom personalities or group interaction, despite our clear instructions to the contrary, and fail even to try to engage with the historical materials. Third, we have not been as successful as we would like in redirecting the class back to the original question: what would be required to establish a just, orderly, and effective international system. Ideally, we would devote more time to careful and extended debriefing. Practically, however, we have almost no additional time to use, given that our university operates on a ten-week quarter system. How to overcome that difficulty remains the most fundamental challenge for further development of this learning exercise.

Notes

1. K. N. Waltz (1954), *Man, the State and War: A Theoretical Analysis* (New York: Columbia University Press).

2. K. Polanyi (1944), *The Great Transformation: The Political and Economic Origins of Our Time* (Boston: Beacon Press).

3. E. H. Carr (1939), *The Twenty Years' Crisis, 1919–1939: An Introduction to the Study of International Relations* (New York: St. Martin's Press).

4. J. M. Keynes (1920), *The Economic Consequences of the Peace* (New York: Harcourt, Brace and Howe).

5. A. Luckau (1941), *The German Delegation at the Paris Peace Conference* (New York: Columbia University Press); K. F. Nowak (1929), *Versailles,* English ed. (New York: Payser and Clarke); *Official German Documents Relating to the World War* (1923), translated under the supervision of the Carnegie Endowment for International Peace, Division of International Law (New York: Oxford University Press); A. Tardieu (1921), *The Truth About the Treaty* (Indianapolis, IN: Bobbs-Merrill); U.S. Department of State (1942), *Papers Relating to the Foreign Relations of the United States: The Paris Peace Conference, 1919* (Washington, DC: U.S. Government Printing Office); B. Baruch (1920), *The Making of the Reparation and Economic Sections of the Treaty* (New York: Harper and Bros.); E. M. House and C. Seymour, eds. (1921), *What Really Happened at Paris: The Story of the Paris Peace Conference, 1918–1919, by American Delegates* (New York: C. Scribner's Sons); R. Lansing (1921), *The Peace Negotiations: A Personal Narrative* (Boston: Houghton, Mifflin); A. S. Link, trans. and ed. (1922), *Deliberations of the Council of Four (March 24–June 28, 1919); Notes of the Official Interpreter, Paul Mantoux* (Princeton: Princeton University Press).

6. D. Lloyd George (1939). *Memoirs of the Paris Peace Conference* (New Haven, CT: Yale University Press).

Part 3 | TECHNOLOGY IN THE CLASSROOM

12 | Creating Active Learning Spaces in the Digital Age

Lev Gonick

Not so long ago, if you asked "What major event took place in the summer of 1969?" during a lecture in an Introduction to World Politics course, the answer was simple. There you were, in the middle of an engaging series of exchanges with your students, highlighting the linkages between science and technology and the arms race, and the answer was, of course, "Woodstock." Well, actually the answer you were looking for was the first landing on the moon during the famed month of August. Woodstock was, at best, part of another discussion on domestic influences on foreign policy issues and the war in Vietnam.

During a more recent class exchange, perhaps you posed the question "What major event took place in the summer of 1989?" In the context of a discussion on science and technology and the arms race, you might have expected to hear about Tiananmen Square, the collapse of the Soviet centralized state, the popular uprisings in Eastern Europe, and the beginning of the end of the Cold War. Those events from that summer, not so long ago, have been seared into the minds of many of us who are now instructors. In retrospect, however, it should not have been surprising that you were met with a deafening silence. Of course, 1989 was a very long time ago for our students. Most have no consciousness of those events in their preteen years. After what may have seemed an eternity, a guy in the corner fidgeting with his headphones tentatively raised his hand. "The big event," he announced, "was the commercial birth of the Internet."

Immediately, the class broke out in a collective sense of affirma-

169

tion. "Why, of course," announced another student spontaneously and with considerable confidence. "We think of the Internet as something that was developed in the '90s but it was actually an '80s invention!" Light bulbs were going off everywhere in the classroom. At that moment you were wondering how to turn this discussion into a lecture on glasnost, the antinuke movement in Europe, and the breakdown of the bipolar world. These were, after all, the key concepts and constructs of the discipline. The Internet was, at best, part of another discussion on the growing influence of technology on domestic policy issues and human rights issues in China.

And then it became clear. Both Woodstock and the Internet were the right answers to the questions about the significance of the summers of 1969 and 1989. These were developments that expressed the zeitgeist of an age. The first step on the moon was, relatively speaking, little more than one small step for humankind. The landing of the first men on the moon was a motif that helped to describe and even reinforce the idea that the "real" world of the 1960s was best understood in terms of states, presidents, power struggles, and the war of ideology linked to, and oftentimes informing, the pursuits of science and technology.

Faculty use events such as the Cuban missile crisis or the landing on the moon to help students develop both the context and the analytical tools for understanding the world around them. Dismissing the answer "Woodstock" effectively reflected a value proposition on the faculty member's part about what context, what framing issues, and what core concepts were important to making sense of the world. In the end, and with considerable hindsight, by the time we began teaching about the summer of 1969 in the 1970s and 1980s, we had reconstructed the meaning and importance of those events to suit the analytical frameworks we were trying to advance. In Popperian terms, while data were following theory, theory was actually constraining our read of the data.[1]

Is it possible to imagine that the half-baked (and only partially correct) student response regarding the summer of 1989 was close to some truth? Oftentimes faculty, fretting on how to bring the discussion around to the "real" events of 1989, do not have enough good sense to let the students try to explain their answers. Only recently, after having a chance to give a number of talks and facilitate discussions on "technology and its discontents," is the answer becoming clearer to me. Technology and its discontents, of course, is a play on Sigmund Freud's last major and most sweeping contribution, *Civilization and Its Discontents*.[2] Freud explained technology's dualism and dynamic. On the one hand, technology was one of the great "civilizing" tendencies in a world largely dominated by self-centered, selfish, egotistical men. On the other hand, Freud contended that the technological and scientific revolution had rendered humans "prosthetic gods" as we mastered science and as technology became ubiquitous and omnipotent. The dialectics of Freud's analysis—a term that has lost all fashion—is of considerable value to understanding the worth of the Internet. At the same time, the growing sense of "surplus powerlessness"[3] that we now experience on a daily basis necessarily tells us something about the general malaise and paralysis of our discipline. Ultimately, the answer to the question "What major event took place in the summer of 1989?" might be "the Internet" and not the end of the framework of superpower politics.

The medium of technology itself is part of the new narrative just as the old medium was a structural element of the dominant ideas that defined the discipline until recently. Hierarchy, bounded rationality, linear reasoning, and the dominance of a single narrative describe the vocation of the traditional instructional environment as much as they do the traditional discipline of international relations. The new technology is a contributing factor to the most substantial challenge to the hierarchy, bounded rationality, and linear reasoning that characterizes the modern era. Indeed, the new technology is a product, perhaps even the logical product, of the scientific era. It is ironic indeed that computer technology—the very essence of science, progress, and rational reasoning—now stands as one of the greatest challenges to the very milieu that nurtured its historic development. In the next section, I review the most significant differentiations associated with emerging technologies and explore their connection to the teaching of world politics.

The Internet as a Paradigm Shift in Pedagogy: Hypertextuality

How do we know what we know? Over the millennia, recorded human history has fallen victim to the limits of technology to record, by and large, linear representations of complex and multidimensional realities. The medium of course is the written word recorded on parchments (whether animal skins or paper). Philosophers of science typically associate the dominance of linear reasoning in Western thought and practice with Cartesian logic. Over the centuries our ability to afford the reader an active opportunity to explore commentary and secondary analysis has been highly restricted. Conventions like footnotes and endnotes are simple, awkward representations and relatively ineffective in providing a method for representing opportunities for discovery.

Embedded in this deep cultural practice is a conception of space and time that anthropologists call "monochronic time"—a course of reasoning that is governed by the linear and direct movement from point A to point B. Monochronic concepts of time and space are typically distinguished from non-Western cultural traditions known as polychronic. Not only our concepts of hierarchy, power, and authority have been deeply impacted by monochronic thinking but also the Western concepts of economic transactions, the logic of the market, and very basic cultural practices.

Textbooks in international affairs, for example, are typically bounded by monochronic reasoning matched only by detective books in terms of the tyranny of the author and linear reasoning. All the complexities of the world and human societies are distilled into analytical frameworks, key categories, and concepts and are turned into restricted lenses through which we are taught to see the world. The very basic issue of English language composition classes is informed by a logic that implies that in order to communicate effectively one has to learn a bounded form of communication largely determined and delimited by the medium.

Hyperlinks on the Internet have had the messy effect of challenging all of those realities. Learning in a hypermedia world is now, more than ever before, the challenge and the responsibility of the learner. The opportunity to discover and to experience the meaning of serendipity and the "a-ha" factor that we used to tell students about when referring to the wonderful experience of scanning the old dusty shelves in the library stacks is more readily available than ever before. Hyperlinks allow the author to create a gateway through which the reader is invited to join new avenues of discovery and insight. Hyperlinks have created a technological bridge joining the monochronic world of the West to the polychronic world of the rest. Multimedia make learning come alive for students challenged by limited proficiencies in written and oral traditions. Multimedia (pictures, sounds, video, music, virtual reality, and even smells) are actually more directly linked to our most acute senses associated with long-term knowledge acquisition. This is helpful on the receptive side of acquiring experience, and in addition the ability to express understanding, insights, and analytical complexities through multimedia has afforded many students with opportunities to develop critical and creative skills that would simply not have been possible if they were limited to written essays and term papers.

Multimedia technology allows students to compile group projects with sound tracks, photographs, and even historical footage on political and historic events. Web browsers bring color pictures, graphs, charts, and even audio files of speeches and music to the Internet. Student authoring on the Web is supported by collaboration, hyperlinks, ease and frequency of feedback, access to learning, and an insatiable commitment on the part of the students to becoming involved in their subject matter. Learning becomes playing, and in turn playing becomes the key factor in fostering a commitment to lifelong learning and an excitement around ideas, people, and the making of history.

In essence, Net technologies advance five key factors that differentiate the new learning era. First, the multisensory nature of the multimedia environment appeals to a broader cross section of learners and calls upon more acute senses than the traditional learning environment. Second, hypertextuality represents the breaking of the linear narrative. Links to footnotes, endnotes, and what the author takes to be a parenthetic insight can be transformed by the learner into a moment, indeed a lifetime, of discovery. The breaking of the tyranny of the author places the burden of learning in a different light than the traditional text. Learners directed to critical analysis and constructivist educational opportunity will seize the opportunities associated with hyperlinks and be richer for the experience. Those less adventurous will continue to be enlightened by the narrative prepared and directed by the author.

Third, the promise of anytime, anywhere asynchronous learning challenges many of the traditional assumptions on how and where learning takes place. Flexibility, convenience, and access to the marketplace of higher education are enabled by the technology. There are tradeoffs associated with the new technology, and the impact in terms of our conceptions of time and space is challenged in fundamental ways.

Fourth, the new technology is, at its core, interactive and largely blind to hierarchy. This creates challenges in the identity and role of the instructor. Students with an active interest in the subject matter can always come more prepared with the most current news than even the most learned scholar. The Net-savvy student learner can almost always extend contemporary case analysis of events in conflict areas, international trade negotiations, or environmental debates.

Truths can and are being challenged by students on a regular basis. Interpretations and analyses of subject matter associated with Professor Smith at AnyCollege USA can be mediated through direct contact between the student and the primary source. Many faculty will have experienced, or are likely to experience in the future, the argument from a savvy student, "After our discussion in seminar yesterday I found and e-mailed Professor Smith from AnyCollege USA and shared my interpretation of his path-breaking work. Here is his response confirming that my analysis was more consistent with his reasoning than the one you suggested yesterday in seminar."

Finally, the very anatomy of the new technology, oftentimes referred to in communication theory literature as "packet switching," is based on the distribution of a message without the need to be directly linked to a messenger. The implications of bouncing or forwarding messages without attribution of authorship are profound in terms of how we communicate and how power flows from those patterns of communication. For those who have used technology in their class, or used e-mail in the course of their daily scholarly research, power and authority have become contested, and our ability to use the new communication structures is both potent and challenging long-held patterns of decisionmaking and processes and norms of our lives.

The central question that needs to be asked is that of how technology can be leveraged to enable best practice in the learning spaces we create, either face-to-face or in cyberspace.

Using Technology as a Lever: Implementing the Principles of Good Undergraduate Teaching Practices

Chickering and Gamson have identified several principles that support good undergraduate teaching practices.[4] In sum, these include increasing student-faculty contact, facilitating cooperation among students, providing prompt feedback to students, emphasizing time on task, communicating high expectations, promoting active learning environments, and, in general, respecting students' diverse talents and ways of learning. These principles not only challenge pedagogical methodology, they ultimately impact the ontology of the international affairs subject matter. Using technology as a lever to realize and even extend best teaching practices has been at the core of many academic and administrative efforts for more than a decade.

Increasing Student-Faculty Contact

The traditional Introduction to International Affairs course is among the larger course offerings in most political science departments. Strategies for combating large-class-size disenfranchisement, alienation, and passive learning environments have been among the major challenges of the active learning community. Although there is something romantic and nostalgic about the fabled priestly environment of one-on-one learning, we continue to strive to reduce classroom size as the sine qua non of learning. Online experiences designed for large classes have allowed greater intellectual contact between faculty and students. Threaded discussions, chat rooms, and e-mail have increased student-faculty interactions. Indeed, both faculty and student alike typically remark that faculty access online surpasses the experience in the lecture hall and faculty office hours. It becomes important, however, to realize that faculty-student contact, though necessary, is not a sufficient condition for enabling good learning. The reality is more muddled.

There is no guarantee that the typical structures that support student-faculty experiences, either online or in class, create positive learning outcomes. What needs to be challenged is the deeply structured view that learning occurs when faculty deposits knowledge into the students' open minds. Most of us learned our subject matter when we were challenged to teach it in front of others. The reality is, however, that we cannot expect to teach anyone anything more than what we ourselves experienced as students. This is a disconcerting admission and challenges some of the core values of academe and our professional lives.

The explosion of access to information has challenged the most basic nature of communication and interaction at the university. The organizing principle for routing traffic in the learning environment has been transformed. Learning from the beginning of time has been of the form known as route directing (I talk to you, she broadcasts to us, "turn taking"). The Net, due to its origins in the script writing of a postnuclear world, was in its very design based on no organization. The message keeps its own gate, is route oblivious, carries its own homing device. The new anatomy of communications architecture contributes to the loss of central control and hierarchical decision-making and authority. This was the central design feature of the Net, a message without a messenger, power without an originating intent to be powerful, influence without an explicit effort to be the influencer. In addition, hyperlinks challenge everything from how to prepare students for writing assignments (perhaps learning to write hypertext-marked-up essays on the World Wide Web?) to the growing reality that access to hyperlinks avails most students equal or even advantaged access to the most important scientific, economic, and political information upon which the professor asserts authority as "expert."

Decisionmakers in the most senior positions in the institution are now accessible in a manner that redefines their ability to make autonomous decisions. In the online classroom, it is very easy for the faculty member to experience "death of the author." Your voice, attached to your message to the class, carries no authority beyond the quality of the message. There is little ability to communicate body language and limited opportunity to actively pursue working on the guilt associated with pulling out answers from students. No longer do classes start when the faculty member walks into the room, quickly establishing new norms, rules, and principles for interaction and etiquette.

Hierarchy, power, and authority are the reinforcing concepts that inform both the subject matter of traditional international affairs and the very structuring of the traditional environment (the classroom) within which we learn about the questions that matter. The implications of technology are not insignificant for either student or instructor. The decline of the presidency, of centralized power in general, the tensions between fragmentation and growing vulnerability to anarchy, and the logic of global capital are mirrored in the daily lives of faculty and students. The same technology and its associated impulses have challenged our own authority in the classroom, and we find ourselves caught between professional practice without rules (the equivalent of fragmentation and growing anarchy) and the assertion of universal truths. Not unlike the introspective soul-searching for meaning in the traditional disciplines of international affairs, it is nothing less than our own identities as faculty that are being challenged by factors informed by technology.

Facilitating Cooperation Among Students

Student collaboration is a key dimension in the Internet age. Many of us who stand in front of the class have already dismissed the technique of student "group" projects because it tends to produce free-rider effects. After all, we are the ones who survived a fairly rigorous and at times painful, alienating, and antisocial process of individual assertion through our efforts to get into graduate school, present comprehensive and dissertation defenses, and ultimately gain tenure and promotion. As many have envisioned, the Internet can be the ultimate clearinghouse for individuals to demonstrate mastery of a given subject matter through some form of outcomes-based assessment. Individuals can interface with their computers until they are prepared to take a competency test, ignoring for the most part the social context within which habits of the mind and the heart take place. Indeed, mastery of subject matter is largely an outdated concept in the age of databases and digital libraries. So too the notion of isolated learning as a measure of individual accomplishment is an outdated conception in the Internet age.

Today, most students will be confronted with social context, team environments, group interaction, and family and community opportunities for collaboration most of their adult working lives. Joining theory to practice becomes a social good and is more times than not a "team" environment whether in the kitchen, factory floor, board room, or community center.

The asynchronous nature of the Net enables individuals to balance personal preferences with the development and production of group outcomes. Chat rooms and listservs support spaces that support active "listening" and relative anonymity that in turn support the bonding of students across traditional cleavages such as class, age, gender, and ethnicity. The Net is color blind, indifferent to gender preferences, and incapable of preidentifying anyone's socioeconomic status. Opportunities exist to leverage this fascinating element of social identity on the Net in order to advocate for tolerance and joint stewardship of important issues that might otherwise be predestined to failure in a real-time environment. Musicians, disabled adults, young Arabs and Israelis, Cypriots from both the Greek and Turkish sides, Protestants and Catholics in Ireland, and rival gang members in downtown Los Angeles have all, to varying degrees and with varying degrees of success, leveraged the technology to foster better communication, opportunities to build better understanding, and many of the necessary (if not sufficient) preconditions for peace and harmony.

Faculty colleagues in institutions around the country have extended the geographical boundaries of the world politics experience to include a limited series of interactions among our students at multiple institutions. In Chapter 14, for example, Jeffrey Seifert and G. Matthew Bonham relate their experiences with videoconferencing and text chat between U.S. and Swedish students during a "virtual conference" on global environmental issues and multilateral peacekeeping. Our ability to make use of the technology to support student-to-student collaboration and interaction has become more sophisticated over the years, but it was as early as 1989 that the asynchronous power of the medium, in terms of anytime, anywhere learning, was apparent and seen as invaluable to extending the opportunity for student-to-student interaction across time and space.

Providing Prompt Feedback and Measuring Time on Task

Computers can certainly provide prompt feedback and measure time on task. Students can take an infinite number of randomly generated practice quizzes and have the computer grade multiple-choice questions. Correct answers are then sent via e-mail to students. Not only are the right answers supplied, but references are included to the readings that deal with a given subject matter where the student may be experiencing some difficulty given his or her response on the computer-aided practice examinations. The material in Chapter 15, "Teaching Human Rights Online: The International Court of Justice Considers Genocide," by Howard Tolley is a good example of a Web-based exercise in which students identify the best legal facts and arguments and then compare their reasoning with the actual opinion of the International Court of Justice judges. This exercise provides prompt feedback to the student and gives the legal rationale for the correct answer.

Keeping students on task is a challenge. Using computers to do class assignments gives the instructor the ability to monitor the students' progress. For instance, a student in a digital course may complain in e-mail that she spent eight hours researching an Internet assignment, claiming that she was "no good at using this new-fangled technology." The instructor can check her time on task and see when she began, when she logged out, and how many times she returned to the project. Faculty will be happy to report, but not be surprised to find, that the student only spent twenty minutes on the assignment. In this case, technology has some monitoring and feedback features that can support some discipline and checking on broad comprehension issues. In addition, simple text-based assignments enhanced with other technology-mediating learning tools—including the use of radio documentaries, analog video editing experiences, short-wave radio diaries, and the integration of film and breaking television news stories—make time on task easier given the engaging nature of the medium. In this book, for instance, Patrick Haney recounts his experience using popular movies to teach issues and concepts in U.S. foreign and national security policy (Chapter 16, "Learning About Foreign Policy at the Movies").

As we move toward portfolio evaluation strategies,[5] computers can provide rich storage and easy access to student products and performances. The computer server can keep track of early efforts, so instructors and students can see the extent to which later efforts demonstrate gains in knowledge, competence, or other valued outcomes. There are still very few international affairs programs or courses, however, that are adopting a digital portfolio approach. Once again the international affairs subject area would appear to be a prime candidate for experimental use of digital portfolios. Innovation and change have become endemic to the field since 1989. Although traditional areas like political philosophy and social science research methods may be less inclined to creativity, international affairs would appear to be a logical candidate for such an initiative.

Communicating High Expectations

Publishing on the Web has always been one of the most attractive ways of communicating high expectations to students. Students who are vested in the course subject matter take pride and ownership in their work's being publicly available and showcased as exemplary.[6] The same logic extends to faculty pages, department Web spaces, and even professional associations. There are some outstanding examples of Web pages of individual faculty members that provide a dynamic invitation to their students and professional colleagues to engage in their digital active learning space. There are fewer departments or associations associated with international affairs that can be pointed to as best practice examples. The two best illustrations of virtual access points on international affairs are the International Affairs Network at the World Wide Web Virtual Library (http://www.ucis.pitt.edu/ianweb/) and Communications for a Sustainable Future (http://csf.colorado.edu).

Promoting Active Learning

There are numerous examples of how technology has promoted active learning in the international relations classroom. International simulation games have been enhanced through the elaborate use of electronic mail to exchange and distribute strategic missives among all the participants. Multisession United Nations summits have been enhanced by the intensive use of e-mail that enabled and supported student attendance to the subject matter of the course well beyond the limited boundaries of the classroom experience. For instance, in Chapter 13, "Face-to-Face in Cyberspace," Lynn Kuzma relates her experiences using a Web-based conferencing tool to simulate a Security Council session between two geographically distant groups.

The only way to make the Net an active learning space is to create great content. After the initial excitement, the Web has devolved into a large number of courses and other offerings being pasted on to the Web and being offered as education opportunities. A poor-quality syllabus on the Web is no better a course offering than the poor syllabus offered on a photocopy. By and large, the Web has not begun to be populated with content that differentiates it from hard copy. The only way to produce exciting content is to find ways to engage the best faculty on the campus to begin to take full advantage of the capabilities of the Web. The university as an institution appears to be predisposed to acquiring technology but regularly fails to invest in the people who will make a difference to the lives of the students who attend the institution. There are but a handful of faculty support environments where faculty can expect to transform their instruction by interacting with support professionals. It has become commonplace for university strategic plans to embrace and even make commitments to becoming the technology university in a given city or region. It is hard to imagine a more exciting subject area for creating great content than for international affairs.

Although texts remain the mainstay for international affairs courses, too few publishers and online education firms have invested in nontraditional active learning content in our disciplines. Count the number of outstanding DVDs (digital video discs) available on the history of the twentieth century. When was the last time you had an opportunity to bring in the United Nations into your classroom? When did your course on trade and development use compressed video conferencing to tie your class into an international symposium on the same topic? Where is the new standard video offering on paths to the twenty-first century? How many case studies have multimedia versions? Where are the virtual reality experiences of the impact of currency crises in Russia and Indonesia from the perspective of peasants and central bank authorities? The Net and technology support active learning. The available portfolio of active learning materials leveraging the technology, however, is still waiting to be developed.

Respecting Diverse Talents and Ways of Learning

Nearly fifteen years ago we discovered that the power of the Net was grounded in our ability to exploit asynchronous learning opportunities. The anytime, anywhere features of the Net have turned into a corporate slogan; however, at the core the Net is the most nonhierarchical and widely accessible space for education—ever. Over nearly fifteen years or so, technology-mediated education has matured and has taken advantage of new technological capabilities. The key differentiation features of the Net include its enhanced capacity to support multisensory learning, hypertextuality, interaction, and democratization of the learning environment. Finally, patterns of communication have been radically altered, leading to both challenges and opportunities. The transformative possibilities of technology, the contribution that technology can make to active learning strategies, and the challenges that the technology puts before the international affairs community both individually and collectively are becoming more evident every day.

Notes

1. See Karl R. Popper (1989), *Conjectures and Refutations: The Growth of Scientific Knowledge*, 5th rev. ed. (London: Routledge); see also Karl R. Popper (1959), *The Logic of Scientific Discovery* (London: Hutchinson).

2. Sigmund Freud (1989), *Civilization and Its Discontents* (New York: W. W. Norton).

3. See Michael G. Lerner (1997), *The Politics of Meaning: Restoring Hope and Possibility in an Age of Cynicism* (Reading, MA: Addison-Wesley).

4. Arthur W. Chickering and Zelda F. Gamson (1991), *Applying the Seven Principles for Good Practice in Undergraduate Education* (San Francisco: Jossey-Bass).

5. See Robin Fogarty, ed. (1996), *Student Portfolios: A Collection of Articles* (Chicago, Il.: IRI/SkyLight Training and Publishing).

6. See Lynn M. Kuzma (1998), "The World Wide Web and Active Learning in the International Relations Classroom," *PS: Political Science & Politics* 31(3):578–583.

13 | Face-to-Face in Cyberspace: Simulating the Security Council Through Internet Technology

Lynn M. Kuzma

Studies have shown that as students become engaged with materials—either as actors, producers, or teachers—they retain information at higher rates.[1] In addition, they increase their ability to think clearly and critically and enhance their problem-solving skills.[2] Ultimately, students learn better when they are active in a process, whether that process comes in the form of a sophisticated multimedia package or a classroom debate on current events.[3] Knowing this, many educators are questioning the utility of the "instructional model," in which teaching is telling and learning is memorizing. This educational approach instills passivity and unquestioning acceptance and establishes an authoritative didactic between teachers and students.

Instead, many educators are adopting teaching strategies that build on a "learning model" that envisions students and teachers working together in active learning environments.[4] Earlier chapters in this book explored two well-established active learning approaches—cases and simulations. Contributors conveyed the educational benefits of the methods of those approaches and assessed their results. The virtues of new educational innovations that incorporate technology into the classroom setting, however, are still under scrutiny.

"Techno-optimists" claim that technology is changing the "what" of learning by "introducing new concepts, techniques, and tools for understanding and also making the world."[5] Technology affects the way we design and create expression, allowing new ways to visualize and integrate data. These radically different forms of inquiry have not been possible until recently. Now that they are here, we should readily embrace them. In sum, techno-optimists view technology as a panacea for what ails higher education. The quicker we adopt technological innovations into our classroom activities, the more student learning will occur.[6]

"Techno-skeptics," on the other hand, contend that educators have adopted a naive optimism regarding technology. They identify the tendency to let technological possibilities drive instructional design. Educators are using "technology for technology's sake."[7] Critics can bolster this argument by asserting that few studies have provided a clear link between the use of technology and student learning goals.[8] What is crucially missing from most technology adoptions, they argue, is any discussion of what is an appropriate use of technology. Whether educators are driven by overly enthusiastic administrators who want their institutions to have all the "bells and whistles" or are seduced by technology's allure, techno-skeptics believe these educators are not questioning technology's educational suitability.[9]

The techno-optimist's enthusiasm needs to be tempered by the techno-skeptic's concerns. Whether responding to technology's appeal or to administrators' demands, educators must embrace a skeptical optimism when considering adopting educational technologies. Educational technologies, in and of themselves, do not automatically foster active learning environments. Educational technology, after all, only refers to the most advanced technologies available in a particular era.[10] In the past, they have included filmstrips, slide projectors, radio, and television. More recently, the Internet and the World Wide Web have joined the list. Each of these devices, however, is simply a *tool* that helps teachers achieve their educational goals.

When applied in the appropriate manner, educational technologies have the potential to greatly facilitate the learning process, because they encourage learning in authentic contexts, through collaboration, and by supporting the use of multiple primary source materials as well as textbooks. Such technologies are not, however, ends in themselves. The effective use of technology to develop learning, communication, and information skills is the result of many factors, chief of which is the teacher's competence and ability to shape technology-based activities that meet students' learning needs. We need to ask ourselves "which technology, how much technology, for whom, and at what cost?"[11]

What is required are new visions of how technological advances can help us create active learning environments. Many in our profession feel, however, that the technology revolution is bypassing them. Most find little time to rethink their current syllabi and integrate technological approaches. Others do not know where to begin.[12] Thus, the experiences of innovators and early adopters,[13] the names given to those who invest time and resources in the application of new teaching methods, should provide guidance as others venture into new instructional terrain.[14] Toward this end, in this chapter I recount one vision of how advances in telecommunication technology can facilitate active learning in an international relations classroom through a simulation of the United Nations (UN) Security Council.

I first describe a traditional Model United Nations (MUN) experience and its educational benefits. I then discuss how two aspects of the simulation, the *preparation* and *participation* phases, were aided by educational technology. In this case, directed learning Web sites enhanced student access to information and created "immersion environments" that facilitated students' ability to assume ambassadorial roles during the simulation. A Web-based conferencing tool and a videoconference session allowed students on remote campuses to simulate Security Council deliberations. Through these experiences, students became active participants in an online learning community not bound by geographic constraints. In essence, a telecollaborative community of practice was assembled.

Educational Objectives

A Traditional Model United Nations Experience

A traditional MUN simulates the activities of a number of international decisionmaking bodies—the Security Council, the General Assembly, the International Court of Justice, and/or the Social and Economic Council. There are two basic components to the MUN experience. Students first go through an intensive preparation process, in which they research the countries they will represent, organize policy papers, draft resolutions, and practice the United Nations' rules of procedure and public speaking.[15] Once prepared, students become country "ambassadors" and travel to a remote location to take part in a multiday MUN simulation and consider items from the UN system's vast agenda.

During the conference, students build collaboration, compromise, and negotiation skills during informal caucus sessions. They hone public speaking abilities during formal debates on the committee floor. Overall, the role-playing during the conference involves participants in the exciting process of synthesizing, and ultimately applying, the information and skills acquired in class and during preparation. Through the two-step process of preparation and participation, students gain greater understanding of our world's problems, comprehend the complexities inherent in the international system, learn the ways and means of global cooperation, and become effective decisionmakers. This "learning by doing" approach creates an enthusiastic and active learning environment.[16]

Perhaps the best outcome of a MUN simulation is that it conveys to students the perceptual differences that arise between countries and cultures and how they lead to international conflict. By role-playing advocates of positions other than that of the United States, students empathize with people of diverse cultures and perspectives. They learn to question their own cultural viewpoints as well. Ultimately, it is hoped that this experience will lead to greater understanding between people, reduce conflict, and successfully resolve many international issues.

These learning outcomes make a simulation of a UN decision-making organ a vital addition to any international relations class. However, the traditional MUN format has two drawbacks. First, to be effective delegates at a MUN conference, students must be able to collect timely and complete information about their assigned countries and the global issues they will discuss. Students and teachers alike, however, are often disappointed with their campus library's holdings. They find that many are not UN document depositories, and others have limited collections. Recently published materials are often outdated by the time they reach library shelves. Students tasked with learning about newly independent countries, for instance, will not find accurate information about the country's government structure.

Second, the expense associated with partaking in a MUN conference for several days is great. Domestic travel is prohibitive for some, and international travel is impossible for most. Hotels may offer conference rates, but even a discounted rate is wildly extravagant to a typical college student. Thus, many are excluded from partaking in a MUN simulation. More disturbing, U.S. citizens rarely get the opportunity to interact with citizens from other countries, given the tremendous expense associated with international travel.

A Virtual Security Council Experience

It is possible, however, to apply the Internet's vast resources and high-performance capabilities to overcome the drawbacks inherent in a traditional Model United Nations experience. I have regularly assembled a "virtual library" composed of "directed learning" Web sites to help students prepare for a MUN simulation. Creation of a Web-based conferencing tool and utilization of a videoconferencing device facilitated student participation in a "Virtual Security Council" simulation from remote locations. Technology was used as an amplification (accessing information) as well as a transformative (changing the student/teacher relationship) device.[17]

Design Parameters and Procedures: Applying Technology to a United Nations Simulation

Amplification: Preparing Students for a Security Council Simulation

A successful simulation is contingent upon knowledgeable participants. A Security Council simulation requires students to master the particulars of global security issues as well as enough country-specific information to assume the character of their assigned country's ambassador. The World Wide Web is a powerful tool that provides access to global information sources and helps prepare students for the simulation.

Online information is current and often more complete than traditional information sources. Using the Web, MUN researchers have instant access to documentation of important international events and agreements. In the past, access to UN proceedings was contingent upon publishers' interest and library budgets. Not so anymore. Students can access UN documents via the United Nations home page.[18] Past and current Security Council resolutions[19] and International Court of Justice (ICJ) rulings[20] are only a mouse click away. Webcasts of the General Assembly's daily proceedings are available for all to hear and see.[21] The Internet also reflects quickly the changing nature of international events. Internet newspapers, nongovernmental organizations, and interested individuals give ongoing accounts of international happenings as they unfold. The *New York Times On the Web,* for example, updates its edition every few hours.[22] Overall, students and scholars will find more complete coverage of global incidents using the Web than through any other source.

What has *not* accompanied the increased access to global information is an organizing device that helps students filter through the muck. Critics of the Web worry that the information glut may pose an even greater challenge than information scarcity ever did.[23] Unlike the information students receive from traditional media—textbooks, television, documentaries, library materials—Web information has not been carefully researched, documented, and selected for publication and presentation. What comes across on the Internet is "undigested" information, provided by "expert and novice alike, scholars and shysters, pedagogues and pedophiles."[24] Scholarly resources, unfounded claims, and advertising are all mixed together on the Web. It is a place where anything and everything goes. Given this, many educators warn that students are not capable of coping with the complexity inherent in the Web: they do not have the analytical frameworks for sorting things out. Some fear that students will be overwhelmed with information, led astray by biased sources, and mistake fiction for fact.

Viewed another way, the public nature of the Web actually affords educators a chance to teach students to become better thinkers. The problems inherent in the Web are opportunities to guide our students in their development of new thinking skills, including effective strategies for sorting relevant information that is most likely to assist in the process of problem solving.[25] Students need to know where to begin, what to look for, what to ignore, and how to make critical judgments about the information's value, reliability, and validity. Since our society is rapidly becoming information driven, an important educational strategy is to help students become effective information managers.[26] To begin this process, educators must construct a middle ground between forbidding students to journey on the information superhighway and giving them the keys to the car without a driving lesson. We need to develop students' "critical literacy,"[27] so they know how to access and organize vast amounts of information.[28]

Toward this end, various educators have devised strategies that effectively integrate the Internet in instruction. One approach is for experts to filter appropriate Internet information. International relations scholars have constructed Web sites that organize reliable information in their respective fields of interest.[29] Sections of the International Studies Association, for example, have created home pages that arrange Internet information germane to their specialties.[30] Educational organizations have built virtual libraries that house information that is searchable online.[31]

Another approach is to ask students to evaluate the Web pages they encounter while doing research.[32] Typically an instructor provides a checklist that requires student to practice recognizing the difference between information, advocacy, and business Web pages.[33] Students are asked to evaluate the accuracy, currency, and authoritativeness of their Web sources. The qualifications of the author, as well as his or her arguments, should also be evaluated.[34] By questioning an author's motives for uploading information to the Web, students learn to read material critically, even skeptically.

These approaches are very helpful to students as they begin to research a specific topic but not as beneficial to students assigned a much larger and more ambiguous task, such as finding out what is in their respective country's national interest. Charged with this undertaking, students often freeze and become unable to proceed. Many do not know where to begin their research, given the immensity of the task. So, oftentimes they begin by doing nothing.

How does one help students prepare for a role-playing situation using the Web's resources? An experimental approach is to construct Web pages that have a "directed learning" element, so students are not "lost in cyberspace." Simply put, a directed learning Web site organizes the Internet's resources according to content categories and then prompts students with specific questions to keep in mind as they explore the information superhighway. Thus, the educator constructs a Web page that has a static frame somewhere on the home page, where questions germane to the topic appear. Readers are constantly aware of what questions they are charged with answering as they search the Internet's boundless resources. These searches are directed, meaning that the instructor designs them so students have a structured frame of reference, a home base from which they venture into cyberspace. During their Internet searches, students are asked to make critical judgments of the information they encounter by the directive Web site. Through this process, students begin to sharpen their "informational" and computer literacy skills.[35]

For the simulated Security Council project, a States Virtual Library (composed of country Web pages for each member of the Security Council) was created and organized around six content categories: general information, culture, politics, foreign relations, military, and economy. Web pages housed links to relevant Internet sites and posed questions germane to the content category.[36] Since the

Web is a multimedia environment, information housed on the country Web pages went well beyond what traditional texts offer. Using the States Virtual Library, for instance, a student gathering information to role-play the Indian ambassador in the Security Council has a variety of data to explore. (Appendix A is the list of questions that accompanied the States Virtual Library.) The delegate can read the *Hindu*,[37] scan current General Assembly resolutions,[38] hear the Indian national anthem, use language translators, review Gandhi's life and times, visit a "virtual mosque," or see video clips of the leaders of Pakistan and India justifying current nuclear tests. This is only a sample of the various possibilities. This type of "immersion environment" greatly enhances a student's ability to prepare for a role-playing simulation. In essence, students "experience" the country they will represent and get a feel for its history, culture, and domestic and international political environments.

How Instructive Were Directed Learning Web Sites?

Twenty-one members of an International Organization class at North Dakota State University used the States Virtual Library to prepare for a regional Model United Nations conference. Overall, the students were very pleased with the Web sites and stated that they were introduced to their respective countries. One student commented, "It really helped me get started. At first I was overwhelmed and did not know where to begin the preparation." Another began her Internet research without using the Web sites and did not make much progress. She stated, "There was so much information out there that I just gave up after one search. Most of the information I came across was travel information. I did not know what to look for. Once I used the Web sites, I had a better idea of what was important and what I should be looking for. The questions really helped. I learned about how the Web worked." Most students remarked that the Web pages helped them begin their initial research.

The directed learning Web sites also increased the students' knowledge of their respective countries and international issues. Due to the fact that students had an organizing device that delivered incredible amounts of information in a "one-stop shop," they spent more time reading, evaluating, and absorbing data. In fact, students who represented countries that did not have a wealth of Internet information compared to other countries—for instance, Djibouti in comparison to the United Kingdom—were quick to complain and felt left out. Overall, students were eager to learn about their respective countries and had access to an abundant amount of information provided in what they considered a fairly painless manner. Given this, students indicated they did more research than they had in the past. I also judged them to be more knowledgeable simulation participants. The most encouraging aspect was that the students brought not only their knowledge to the simulation; they also carried maps, treaties, speeches, resolutions, and statistical tables. More important, they carried the air of confidence that comes from being prepared.

Transformation: Participating
in the Virtual Security Council Simulation

Educators have begun experimenting with ways in which traditional simulations can be enhanced with computer technology.[39] The key is to analyze the structure of a traditional simulation, break it into components, and then decide which parts can be aided by technology. A Security Council simulation has two components. The first is a formal session, in which the fifteen-member council meets at a specified location during an appointed time. This session is structured by an agenda. Representatives address the body according to a speakers' list and interact with each other under the guidelines of parliamentary procedures. Decisions are made using specified voting rules. The second component is informal caucus sessions. These deliberations occur when members decide to suspend the formal Security Council session so they can meet freely with any delegate. During this time, members build coalitions around working resolutions and practice the art of consensus and compromise. Oftentimes it is in the informal caucus sessions that the bulk of the Security Council's work gets done.

To simulate the formal aspects of the Security Council deliberations using technology, a videoconference was scheduled for two three-hour sessions one Saturday afternoon. Students at North Dakota State University were linked via teleconference rooms with students from the University of Cincinnati. They were charged with re-creating the 1993 Security Council decision to establish safe havens in the former Yugoslavia. They also discussed whether an ad hoc war crimes tribunal should be created. Two students from North Dakota State University were cochairs and ran the formal session. Students from either school were recognized according to a speaker's list. Both teams could hear and see each delegate deliver speeches, follow procedures, and partake in voting. This created a face-to-face, real-time collaborative learning and mentoring situation between geographically distributed groups.

To simulate the informal caucus sessions using technology, a Web-based conferencing tool was designed to allow participants to converse on topics that defined the Security Council's agenda. On-line asynchronous text exchange enabled students to send diplomatic messages to country teams and submit resolutions to the chair. Once approved, resolutions were posted for discussion in the formal Security Council videoconference session.[40] Each student in North Dakota was furnished with a laptop computer that facilitated this interaction. Students in Cincinnati, however, did not have this ease of access. They shared computers that were housed in the general proximity of the teleconference room.

Flesh to Silicon?

Since the same group of students from North Dakota State University participated in a traditional Model United Nations and the Virtual Security Council sessions, they were able to compare and contrast the "real" with the "virtual" simulation experience. Overall, they judged the videoconference a great success. The technical aspects worked well after kinks with the Web-conferencing tool were ironed out. The students were enthusiastic, knew their country roles, and applied complex arguments. One student stated, "It was a very valuable experience. I didn't know much about the Security Council or the Bosnia issue, so I really learned a lot." Another stated, "I was really nervous at first about seeing myself on television. It was rather distracting. But, after I got used to it, it was as if the people in Cincinnati were in the room with us."

My experience with the Virtual Security Council simulation led me to conclude that some simulated bodies work better than others at a distance. A decisionmaking body that relies heavily on informal caucus sessions and interpersonal interactions, such as the Security Council, is harder to simulate via videoconferencing. Although each student's having access to a personal computer helped students on remote campuses interact, a communication barrier was apparent. Campus groups tended to caucus among themselves during the informal sessions. Few cross-campus interactions were initiated. Connectivity fell far short of the intended outcome. This, of course, is understandable. The members of each campus group had built personal relationships during their classroom experience. They felt more comfortable with each other than with students from a remote campus whom they had never seen. The same phenomenon occurs during the first interactions of a traditional MUN session. By the end of the virtual simulation, however, students on the two campuses were still literally and figuratively miles apart.

In the future, person-to-person videoconferencing capabilities may facilitate more extensive informal caucusing between distant individuals. For instance, a software program called CU-See-Me allows individuals with Internet access to connect while using personal computers.[41] Students have the ability to see and talk to those on remote campuses in a more intimate setting. They can also send and view documents while online.

Simulations of formal decisionmaking bodies may work better at a distance. A simulation of the ICJ held between the two schools during the previous month functioned better. Oral arguments, judges' questions, advocate rebuttals, and then closing statements created a flow of events that was captured better using a videoconferencing tool. The action in this case focused upon one or two individuals at a time in a formal setting. There was no need to construct coalitions or make compromises. The ICJ simulation lasted an hour, rather than a day. Overall, it was more manageable.

This raises the question of whether it is worthwhile to "replace flesh with silicon."[42] The students gave high marks to the videoconference and felt that they learned a great deal. They would not, however, have chosen to partake in a videoconference rather than a real MUN. The experience with the simulation of the Virtual Security Council was that the interpersonal and extracurricular activities that students experience at a three-day conference could not be simulated over the Internet. It would be impossible to simulate sitting up all night working on resolutions by the pool at a hotel with fellow MUN delegates.

As we discovered, the point of videoconferencing is to augment physical, hands-on learning and face-to-face encounters, not to replace them. Given the choice between a videoconference, a classroom simulation, and nothing at all, the students chose the videoconference hands down. Yet, in the not-so-distant future, travels in cyberspace (video- and teleconferencing, simulations, interactive video) may be cheaper, more effective, and easier to conduct than the real thing. This will allow educators to supplement their International Relations classes with many different types of simulations involving individuals anywhere in the world.

Overall Assessment of the
Virtual Security Council Project

The early success of the Virtual Security Council Project can be attributed to a group of dedicated individuals at the Information Technology Services at North Dakota State University. Educators who begin to integrate technology with their educational goals should contact the technology specialists at their respective colleges and universities. Most will be able to help develop course work using information technology. Asking for their help is half the battle, and one does not have to produce a project as large as a Virtual Security Council to benefit from the expertise of these professionals.

When investing in the development of educational information technologies, keep in mind that there will be a need for sustained investment of personnel (faculty and technical support) and financial resources. Infrastructure fosters innovation. For instance, the use of e-mail expanded once-local area networks connecting desktop machines to the Internet, and easy-to-use e-mail software packages became available. As one commentator noted, "It may seem an easy matter to add an e-mail address or Web-based assignment to your syllabus, but it makes sense to do so only if the instructor—and the student—have easy access to a network providing the necessary tools."[43] Educators attracted to developing technology-based projects should determine the availability of the resources at their college or university.

Those interested in videoconferencing tools should be aware that the cost can be prohibitive. An integrated services digital network line, which must be specially ordered from telephone companies, generally conveys data at 128 kilobits a second. This allows users of most videoconferencing systems to see up to fifteen frames of live video a second. That is only about half the speed of the full-motion video that television viewers are used to. That generally suffices, however, for capturing the proceedings of a typical simulation. Depending on the technology used, phone fees can be approximately eighty dollars an hour or sixty cents a minute. Thus, the longer the videoconference, the greater the cost. Compared to the costs associated with a traditional MUN conference (travel, registration fees, hotel, food), the teleconference is nevertheless a comparative bargain.

In the near future, the cost of videoconferencing should dramatically decrease. Recent videoconferencing product offerings, coupled with newly adopted transmission standards, have radically changed the financial equation for delivering live, interactive video to the classroom. Many manufacturers now make available very affordable desktop and small classroom videoconferencing systems at a much lower price than previously available while maintaining a level of quality, connectivity, and ease of use that support effective classroom use. Software that uses the Internet instead of phone lines is readily available. Educators may incorporate less formal, but equally useful, applications of interactive video as part of the classroom experience.

Conclusion

After I witnessed the videoconference simulation of the Security Council, the phrase "the future is now" ran through my head. The advances in computer and telecommunications technology are truly astounding and only promise to get better. They allow a new way of thinking about active learning and connecting students across the country and around the world. In this environment, the role of educators is changing from dispenser of knowledge to facilitator of the learning experience. As educators push the limits of technology and—we hope—our students' learning experiences, it is important to remember that the tools we bring to bear are just that, tools. They should not be seen as ends in themselves. Learning goals and objectives are always the primary motivator of these innovative techniques and should continually inform them. Experimentation and assessment are vital phases of a process by which we search for effective ways for our students to learn. Sharing such experiences is a way we can all learn.

Appendix:
Study Questions for Simulation Participants[44]

General Information:
- Which states are prominent neighboring states to your nation?
- Are there any significant aspects of your state's history that influence the way it operates today and its priorities for the future?
- Did your state experience colonialism or was it a colonial power?

Political:
- What form of government characterizes your nation—democracy, authoritarian, or totalitarian?
- Overall, would you say that your country's government rules legitimately? Is it very secure, or are there rival groups contending for power?
- What role does your country's government play in the economy? In society?

Economy:
- Which industrial revolution has your country experienced (pre-industrial, 1st, 2nd, 3rd)? What type of economic system (capitalism, socialism, communism) does it employ? What are its major exports? To which countries do they go? What are your country's major imports? These goods come from which states? Who are your country's major trading partners?
- What is the population, population density, and population growth rate of your state? What influence have they had on your state's economy and its available resources?
- What natural resources does your nation possess? How has the lack or abundance of various resources influenced your state's economy and its relationship with other states?
- How does your state stand in terms of pollution, energy consumption, and other environmental problems? What actions have been taken to help or hurt the environmental situation?

Foreign Relations:
- In which international governmental organizations does your state have membership? How does your state view the role and impact of these and other international organs?
- What kind of technical and economic aid does your country give or receive? Why?
- Who are your nation's significant allies and enemies? Why? What effect have they had on your state's economy and political system?
- What is the status of your state's financial contributions to the UN?

Cultural:
- What religion(s) do the citizens of your state practice? Do any have a significant influence on your government and the policies it may pursue?

- What are the prominent majority and minority ethnic, religious, and political groups in your state? Are there conflicts among these groups? What influence do they have on the political system and public policy?
- What are some of the customs and attributes that characterize your state's culture? What effect could this have on your state's dealings with other countries?

Military:
- What are your state's defensive and offensive military capabilities? How often does your state employ its military capabilities? Does it tend to use them domestically or for advancement of foreign interests?
- Does your country possess nuclear arms? Is your state more interested in acquiring or selling arms? From or to whom?

Notes

1. James E. Stice (1987), "Using Kolb's Learning Cycle to Improve Student Learning," *Engineering Education* 77(5):291–296.

2. John D. Bransford, Robert Sherwood, and Tom Sturdevant (1987), "Teaching Thinking and Problem Solving," in *Teaching Thinking Skills: Theory and Practice*, ed. Joan Boykoff Baron and Robert J. Sternberg (New York: W. H. Freeman and Company); Robert H. Ennis (1987), "A Taxonomy of Critical Thinking Dispositions and Abilities," in *Teaching Thinking Skills: Theory and Practice*, ed. Joan Boykoff Baron and Robert J. Sternberg (New York: W. H. Freeman and Company).

3. Paul Mather (1996), "Critical Literacy: The WWW's Great Potential." Available online at http://ei.cs.vt.edu/%7Ewwwbtb/book/chap6/critical.html.

4. For a discussion of the learning paradigm, see Robert B. Barr and John Tagg (1995), "From Teaching to Learning—A New Paradigm for Undergraduate Education," *Change* 6 (March-April):13–25.

5. Roy Pea (1998), "The Pros and Cons of Technology in the Classroom," *Tapped In.* Center for Technology in Learning. Available online at www.tappedin.org/info/teachers/debate.html.

6. William Geoghegan (1996), "The Coming Ubiquity of Information Technology," *Change* 7 (March/April):26–28; Sheryl Burgstahler (1997), "Teaching on the Net: What's the Difference?" *Technological Horizons in Education Journal* 24 (April):61–64; John E. Reid Jr. (1997), "Preparing Students for the Task of Online Learning," *Syllabus* 10(7):38–39; Peter J. Dunning (1996), "The University's Next Challenges," *Communications of the ACM* 9(5):27–31; Donna Hunter (1996), *Cybercolleges.* Available online at www.cnet.com/Content/Tv/CNETCentral/Links/colleges.html.

7. H.F.W. Stahlke and J. M. Nyce (1996), "Reengineering Higher Education: Reinventing Teaching and Learning," *Cause/Effect* 19(4):48. Available online at www.educause.edu/ir/library/html/cem9649.html.

8. Donald L. Jordan and Peter M. Sanchez (1994), "Traditional Versus Technology-Aided Instruction: The Effects on Visual Stimulus in the Classroom," *PS: Political Science and Politics* 27(1):64–67; G. David Garson (1998), "Evaluating Implementation of Web-Based Teaching in Political Science," *PS: Political Science and Politics* 31(3):585–590.

9. H.F.W. Stahlke and J. M. Nyce (1996), "Reengineering Higher Education"; Ed Neal (1998), "Does Using Technology in Instruction Enhance Learning?" The Technology Source. Available online at horizon.unc.edu/TS/commentary/1998–06.asp.

10. Roy Pea (1998), "The Pros and Cons of Technology in the Classroom."

11. Kathleen Fulton (1998), "Learning in a Digital Age: Insights into the Issues and the Skills Students Need for Technological Fluency," *T.H.E. Journal*. Available online at www.thejournal.com/journal/magazine/98/feb/298feat5.html.

12. For a discussion on what inhibits educators from adopting technology, see LeAne Rutherford and Sheryl Grana (1998), "Retrofitting Academe: Adapting Faculty Attitudes and Practices to Technology," *T.H.E. Journal*. Available online at www.thejournal.com/journal/magazine/95/sep/feature4.html.

13. Everett M. Rogers (1995), *Diffusion of Innovation*, 4th ed. (New York: The Free Press).

14. See Gary M. Klass (1995), "Bringing the World into the Classroom: POS302L—The Race and Ethnicity Seminar Discussion List," *PS: Political Science and Politics* 28(4):723–725 on how to create Internet discussion groups in class. See also Martha Bailey (1995), "USENET Discussion Groups in Political Science Courses," *PS: Political Science and Politics* 28(4):721–722 and David Alexander Bowers (1994), "Using Prodigy and Other Online Services in the Political Science Classroom," *PS: Political Science and Politics* 27(4):708–712 for other examples of technology's use in the classroom.

15. See Model United Nations Online (http://www.munol.org).

16. For more information on the Model United Nations experience contact the UN/USA. Available online at http://www.unausa.org.

17. Patrick J. Haney (1998), "Integrating Cases and Technology in the Classroom" (presented at the annual meeting of the International Studies Association, Minneapolis, MN).

18. Available online at www.un.org.

19. Available online at www.un.org/Docs/sc.htm.

20. Available online at www.icj-cij.org/.

21. Available online at www.un.org/av/.

22. Available online at www.nytimes.com/.

23. Neil Postman (1995), "Virtual Students, Digital Classroom," *The Nation* (October 9):377–382.

24. Kathleen Fulton (1998), "Learning in a Digital Age." Available online at www.thejournal.com/journal/magazine/98/feb/298feat5.html.

25. James W. Pellegrino (1995), "Technology in Support of Critical Thinking," *Teaching of Psychology* 22(1):12.

26. See Paul Mather (1996), "Critical Literacy: The WWW's Great Potential." Available online at ei.cs.vt.edu/%7Ewwwbtb/book/chap6/critical.html. See also Hope N. Tillman (1997),"Evaluating Quality on the Net." Available online at www.tiac.net/users/hope/findqual.html.

27. Kathleen Stumpf Jongsma (1991), "Critical Literacy," *The Reading Teacher* 44(7):518–519; Christine Mann (1994), "New Technologies and Gifted Education," *Roeper Review* 16(3):172–176; Barbara D. Farah (1995), "Information Literacy: Retooling Evaluation Skills in the Electronic Information Environment," *Journal of Educational Technology Systems* 24(2):127–133.

28. Jan Alexander and Marsha Tate (1996), "The Web as a Research Tool: Evaluation Techniques." Available online at www.science.widener.edu/~withers/evalout.htm.

29. For example, The World Lecture Hall contains links to pages created by faculty worldwide who are using the Web to deliver class materials. Available online at www.utexas.edu/world/lecture/pol/.

30. Available online at www.isanet.org/.

31. For instance, see Yale's United Nations workstation. Available online at www.library.yale.edu/un/unhome.htm.

32. Lynn M. Kuzma (1998), "The World Wide Web and Active Learning in the International Relations Classroom," *PS: Political Science and Politics* 31(3):578–584.

33. "Evaluating Web Sites on the Internet." Available online at milton.mse.jhu.edu:8001/research/education/net.html.

34. Kari Boyd McBride and Ruth Dickenstein (1998), "The Web Demands Critical Thinking by Students," *The Chronicle of Higher Education* (March 20). Available online at chronicle.com.

35. Barbara Farah (1995), "Information Literacy."

36. The States Virtual Library is accessed through the Virtual Model United Nations Web site at North Dakota State University, which is available online at www.ndsu.nodak.edu/instruct/wwwinstr.vun.

37. Available online at www.webpage.com/hindu/index.html.

38. Available online at www.un.org/ga/.

39. Vernon J. Vavrina (1992), "From Poughkeepsie to Peoria to the Persian Gulf: A Novice's ICONS Odyssey," *PS: Political Science and Politics* 28(4):700–702; Starkey and Wilkenfeld, "Project ICONS: Computer-Assisted Negotiations for the IR Classroom," *International Studies Notes* 21(1):25–29.

40. Available online at wow2.cc.ndsu.nodak.edu/users/un/login.qry.

41. Available online at cu-seeme.net/.

42. Roy Pea (1998), "The Pros and Cons of Technology in the Classroom," p. 4.

43. Larry Johnson (1996), "In Response to Kenneth Green," *Change* (March/April):31.

44. This appendix is informed by the study guide developed by Barry Miller in 1995 for his students at Fayetteville-Manlius High School in New York before their participation in the Central New York Model United Nations held at Syracuse University.

14 | Learning Through Digital Technology: Videoconferencing, Text Chat, and Hypertext

Jeffrey W. Seifert and G. Matthew Bonham

The explosion of computing power and the proliferation of electronic technology have brought the World Wide Web into the classrooms of colleges, universities, and professional schools.[1] The results of these applications are not equally effective. We have argued elsewhere that "Webified" courses do not effectively improve learning. By *Webify*, we mean the "conversion of printed materials such as syllabi, handouts, and readings into basic HTML documents with little interactivity or other features, which the World Wide Web is capable of supporting."[2] In our view, students do not perceive Webified course material as enhancing their learning experience and are not impressed or motivated by relatively simple applications of a robust medium such as computer technology. Our research was based on a survey of 112 students taking Critical Issues for the United States, a multidisciplinary course designed to fulfill the social sciences component of Syracuse University's Arts and Sciences Core Curriculum. The research revealed that few students visited the course Web site on a regular basis and that fewer than half of them reported using the site to explore course-related ideas. In light of the low number of reported site visits, it was not surprising that "only three of the students cited materials related to the World Wide Web, or the course site specifically, as something that could have made the learning experience of the course more valuable."[3]

Traditionally, students have been spoon-fed in the usual kind of lecture courses. Webified courses also belong to that tradition. The biggest benefit, according to Craig Merlic, who chairs a committee at the University of California at Los Angeles that is evaluating the Instructional Enhancement Initiative, is that the Web makes it easier to distribute materials to students.[4] In other words, the Webification of a course is primarily a convenience for the students. If the instructor puts course materials online, the students no longer have to visit the bookstore or the reserve room in the library.

In addition to Webifying courses, academic institutions should move quickly to promote active learning. The use of case studies and role-playing simulations helps to shift responsibility for learning to students, but more can be done, especially outside of the classroom. This is particularly true in international affairs education, where the potential benefits are enormous. By taking full advantage of computer technology, educators can promote active learning through collaboration with colleagues who reside anywhere in the world.

Recently, scholars in the field of international relations have noted the "unbundling of territoriality" in the global system. For example, Ruggie has written about a "nonterritorial 'region' in the world economy—a decentered yet integrated space-of-flows, operating in real time, which exists alongside the spaces-of-places that we call national economies."[5] The unbundling has been made possible in part by computers and developments in the communications environment that favor "the complex diffusion of production across territorial/political boundaries by facilitating multilocational flexibility, transnational joint-ventures, and both global localization and 'local' globalization."[6]

Similarly, advances in computer and communication technology have resulted in an unbundling of territoriality in international affairs education. The World Wide Web, for example, creates a virtual space where distance becomes unimportant. Using computer technology in a real-time format, faculty and students who have similar interests can meet each other and exchange perspectives and information in a meaningful way. Using asynchronous communication, they can also exchange messages without regard to the limitations of time and time zones. As a consequence, collaboration at a distance becomes both feasible and efficient, and students can "work without having to be in residence at a geographical or spatial site."[7]

Educational Objectives

We were motivated by three objectives in the design of our application of digital technology to international affairs education. These objectives, described below, were derived from our experiences teaching international affairs in the classroom, including core courses designed for students in a professional M.A. in International Relations Program as well as skills-oriented workshops in environmental advocacy, international economics, and role-playing simulation. The objectives also reflect our interest in discourse analysis and the larger body of postmodern thought, with its emphasis on the decentered self, the sense of "juxtaposition and superimposition, and nonlinear, pastiche-like orderings of space."[8]

Incidental and Contextual Learning

Our first objective involves abandoning the conceptual system based on the idea of linearity[9] in order to facilitate implicit, incidental, and contextual learning.[10] As learners move through a text, they should not be locked into the perspective of the author but rather should be guided by their own interests, jumping back and forth, omitting material, skimming detail, or going deeper than the author intended. By departing from the author's organizing framework and following a nonlinear strategy, learners are better able to integrate the course materials and information into their own conceptual frameworks. Words (or blocks of words) and images can be interlinked, creating multiple paths that encourage the integration of information.[11] This approach not only facilitates understanding but also helps students learn how to work in a world that is neither linear nor disciplinary.

Our interest in nonlinearity and the intertextual stems in part from the writings of prominent postmodern theorists. For example, Barthes has proposed a form of text that is a web of language linked to other discourses.[12] Likewise, Derrida viewed text as having "the structure of an interlacing, a weaving, or a web, which would allow the different threads and different lines of sense or force to separate again, as well as being ready to bind others together."[13] Foucault also conceived of text in terms of networks and links.[14] A text for Foucault is a node within a network of "often contradictory taxonomies, observations, interpretations, categories, and rules of observation."[15] For these postmodern writers, meaning, itself, is derived from webs of discourse and the "interrelationship of texts."[16]

Independent and Active Learning

Our second objective is to promote independent and active learning by students. Both traditional lecture courses and many courses that utilize computer technology, the Webified courses, treat students like passive objects whose purpose is to absorb "knowledge." Instead, we would like to transfer "to students much of the responsibility for accessing, sequencing, and deriving meaning from information."[17] Having taken this responsibility, students will move from being spectators to real involvement with their teachers, classmates, and others who share their interests. In other words, we hope to use computer technology to empower students to pursue their interests.

This notion of empowerment is reflected in the postmodern understanding of what it means to be an author of a text. Barthes described the "author" as follows: "This 'I' which approaches the text is already itself a plurality of other texts, of codes which are infinite."[18] Or as Snyder put it, "The 'author' of a text is therefore as intertextual a phenomenon as the text itself."[19] Although the author has lost power, the reader has gained it through his or her ability to navigate a text, annotate sections of the text, and create new links to other texts. In other words, the reader "can become an active, independent, and autonomous constructor of meaning."[20]

Collaborative Learning

Our third objective is to encourage collaboration with others, including learners in distant locations. Learners should be able to work with each other successfully not because of geographical propinquity (for example, sitting next to each other) but because they share an interest in a particular subject matter. In other words, students will be able to work together in virtual space based on interest rather than spatial site.[21] "The result is a much more decentered, multiperspectival universe of imagined communities."[22]

Collaborative learning fits into what can be called, after Bakhtin, the dialogical approach to meaning.[23] According to the dialogical approach, meaning emerges from the interaction between the self and the other. "While no 'I' controls meaning, there is an endless set of episodes in which a 'we' is involved in constituting meaning. Within this view a person's acceptance of a particular understanding is a result of an interaction, actual or symbolic, between that person and another."[24]

In our own research on the nuclear test ban treaty, for example, we found evidence for the process of collaboration in the construction of meaning. Although the negotiators from the United States and the Soviet Union had radically different representations of the world, they were able to work together to construct a "shared discursive space, which amounts to their building a shared reality." This collaborative effort may have facilitated the success of the negotiations and the emergence of new knowledge structures.[25]

Design Parameters

On the basis of these three educational objectives and our theoretical perspective, we worked to design a learning environment that became progressively more contextual, active, and collaborative. The core components of our efforts to create a more independent and active graduate education involved three learning activities. Although all three educational objectives are represented in each of the learning activities described below, each of these activities was designed with a particular objective in mind.

A major goal of each of these learning activities was to provide a successful virtual learning experience, or what Klass refers to as a "third-stage" cybercourse. Klass analyzed forty-one political science "cyberclasses"—courses with their own Web sites. He found that the typical course site was a "digital resting place for a variety of course materials that could just as easily—sometimes more easily—be distributed to students in printed format."[26] Klass coded 53.7 percent of the sites as first-stage cyberclasses, that is, they consisted of only a syllabus and hyperlinks to other Web sites; 39.0 percent as second-stage cyberclasses that included activities that were Internet dependent, such as interactive e-mail, computer-assisted simulation, or role-playing exercises involving use of the Internet; and 7.3 percent as third-stage offerings or virtual courses "without physical (or sometimes temporal) boundaries." Although we do not advocate the replacement of all traditional on-campus courses with virtual courses, we do believe that virtual and active learning activities provide an enhanced instructional environment that expands the classroom.

A Second-Stage Cyberclass

The first activity that was part of our strategy to advance graduate education through digital technology involved a three-credit graduate course, Theories of International Relations (PSC 651), taught by Bonham in the fall semester.[27] The course is a survey and critique of approaches to understanding international relations, with a focus on policy decisionmaking and international negotiation. Originally conceived of as a traditional "talk and chalk" class, supplemented by case studies and simulations, PSC 651 has been redesigned into an advanced second-stage cyberclass. As one of the first courses most students take in the International Relations Program, it serves as an opportunity to set the tone, encourage students to become familiar with the interests of their colleagues, and fulfill our first objective of facilitating implicit, incidental, and contextual learning. For example, the course site provides optional hyperlinks to a variety of related Web-based materials so that students can follow their own interests and not be strictly bound to the course material. By providing a common framework through lectures, readings, and active learning opportunities such as participatory case studies, simulations, and the course site, the groundwork is laid for future collaborative exercises both inside and outside the classroom.

Professional Policy Workshops

The second strategic activity involved a series of three one-credit professional policy workshops. Offered in the spring semester, these workshops were designed to fulfill our second objective—to promote independent and active learning by students. Each workshop emphasized a different skill area that can be used toward the global information policy concentration of the International Relations Program. The skill areas included environmental advocacy, international economic analysis, and role-playing simulations for conflict analysis. Each workshop consisted of two all-day weekend meetings. Students worked on assignments between the workshop meetings and submitted final versions of the assignments later in the semester. For the purpose of this chapter, we will concentrate on the Environmental Policy Advocacy workshop.

Offered first in the series of workshops, this class had the objective to "train participants in the use of computer-based (digital) tools for promoting environmental policy advocacy." The technical emphasis of the class was on PowerPoint presentations, Web publishing using Hypertext Markup Language (HTML), and interactive videoconferencing skills. These skills were taught within the context of advocating effective environmental policies. This workshop combined hands-on technical lab sessions with role-playing exercises and discussions on presentation skills and effective Web page design.

Although there were no technical prerequisites for the class, students who possessed basic computer skills tended to get more out of the workshop than did those who were less computer literate. Moreover, the skills learned in this workshop could be applied in the other workshops as well as in the third learning experience, a virtual conference.

The Virtual Conference

The third active learning activity that involved students was a virtual conference with students at another university. The Virtual Conference on Challenges to Global Governance was held in the spring 1998 semester with faculty and students of the Department of Peace and Conflict Research at Uppsala University in Sweden. The purpose of the virtual conference was to bring together students interested in global environmental issues and multilateral peacekeeping, who would probably not otherwise come into contact with one another owing to their geographic separation. Fulfilling our third objective, to promote collaborative learning, the virtual conference was actually the combination of three separate activities: two interactive videoconferences and a Web-based text chat session. The most technologically advanced of the three learning experiences, the virtual conference represented a third-stage cyberclass that was without physical and, to a lesser extent, temporal boundaries. The virtual conference was not part of any formal course but instead was offered as a voluntary enrichment activity for interested students.

Procedures

The Theories of International Relations Class

PSC 651 was the first and most traditional learning activity of our plan. The class met once a week for three hours. With over thirty students enrolled, the class could not be effectively taught as a graduate seminar. PSC 651 was thus an especially good target to be redesigned to include a number of incidental and contextual learning opportunities, both inside and outside the classroom.

The focal point of PSC 651 was its course site.[28] The PSC 651 course site provided students with a hypertext syllabus that included information about assignments, office hours, audio and video clips, and links to outside source materials. In addition, weekly video updates by the instructor were posted to the course site to remind students of important dates and inform them of any new materials added to the site. The course site was closely integrated with the in-class activities to create a comprehensive whole.

For example, to supplement the unit on cognitive dynamics, in addition to the readings and lecture, students were required to visit the Web site of the University of California at Berkeley's Institute of International Studies and to view Harry Kreisler's interview with Robert McNamara.[29] The purpose of this assignment was to provide the students with a contextual learning experience on how personality can influence foreign policy decisions. The unit on small groups incorporated digitized recordings of President Johnson's discussions about the Vietnam War, made available on *The Challenges of Democracy* textbook Web site.[30] The wealth of multimedia material on the Cuban missile crisis offered a special opportunity for students to look beyond regular lectures and readings. On the PSC 651 course site, short digitized clips from a documentary video, "The Missiles of October," were available as well as links to the recently released digitized tapes of the Executive Committee deliberations.[31]

For the unit on crisis management, an in-class simulation exercise on the TWA 847 hijacking incident was used to facilitate contextual learning. In the simulation, the students played such roles as the vice president, members of the Joint Chiefs of Staff, and the national security adviser. The course site provided background information for the simulation as well as video clips from the past year's simulation.

In addition to these in-class exercises, one of the graded assignments was designed to facilitate implicit, incidental, and contextual learning. The assignment that helped fulfill our objective was a position paper on the Anti-Personnel Land Mine Treaty. The assignment required students to write a four-page position paper with an executive summary for a high-level National Security Council staff member. In the paper they were to discuss three possible options and their recommendations. By choosing an issue that was currently being debated, the assignment provided the students with a chance to learn a task they might be required to perform in their careers, within the context of real-world events.

Although the PSC 651 course site represents a continual work-in-progress as new features providing greater interactivity are added, a number of practical and technical considerations need to be addressed before it becomes a third-stage or virtual course. One of these considerations is the skill level and frame of reference of the students with respect to Web-based learning. Although each successive cohort of students is more computer literate and oriented toward the Internet, most students in the International Relations Program have not engaged in active learning online. Moreover, each entering cohort of students has a significant number of international students, some of whom come from countries where technological opportunities are limited. To that end, three one-credit professional policy workshops were offered to teach the students technical skills in the context of international relations.

Environmental Policy Advocacy Workshop

The Environmental Policy Advocacy Workshop met during the second weekend of the spring 1998 semester. It was purposely held early in the semester so that the students had the opportunity to use the tools of the workshop in their other classes. The workshop was held in an electronic classroom called the Global Collaboratory. The fifty-five-seat Global Collaboratory is outfitted as a production-ready studio with four cameras, studio lighting, and a teaching cart. The teaching cart holds a computer connected to the school's network, a videocassette recorder, and a document camera, the content of which is shown on a rear-projection screen at the front of the room. Before the class met, students were encouraged to visit the course site to review the main features of the technologies used in the workshop.

The workshop began with an introduction and overview of the philosophy of the course and why it was relevant to those seeking professional careers in international affairs. We then moved to the PowerPoint portion of the course. Here we not only covered a technical demonstration of how to create presentations in PowerPoint 97 but also discussed important design issues and gave examples of both effective and ineffective PowerPoint presentations.

In the next part of the class, we introduced the World Wide Web and HTML. Topics covered included the history of the Internet and why it has grown exponentially, simple Web page design, technical considerations, and Internet legal issues, such as copyright, encryption, and privacy. We also did a technical demonstration, similar to the PowerPoint demonstration, on how to create a Web page using common HTML commands in an HTML editor called Webber. Although students were encouraged to take advantage of the new what-you-see-is-what-you-get editors and conversion filters in popular software programs that require no knowledge of HTML to create a Web page, it is our view that students need to learn the basics of writing their own HTML code, so they will be empowered to either fix problems or go beyond simple conversions to create more dynamic Web sites.

We then continued our focus on the Internet by showing the students different Web publishing techniques and taking a more in-depth look at examples of effective and ineffective uses of the Web to advocate policy positions. We also showed the students some of the most elaborate Web sites we could find as examples of what the future of the World Wide Web will hold for international relations.[32]

The students were then taken to a computer lab for a hands-on experience. Here they began to work on their PowerPoint and Web page presentations for the following day. Although we were present in the lab to answer questions and provide technical support, the students were encouraged to explore the functions of the software on their own and to work with their colleagues to overcome any problems. The goal of this approach was to show them that they could not "break" the computer and to more closely simulate a real-world work experience where they would have to collaborate with co-workers.

Before going into the lab, the students were given their two-part assignment: making two presentations to the class. The first was a PowerPoint presentation to the executive committee of a fictitious or real organization, pitching the need for a Web-based campaign on a particular issue. The rest of the class acted as the executive committee. In the afternoon the students presented their second assignment—their Web sites for critique and review. This was the most important part of the workshop because it was an interactive exercise. After working independently on their chosen topic, the students were able to practice their presentation skills and receive immediate feedback on their projects in a simulated work environment. At the end of class on Sunday, the students were given three weeks to revise their presentations in light of the class critique and submit them with a short written assignment, detailing the rationale for the design of their presentations, for a final grade.

In addition to covering PowerPoint and HTML, we introduced interactive videoconferencing. We discussed the growth of the technology and different ways it is being used in business, government, and education. A couple of weeks after this initial weekend class meeting, the students reassembled to participate in a simulated videoconference that was videotaped for later critique. For this simulation the students were broken into two groups and given roles in advance. The subject of the spring 1998 videoconference was the use of technology in university education. One group, representing a private company that sells technologically based education solutions, met in the Global Collaboratory. The other group, representing a university, met in another videoconferencing room across campus. Using PictureTel machines over integrated services digital network lines, the students engaged in a one-hour discussion. The students reassembled a week after the videoconference to review highlights of the taped simulation and engage in an analysis and critique session. Besides providing students with an opportunity to experiment with a cutting-edge technology, this exercise served as an introduction to the third learning experience, the virtual conference.

The Virtual Conference

The Virtual Conference on Challenges to Global Governance was an enrichment activity designed to promote collaborative learning. A Web site was created as a central information point between the two sides.[33] The site included video clips and transcripts of the conference activities, links to the participant schools, and discussion forums. The virtual conference began with an "ice-breaker" videoconference in October between the faculty of the participating schools. It was during this videoconference that the participants decided that the future activities should focus specifically on environmental and peacekeeping issues.

The second videoconference took place in February, led by three faculty members from Syracuse University and two faculty participants from Uppsala University. In addition, fifteen students (eight from Syracuse and seven from Uppsala) participated. Beforehand the participants were encouraged to visit the conference Web site and view selected video clips from the first videoconference. The second videoconference led off with a discussion on global environmental concerns, especially as they related to cooperation and conflict. A number of issues were touched on, including chemical and nuclear weapons disposal, population growth and natural resource depletion, water scarcity, and indigenous conflict management approaches to natural resources. The underlying interest in all of these issues that gave hope for future collaboration between the two groups was the conflict caused among the local, national, and global levels in response to various efforts to address environmental issues. After this common ground was established, the discussion moved to the topic of peacekeeping.

With this shift the pace and participation by the students picked up noticeably. Although several issues were discussed, the conversation quickly focused on the movement away from global organizations toward regional organizations for peacekeeping operations. Many hypotheses were offered and debated to explain this important change in international relations. As the videoconference drew to a close, it was agreed that the Web-based text chat exercise would focus on peacekeeping.

Due to semester schedule differences between the two universities, the Web-based text chat could not be held until mid-April. After agreeing to a time that would take into account the six-hour time difference, the text chat meeting was held in a virtual classroom, created by the AskERIC team at Syracuse University, that utilized collaborative software called The Palace. Using The Palace software, we were able to have a virtual classroom, complete with a whiteboard and the ability to stream Real Media software. One of the advantages of using The Palace was that it allowed the participants to use avatars to represent themselves in the classroom. In this case, we digitized a head-and-shoulders picture of each participant to "wear" on screen during the text chat. The text chat session lasted approximately one hour and focused on the role of the United Nations in peacekeeping operations. The event closed with a call to look into possibilities for faculty and student exchanges.

The final outcome of the virtual conference consisted of a hypertext transcript of the videoconference and a log of the text chat, both of which were posted on the conference Web site. The transcript contained images of the participants as well as short video clips of their contributions. In addition, comments of the participants in the videoconference were hyperlinked to related comments by the same speaker in the log of the Web-based text chat.

Assessment

The learning activities described in this chapter represent a constantly evolving strategy to advance graduate education through digital technology. In an earlier study we found support for our hypothesis that "students do not view 'Webified' course materials as enhancing their learning experience."[34] Consequently, assessing the value and effectiveness of these activities represents an important part of our efforts to improve the way international relations is taught. Based on responses to students' questionnaires and the end products produced by the learning activities, overall we can say that the activities fulfilled their respective educational objectives. However, as our surveys showed, there are still many improvements to be made and new objectives to be met.

The Theories of International Relations Class

The objective of redesigning PSC 651 into an advanced second-stage cyberclass was to facilitate implicit, incidental, and contextual learning. This was done primarily through the course site and active learning activities in class. A course evaluation and survey instrument was administered at the end of the semester. We collected completed surveys from all thirty-two students in the class, although in some cases not all of the questions were answered.

One of the questions asked the students how many times they visited the course site. Of the thirty-one usable responses, the majority of the students (51.6 percent) visited the course site 6–10 times during the semester. The mode was 10 visits. The lowest number of reported visits was 3; the highest was 30. A related question asked the students to rate the course site as a whole, using a scale of 1–5, where 1=poor and 5=excellent. The majority of the students were very positive about the course site. Half of the students (50 percent) assigned the site a value of 4, and one-third (33.3 percent) assigned it a value of 5. The remaining students rated the site with a score of 3. There were no responses below a value of 3.

Despite these relatively high ratings, however, many of the students did not take full advantage of the course site's features. One part of the survey listed twelve items that were either part of the site or hyperlinked from it. Students were asked if they had visited those locations and, if so, to rate them. The majority of the students (64.8 percent) had visited half or fewer of the locations; only 6.3 percent of the students had visited ten of the locations. None of the students visited all twelve; the most often reported number of visits was six. Finally, students were asked to "rate the effectiveness of this course site *as compared to others you have used for other courses*." Here we used a five-point Likert scale. They could also respond that they never used a course site before. The majority of the students (65.5 percent) rated the PSC 651 course site as either more effective or much more effective than other course sites they had used. Only 6.9 percent of the students rated it as less effective, and none rated it as much less effective. Interestingly, only 17.2 percent of the students stated they had never used a course site before. This would suggest that the majority of graduate students have enrolled in some form of a cyberclass (probably a noninteractive Web site, a stage-one cyberclass) during their academic careers. These findings provide further support for our earlier work that showed students are more engaged by interactive course sites than Webified course materials.

Environmental Policy Advocacy Workshop

The object of the professional policy workshops was to promote independent and active learning. This was done primarily through hands-on lab sessions, demonstrations, and student presentations. A course evaluation and survey instrument was administered at the end of the second day of the weekend session to thirteen students.

With the exception of one student whose response was "not sure," all of the students claimed the class was useful for their professional development. Most of the students also gave high ratings to the active learning parts of the class. On a four-point scale, where 4=excellent, 3=good, 2=fair, and 1=poor, 69.2 percent of the students rated the hands-on lab session a value of 4, and the remaining students rated it a value of 3. Using the same four-point scale, the majority of the students rated the in-class presentation exercise a value of 4; 30.8 percent of the students rated it a value of 3.

Perhaps the most convincing evidence that the students benefited from and are receptive to this style of learning is the students' own words. At the end of the survey we had three open-ended questions under the heading "Suggestions for Improvement." We received several comments that support our interest in active learning and lead us to believe that the students benefited from our approach. One student responded, "This is so exciting—we need more training classes like this." Another student, noting the technical nature of the class, said "This is an intimidating area which the instructors managed to make manageable." Finally, another student reported that "I really enjoyed myself and felt I learned a lot." We believe, based on the high quality of the students' work and their generally positive feedback, that the workshop was a successful active learning experience in terms of our objectives.

The Virtual Conference

The objective of the Virtual Conference on Challenges to Global Governance was to promote collaborative learning. Although we were unable to conduct a more formal survey of the participants, the outcomes of the events reflect the success of the learning activity. The virtual conference brought together faculty and students from two universities who had previously had no contact with each other. Moreover, this was not one isolated meeting but three separate collaborative sessions that have laid the groundwork for future exchanges. The transcripts of both videoconferences and the Web-based text chat session also support the idea that collaborative learning took place. Student interaction was greater during the text chat as compared to the second videoconference. The immediacy and ability to have multiple conversations occurring at once, even though at times confusing, allowed for more interactivity and for the two sides to develop a rapport with each other. The participants were able to find common ground between their differing perspectives and conduct an informative dialogue. The students engaged in a discussion on par with what might be experienced in a graduate seminar but with the added benefit of having done so with people from another university on a topic of specific interest to them.

Conclusion

Having met all three of our educational objectives, our next step will be to give students the opportunity to do routine work in hypertext and hypermedia in the context of a collaborative environment. Although the Web sites the students developed in the workshops contained hyperlinks, they did not utilize fully the unique properties of hypertext, such as nonlinearity, decentering, and virtual presence.[35] For the most part their work still resembled single-author, linear structure monographs.[36]

The Virtual Conference on Challenges to Global Governance points the way to the kind of digital environment in which our current students will be working in the twenty-first century. They will be collaborating with people who share their interests, without regard to the limitations of distance and time zones. The collaboration will utilize a variety of computer-based technologies, such as interactive videoconferencing and Web-based text chat. The students will produce documents that are truly intertextual; that is, the documents will be hyperlinked to each other as well as to external resources. To facilitate collaboration with colleagues in different physical locations, they will have access to a Web-based environment for communicating with each other and trading documents as well as self-organizing frameworks for storing and accessing documents, hypertext, and hypermedia. Before they leave the International Relations Program, students will have created a kind of virtual portfolio of documents, including hypertext and hypermedia objects, and links to relevant resources on the Web, organized on the basis of their own understandings of the topic. As a result, their scholarly performance will have become "a form of continuing seminar," which is "interactive, dialogic, and self correcting."[37]

Notes

1. This is a revised version of a paper prepared for delivery at the annual meeting of the American Political Science Association, Computers and Multimedia Section, Boston, MA, September 3–6, 1998. We also have prepared a hypertext version that is available at the following Web site: http://www.maxwell.syr.edu/ir/apsa98.htm.

2. J. W. Seifert and G. M. Bonham (1997), "Using the World Wide Web: Expanding the Classroom or a Virtual Distraction?" (prepared for delivery at the annual meeting of the American Political Science Association, Computers and Multimedia Section, Washington, DC, August 28–31).

3. Ibid.

4. J. Young (1998), "A Year of Web Pages for Every Course: UCLA Debates Their Value," *Chronicle of Higher Education* (May 15):A29.

5. J. G. Ruggie (1993), "Territoriality and Beyond: Problematizing Modernity in International Relations," *International Organization* 47:172.

6. R. J. Deibert (1997), *Parchment, Printing, and Hypermedia. Communication in World Order Transformation* (New York: Columbia University Press), pp. 204–205.

7. George P. Landow (1992), *Hypertext. The Convergence of Contemporary Critical Theory and Technology* (Baltimore, MD: The Johns Hopkins University Press), p. 129.

8. R. J. Deibert (1997), *Parchment, Printing, and Hypermedia,* p. 201.

9. George P. Landow (1992), *Hypertext,* p. 2.

10. I. Snyder (1996), *Hypertext. The Electronic Labyrinth* (Carlton, South Australia: Melbourne University Press), p. 103.

11. J. W. Seifert and G. M. Bonham (1997), "Using the World Wide Web."

12. R. Barthes (1979), "From Work to Text," trans. J. Harari, in *Textual Strategies,* ed. J. Harari (Ithaca, NY: Cornell University Press), p. 76.

13. J. Derrida (1973), *Speech and Phenomena*, trans. D. B. Allison (Evanston, IL: Northwestern University Press), p. 131.

14. I. Snyder (1996), *Hypertext: The Electronic Labyrinth*, p. 49.

15. George Landow (1992), *Hypertext*, p. 25.

16. J. Der Derian (1989), "The Boundaries of Knowledge and Power in International Relations," in *International/Intertextual Relations*, ed. J. Der Derian and M. J. Shapiro (Lexington, MA: Lexington Books), p. 6.

17. I. Snyder (1996), *Hypertext: The Electronic Labyrinnth*, p. 103.

18. R. Barthes (1979), "From Work to Text," p. 10.

19. I. Snyder (1996), *Hypertext: The Electronic Labyrinth*, p. 63.

20. Ibid., p. 62.

21. George Landow (1992), *Hypertext*, p. 129.

22. R. J. Deibert (1997), *Parchment, Printing, and Hypermedia*, p. 198.

23. M. M. Bakhtin (1981), "Discourse and the Novel," in *The Dialogic Imagination*, trans. M. Holquist and C. Emerson (Austin: University of Texas Press), pp. 257–422.

24. M. J. Shapiro, G. M. Bonham, and D. Heradstveit (1988), "A Discursive Practices Approach to Collective Decision-Making," *International Studies Quarterly* 32:399.

25. G. M. Bonham, V. M. Sergeev, and P. Parshin (1997), "The Limited Test-Ban Agreement: Emergence of New Knowledge Structures in International Negotiation," *International Studies Quarterly* 41:238.

26. G. Klass (1996), "A Survey of Political Science Cyberclasses" (prepared for delivery at the annual meeting of the American Political Science Association, Computers and Multimedia Section, San Francisco, August 30), p. 1.

27. The International Relations Program at the Maxwell School of Citizenship and Public Affairs of Syracuse University offers both undergraduate (B.A.) and graduate (M.A., Ph.D.) degrees. The activities and students described in this chapter are part of the professional M.A. program, which emphasizes bringing together theory and practice to prepare students for professional careers in international affairs. PSC 651 is one of three required core courses. Two-thirds of each entering class of approximately fifty students take this course during their first semester at Maxwell.

28. http://www.maxwell.syr.edu/faculty/gmbonham/psc651.htm.

29. http://globetrotter.berkeley.edu/McNamara/.

30. http://oyez.nwu.edu/history-out-loud/lbj/vietnam/.

31. http://oyez.nwu.edu/history-out-loud/jfk/cuban/.

32. Some of the sites we examined included the Sierra Club (http://www.sierraclub.org), CNN (http://www.cnn.com), the World Bank Group (http://www.worldbank.org), the United Nations (http://www.un.org), and the Electronic Embassy (http://www.embassy.org).

33. http://www.maxwell.syr.edu/ir/globgov.htm.

34. J. W. Seifert and G. M. Bonham (1997), "Using the World Wide Web."

35. Ibid.

36. J. T. O'Donnell (1998), *Avatars of the Word. From Papyrus to Cyberspace* (Cambridge: Harvard University Press), p. 133.

37. Ibid., p. 136.

15 Teaching Human Rights Online: The International Court of Justice Considers Genocide

Howard Tolley Jr.

The Teaching Human Rights Online project (THRO) employs instructional technology to make case problems interactive. The "ICJ Considers Genocide" Web site[1] enables students to play the role of a judge at the International Court of Justice (ICJ). The case brought by Bosnia in 1993 charged genocide, called for an end to the United Nations (UN) Security Council arms embargo, and sought damages from Serbia and Montenegro, the former Yugoslavia. Students can review the facts, research the law, and consider opposing arguments that support one side or the other. The prototype Web case can be used in three ways—as an interactive assignment for individuals, as a vehicle for asynchronous exchange of advocacy briefs prior to in-class simulation, and for a simulcast between competing student teams in distance learning centers at different universities. In this chapter I describe how the first two applications develop understanding of human rights and critical thinking skills.

Educational Objectives

Studies demonstrating how the case method enhances learning suggest that computerized problem-solving exercises should also promote critical thinking. The Pew Case Studies in International Affairs have brought to the undergraduate classroom teaching methods that worked well in law schools and colleges of business.[2] "Thinking like a lawyer" of course entails more than calculating the dollars in a contingency fee award: legal reasoning fosters a rational-analytical approach to problem solving.[3] The first step involves the definition of a problem or a decision. The second step requires the diagnosis of the possible reasons for the problem. The third step includes a search for alternative solutions to the problem. Finally, the fourth step involves a comparison of the various alternatives and a choice of the most appropriate one.[4]

The ICJ problem requires students to learn about a contemporary human rights dispute in order to resolve legal issues. Three ambitious goals are (1) to improve knowledge of ICJ procedures, treaty law, and the genocide convention; (2) to develop analytical skills by applying case precedents to a new problem; and (3) to promote collaborative learning with computer-mediated communication. "The ICJ Considers Genocide" combines the critical thinking elements of a Pew Case Study, computer-assisted conflict analysis,[5] and the cross-cultural communication features of the International Communications Negotiation Simulation (ICONS).[6]

By placing factual and legal information in the context of an actual case, the exercise seeks to develop six cognitive skills identified by Bloom:[7]

1. Knowledge: learning facts about the Balkans conflict and rules governing genocide, world court jurisdiction, treaties, and customary norms on genocide.
2. Comprehension: determining which facts and rules support Bosnia's claims and which favor Yugoslavia's defense.
3. Application: selecting appropriate evidence and legal authority to identify the strongest arguments possible for both Yugoslavia and Bosnia.
4. Analysis: reasoning by analogy from prior ICJ cases to reach distinct judgments on each of the different claims raised by Bosnia.
5. Synthesis: reexamining the precedents and arguments to identify an original solution distinct from the outcome advocated by either party.
6. Evaluation: assessing the rationale offered by ICJ judges writing opinions on the dispute.

Evaluating the rival claims obliges students as decisionmakers to comprehend facts, apply legal norms, and analyze different options. The goal is not only to understand the Balkan conflict and international human rights law but also to learn critical thinking skills. Romm and Mahler noted that higher-level cognitive problem solving overlaps the separate affective domain identified by Bloom. Simulation and role-playing are especially educational, as "valuing can be achieved when students actually play a character. By experiencing a character as oneself they go beyond a mere accepting of the character's point of view that is typical of 'responding', into an active involvement, internalization and commitment to it."[8]

Assigning students an unpopular role promotes understanding of alternative values. As advocates for a human rights or authoritarian position that they categorically reject, students may become less certain of their knowledge and more willing to entertain new ideas, learn by questioning, and entertain a range of possibilities. Whether or not they ultimately modify deeply held personal beliefs, the exercise can provide fresh information and the ability to rebut an adversary. Students must identify unresolved issues, recognize relevant facts and legal authority, and reason by analogy. The case method and Socratic dialogue challenge students to balance competing norms and to explain reasoned conclusions.

The case can also be a vehicle for developing oral and written communication skills in combination with assigned position papers and class debate. As a homework exercise or during class, students can write short answers making judgments about competing claims. Small class discussion groups of four to six students can then compare their ideas and explore disagreements. Next, selected representatives from each group can explain their reasoning to the full class. Those explanations should lead to a guided debate that clarifies differing value judgments.

Finally, the problem can help develop student research skills. The Appendix, "Active Teaching Resources," guides students to primary source materials on the case. The problem was completed in August 1996, the point at which the ICJ released its second judgment in the case. Students could be assigned to investigate subsequent developments as the parties present evidence for the court to determine whether Bosnia is entitled to damages.

Case Design

Using a Web browser, students can play the role of an ICJ judge to decide Bosnia's claims. The interdisciplinary problem should be

appropriate for undergraduate students in philosophy, history, political science, psychology, and international relations; for students in
professional classes in law and education; and for high school social
studies students. As distance learning and Internet access become
routinely available, the interactive problem should meet a growing
demand for active learning materials in such classes as International
Law and Organization, Ethics and International Relations, Comparative Government, Human Rights, Modern European History, Critical
Thinking, Philosophy of Law, Educational Philosophy, and Social
Change.

The 4,500-word Web site is illustrated with several color
images—national flags, a regional map, and a photograph of the ICJ
justices. By identifying all the best facts and arguments that support
each side, a participant can earn a perfect score of 100.[9] After receiving a score, students are asked to decide two issues and to provide a
written rationale justifying opinions for Bosnia and/or Yugoslavia.
Participants may then compare their reasoning with the actual opinion of the ICJ on each issue before writing a personal conclusion
reflecting on the court's judgment. A Teaching Note is also available
online. Individuals who want to use the Teaching Note are requested
to submit information about intended use and may then download it
from the Web. The entry screen presents the Case Problem Outline,
with highlighted links in italics.

The ICJ Considers Genocide

I. First. . .
   Introductory Background and Context
   Get More Facts
   Review Legal Authorities
   Consider Possible Arguments
II. Then. . .
   *Select arguments, facts, and authority for each side and receive a
   score*
   *Write your opinion on two issues, read what the court decided,
   and write a critique*
Acknowledgments and Feedback
A Note on Scoring
Reference Links for Further Research

After reviewing the background material, the student com-
pletes a form testing comprehension that is immediately scored
online.

Identify the Best Arguments for Each Side

Check the boxes below to indicate for each item which supports Yugoslavia and which supports Bosnia. Your score will be determined by how well you understand which items support each side.

The strongest **arguments** for each state's position are: Bosnia Yugoslavia

1. Bosnia was not a party to the Genocide
   Convention during the alleged violation   ☐   ☐
2. The Security Council arms embargo violates
   Bosnia's right to self-defense   ☐   ☐
3. Only the Security Council may order provisional
   measures after war has begun   ☐   ☐
4. The fighting in Bosnia is a civil war, not an
   international conflict   ☐   ☐
5. Ethnic cleansing is a form of genocide   ☐   ☐
6. The Genocide Convention applied to Bosnia from
   its independence day   ☐   ☐
7. The Genocide Convention does not apply to
   casualties in military conflict   ☐   ☐

The **facts** that support each state's case are: Bosnia Yugoslavia

1. The indictment of Yugoslav soldiers by the
   War Crimes Tribunal   ☐   ☐
2. Security Council resolutions that condemn
   ethnic cleansing   ☐   ☐
3. Evidence that Yugoslavia's army units never
   entered Bosnian territory   ☐   ☐
4. Bosnian Muslims' killing and deportation of
   Serbs, destruction of religious monuments   ☐   ☐
5. U.N. human rights Special Rapporteur's finding
   that Serbian ethnic cleansing did not appear to be a
   consequence of the war, but rather its goal   ☐   ☐
6. The UN Secretary General accepted Bosnia as a
   successor treaty party rather than as a new state
   acceding to the Genocide Convention   ☐   ☐

Prior **legal doctrines** that support each state's case are: Bosnia Yugoslavia

1. ICJ decision against Libya's challenge to Security
   Council sanctions   ☐   ☐
2. ICJ decision on provisional measures on behalf
   of Nicaragua   ☐   ☐
3. Rules governing when states obtain treaty rights   ☐   ☐
4. UN Charter Article 51 on the right to self-defense   ☐   ☐
5. Standard of proof required to establish
   genocidal intent   ☐   ☐

Submit Form

Score

You earned a total of _____ points of a possible 100.

For Bosnia the strongest arguments are numbers 2, 5, and 6; the facts supporting Bosnia are 1, 2, 5, and 6; and prior legal doctrines that favor Bosnia are 2, 4, and 5.

For Yugoslavia the strongest arguments were numbers 1, 3, 4, and 7; the facts supporting Yugoslavia are 3 and 4; and prior legal doctrines that favor Yugoslavia are 1 and 3.

After receiving the individual score, the student must use skills of analysis and application to make two judgments in the case and explain the reasoning for each. Once those written opinions have been recorded, the student should review the actual ICJ decision/rationale and may write a concluding critique.

Judgment and Rationale

Now it is your responsibility as a judge to write your opinion about two issues confronting the court and explain your reasons in the space provided.

1. Should the court find that the Security Council arms embargo violated Bosnia's rights to self-defense under the UN Charter?

2. Was Bosnia a party to the Genocide Convention from the date of its independence or only after its formal accession took effect?

Submit Answers

After submiting your answers, review what the ICJ actually decided, consider the judges' reasoning, and write a critique of their rationale.

Most students complete the problem in less than forty-five minutes. No additional research is required to answer the case questions. An appended reference section identifies varied sources that students may consult about human rights law. Wherever possible, the bibliography promotes online access to materials via computer by offering uniform resource locator addresses for appropriate Web sites.

"The ICJ Considers Genocide" is a learning tool, not an evaluation instrument. Students can with a few clicks of the mouse jump ahead in order to discover the scoring formula and model written answers. There is no access charge, so any "cheating" cost is limited to a lost learning opportunity. Those who follow the script can profitably use the problem at several levels. An Instructor's Manual (obtained online by submitting a request form) provides discussion questions for a single class session and guidelines for additional asynchronous text and teleconference interaction.

Classroom Implementation

Instructors can use the interactive problem either as an individual or a group assignment in preparation for a single class meeting or for a more elaborate simulation exercise. As an individual assignment, students can work the problem independently and receive immediate feedback online to both forced choice and written answers. As a collaborative learning tool, the case may be used by instructors for role-playing after Internet text exchange between their own students and with classes at other institutions, both in the United States and abroad.

Discussion at a Single Class Meeting

The case forces students to select between competing authority and values to resolve a dispute that has no single answer. William Perry's work on the stages of intellectual development revealed the need to cultivate uncertainty in undergraduates' worldview.[10] High school graduates bring to college a dualistic mind-set and expect to be taught the truth. "Professor, what is the correct answer?" "How can there possibly be more than one way to solve that problem and still get it right?" Dualists with simplistic views of truth and justice regard attorneys as unprincipled hired guns. The case method complicates that reality.[11]

Craig Nelson labeled the elementary stage of cognitive development the "Sergeant Friday" approach, using "just the facts" to establish an unequivocal truth.[12] At the intermediate level of cognitive development, Nelson described a "Baskin Robbins" mode when student relativists find some validity in every individual's unique tastes and have little basis for making value judgments. At the highest level of moral reasoning, the course instructor may enlist advanced students in evaluating universal principles, cultural relativism, and situational ethics.

In an undergraduate class of "Sergeant Friday" thinkers, a split decision illustrates the type of "Baskin Robbins" uncertainty that would demonstrate development of intermediate-level critical thinking skills. Reasonable minds may differ on how the ICJ should decide Bosnia's claims. What appears correct from a humanitarian perspective may seem erroneous to a rule of law advocate.

As a homework assignment, instructors should require students to bring printouts of their responses, score, and written answers from the interactive exercise to class. Students should make difficult choices on their own without first checking out the answers/analysis provided online. By awarding an equal pass to every student who turns in a completed printout, the instructor can promote a more genuine student effort to understand the material. Those who do poorly should be encouraged to repeat the exercise and learn from their errors, but submission of a 100 score ought to be awarded the same passing grade as a 50. The recommended student evaluation questions below may be used either for in-class discussion or on a written test of students' ability to apply concepts learned by doing the Web exercise. An instructor who wants to use the Internet case to grade students on how well they answer the problem questions will need to limit access to the answers provided online.

Before students turn in their papers, the instructor may use class time to have work groups reorganize the three sections of eighteen forced choice items into four different issue areas. Which of the different facts and prior legal doctrines address which arguments? Students in each class group should compare their answers, noting areas of consensus and disagreement. A designated reporter from each group may then give an oral summary to initiate discussion by the entire class. If desired, a printout of the selection page can be prepared as an overhead transparency to assist when groups report their analysis to the entire class.

Argument: The arms embargo violates Bosnia's right to self-defense.

- Only the Security Council may order provisional measures after war has begun
- ICJ decision against Libya's challenge to Security Council sanctions
- ICJ decision on provisional measures on behalf of Nicaragua
- UN Charter Article 51 on the right to self-defense

Argument: The Genocide Convention applied to Bosnia from its independence day.

- Bosnia was not a party to the Genocide Convention during the alleged violation
- The UN Secretary General accepted Bosnia as a successor treaty party rather than as a new state acceding to the Genocide Convention
- Rules governing when states obtain treaty rights

Argument: The fighting in Bosnia is a civil war, not an international conflict.

* Evidence that Yugoslavia's army units never entered Bosnian territory

Argument: Yugoslavia is responsible for ethnic cleansing, a form of genocide.

* The Genocide Convention does not apply to casualties in military conflict
* The indictment of Yugoslav soldiers by the War Crimes Tribunal
* Security Council resolutions that condemn ethnic cleansing
* Bosnian Muslims' killing and deportation of Serbs, destruction of religious monuments
* Human rights special rapporteur finding that Serbian ethnic cleansing did not appear to be a consequence of the war but rather its goal
* Standard of proof required to establish genocidal intent

Once the class has sorted out which legal doctrines and facts apply to each argument, students should identify for each issue the items that support Yugoslavia and those that support Bosnia's claims. The instructor may then lead the students into a critique of the ICJ decision on the first two issues by evaluating the conflicting material. Did Yugoslavia have the superior argument on the arms embargo, and was Bosnia entitled to benefit from the Genocide Convention prior to the government's formal accession?

The exercise works best when all students have the same basic information. Some individuals may know more about the situation or about developments since the case was written. Any additional information that influences students' reasoning should be shared with all. In order to develop analytical skills, students should write papers assessing the strengths and weaknesses of the arguments for both sides. Students might consistently favor one party or attempt a synthesis of the rival positions. All choices should be carefully reasoned and cogently explained.

Optional Simulation at a Second or Third Class Meeting

In pilot tests with classes at the University of Cincinnati, students learned more from the exercise when assigned roles to play in a simulated ICJ hearing of oral argument by opposing counsel. The following recommended one-week schedule of three fifty-minute classes could be combined into two seventy-five minute sessions for classes that only meet twice a week.

The course syllabus or other advance handout should specify the simulation date, offer a preliminary introduction to the different roles, and provide a response form (if students are invited to express a preference for a particular role as counsel or judge). The instructor then assigns individuals to prepare oral argument as opposing counsel and instructs judges to prepare questions. Cocounsel should prepare and distribute advocacy briefs in advance, using a class e-mail address if possible.

Depending on the number of issues identified and the number of judges participating, the simulation can work with as few as three students, and it is possible to involve up to twenty-five. Here is a format for eleven students playing three judges and two cocounsel for each side on two of the four possible issues. The remaining two issues can be used in class discussion to assist those preparing for the simulation.

Advocates for Bosnia:
Two Cocounsel: Issue of Security Council arms embargo.
Two Cocounsel: Issue of whether Bosnia was a party to Genocide Convention.

Advocates for Yugoslavia:
Two Cocounsel: Issue of Security Council arms embargo
Two Cocounsel: Issue of whether Bosnia was a party to Genocide Convention

Judges of the ICJ:
President of the court (from Algeria)
Two ad hoc judges appointed by Bosnia (from UK) and Yugoslavia (a Serbian)

First Session, Monday:
- Lecture on Balkans' political history through the 1995 Dayton Peace accords, individual war crimes prosecutions in The Hague, and Bosnia's genocide case at the ICJ.
- Review instructions for all to do the Web exercise. Assign all

to print out pages indicating the choices made, scoring results, and their written answers.

• Follow-up e-mail to class from instructor identifying roles, repeating instructions.

Second Session, Wednesday:

• Identify one issue for discussion: Is it a civil war or international conflict? Overhead transparency to display response form listing choices of facts and legal authority that students should have brought to class as a printout. Discuss which facts and authority relate to the civil war issue and which items support Yugoslavia or Bosnia.

• Identify a second issue for analysis: Is Yugoslavia responsible for genocide? Discuss which evidence and legal precedent support each party's position on ethnic cleansing.

• Restate the two remaining issues to be argued by counsel at next class session. Instruct cocounsel to write advocacy briefs by selecting the best evidence and legal authority for their client from the list. No additional research required beyond creative analysis using previously assigned text readings. Clarify roles of cocounsel and ICJ judges, noting availability of the July 1996 ICJ opinion online for those interested. Group work at conclusion of class to discuss advocacy briefs for class e-mail distribution prior to noon Thursday.

• Collect page printouts of all students' scores from individual Web role-play.

Third Session, Friday:

• Role-play oral argument. Five minutes for each side on each issue, with more time as needed for questioning by judges. Brief caucus of cocounsel, then three-minute closing argument per side. Judges vote separately on each issue, announce results.

• Debriefing: Return student score pages for in-class correction of errors using overhead transparency. Identify additional arguments and evidence not included in the Internet materials.

• Give wrap-up minilecture on ICJ split decisions of 1993 and 1996 and remaining issues.

• Consider and discuss analogous relationships—U.S. Supreme

Court judicial review of Congress, European Court of Justice and Parliament. Consider significance of distinction between civil war and international conflict.

- Present and discuss hypothetical analogy arising from genocide in central Africa.
- Preview how the analytical approach used may be tested on future written exam. Prepare exam questions such as those given in the Rwanda problem in the box, "Winter 1997 Assessment of ICJ Genocide Computer Role-Playing and Case Simulation," to assess whether the exercise fulfilled the learning objectives.
- Circulate and discuss the evaluation form given in the box, "Student Evaluation of Computer Role-Playing and Case Simulation, 1977–1998," to obtain students' written assessment of the exercise.

Assessment

Peer Review

Experienced case authors from several disciplines have contributed to the ICJ prototype since it went online in 1996, although few of those authors had personally employed Web-based instruction. Pew Faculty Fellows reviewed the exercise at the 1997 and 1998 International Studies Association meetings of the section on Active Learning in International Studies. A weeklong Pace University workshop on case writing led to considerable improvements. Blind review conducted by the North American Case Research Association and the World Affairs Case Research Association resulted in presentations and further improvements at two professional meetings.[13] THRO will arrange comparable peer review for any original cases submitted to the project and has an International Standard Serial Number to publish work in an electronic journal.[14] The project will also assist authors of published cases to reformat their work as interactive human rights exercises for THRO.

After discovering the exercises on the Web, several course instructors have used the first prototype cases with their students; repeated use and adoption by more faculty will be a future measure of success.

Learning Outcomes

Assessment is hot in higher education. The American Association of Higher Education's Teaching Learning and Technology Affiliate's Flashlight Project has developed a tool kit for Gathering Student Data About the Value of Educational Uses of Technology (created and funded by Annenberg Corporation for Public Broadcasting Project). The five hundred survey items and accompanying handbook might be adapted for use with both U.S. students and overseas participants. One or more additional tools for measuring students' cognitive and moral development may be selected from the Cornell Critical Thinking Test, the California Critical Thinking Skills Test, the Reflective Judgment Interview, and the Defining Issues Test.[15] A growing interest in "global competence" indicates a need for original measures to assess whether the planned transnational videoconferences improve cross-cultural communication skills.[16] According to Dewey, the use of interactive problems should also benefit the instructor: "[T]he alternative to furnishing ready-made subject matter and listening to the accuracy with which it is reproduced is not quiescence, but participating, sharing in an activity. In such shared activity, the teacher is a learner, and the learner is, without knowing it, a teacher."[17]

Research in several disciplines has found improvement in student learning from computer-mediated communication. Matthew Bonham and Jeffrey Seifert identified three levels of computer use in a survey of students who experienced a range of frustration and success on the Web.[18] An article in the electronic peer-reviewed *Journal of the Asynchronous Learning Network* assessed the successes and failures of "CyberProf."[19] A Dutch research group used a pretest-posttest design to evaluate learning outcomes of computer-based role-playing and found significant dividends for interpersonal skills training.[20] Other research in political science, critical thinking, computer education, and other fields has also shown benefits.[21]

Two minimally sophisticated evaluation tools have been used to measure the effectiveness of the ICJ problem after several trials with undergraduate classes: a questionnaire survey to obtain students' evaluation of their experience with the interactive case, and test questions to assess their mastery of problem-solving skills and substantive content based on their work online. Generally positive student feedback confirmed an expectation that students would enjoy new learning with new technology. Disseminating their written work on the Internet and arranging a competitive simulation with another institution increased students' efforts to master the material.

Formative Evaluation

THRO role-playing exercises seek to realize Bloom's taxonomy of educational objectives, the rational-analytical model of John Dewey, and the cognitive developmental theories of William Perry. Success will require formative evaluation during pilot tests of prototype problems subject to ongoing revision and improvement.[22] Following the first in-class simulations of the ICJ prototype case, fifty students were asked to "grade" the exercise on an A to F scale:

Student Evaluation of Computer Role-Playing and Case Simulation, 1977–1998 (percentage)	A	B	C	D	F
1. Enhancing *knowledge and comprehension* of the ICJ, Bosnian situation, treaty law, etc.	65	33	2		
2. Developing critical thinking skills of *questioning, analysis,* and *application*	60	31	8		
3. Promoting effective collaboration with other students in problem solving	45	36	18		
4. Fostering improved electronic, written, and/or oral communication skills	55	40	4		
5. Stimulating interest in and effort to understand international law and organization	61	32	7		
6. Overall value of the project as presented by the instructor for your major	57	34	4	4	

Other evaluation questions asked students to evaluate four teaching problems—two hardcopy Pew case studies and two Web interactive exercises—as well as the assigned course text, lecture/discussion, in-class negotiation/simulation, and the electronic communication tools. The text received the lowest marks, and the Pew hardcopy problem on the Falklands/Malvinas was most highly rated. Students recommended future use of both formats, finding advantages and disadvantages in each approach. The text-based problems were more expensive and lacked the Internet research links, but access and use were easier. One student wrote: "I have a hard time reading off a computer screen. The electronic problems sometimes were too massive and [it] was hard to keep track [of] where info was." The new technology generally received high praise, as reflected in the following comments.

Knowledge/Comprehension

I liked . . . the Bosnia example because it is always in the news and is hard to understand. This exercise cleared up many of my questions not answered by the mainstream media.

Best feature of case is it allowed me to apply facts and law to actual cases. Gives a fuller, more in-depth knowledge. . . . I can repeat facts, but not fully understand the concept. Helps to prepare for career, in organization, presentation, and delivery. Helps to identify important facts and understand concepts. Helps with critical thinking.

Collaborative Problem Solving

- The most valuable piece to this class was the tremendous amount of class participation. I now have twenty new friends.
- Does stimulate learning and creates an atmosphere of camaraderie among classmates who must work together! It was time well spent for case studies are the best approach. Survey courses don't teach enough hands-on material.
- Case problems allow the class to visualize specific proceedings of the ICJ and the UN. That's better than a lecture in that we see how things work instead of just hearing how they work.

Critical Thinking

- I found the case problems to be of great value. They required critical thinking and interaction w/classmates which are both pluses in the educational process.
- This is as close to real life [as] we can get. It stimulates critical thinking and extends interest for extra research in every subject.
- I enjoyed it very much. You always learn more when you actually get involved hands on and not just concentrating on memorizing.

Communication Skills

- E-mail was probably the most useful tool. When events occurred outside of our small window of meeting time, it was easy to be kept abreast. Cooperation w/others was a somewhat tenuous situation for me.
- The Internet use was good. I enjoyed being able to turn stuff in from home.

- Internet cases had the advantage of bibliography and Internet links for further reference.
- I think the electronically oriented aspects of the class have added to the class. Allowing interaction between students prior to in-class debates is very helpful.

Stimulating Interest

- Internet is cheaper. . . . I personally learned far more from the in-class simulations than I did cramming for a midterm!
- I preferred the electronic format because it offers more in terms of specific laws and applicable information than the standard hard copy.
- The best thing was the scoring process; it's fun to see in a role-playing situation if in fact one's choices were correct.
- The role-playing is the part of this class I always learn the most from. This was great. Getting involved and knowing specifics is a more interesting way of learning.

Winter 1997 Assessment of ICJ Genocide
Computer Role-Playing and Case Simulation

A question on the final exam tested students' ability to apply lessons from the ICJ genocide role-playing to a quasi-hypothetical situation in Africa.
Problem: After Hutu genocide against Tutsis in Rwanda, the Tutsis won control of Rwanda's government. Hutu refugees fled to neighboring Zaire where UN workers provided humanitarian relief. Native Tutsis in Zaire have now killed many refugees as part of a military campaign to secede and become independent. The government army has counterattacked.

Exam Questions	% of 30 Students with Correct Answers
1. What could the UN do to punish individual Tutsis in Zaire for acts of genocide?	50
2. If requested by Zaire, could the ICJ order the UN workers to leave the country?	43
3. Could the ICJ hold Rwanda's Tutsi government responsible for genocide against Hutus in Zaire?	63
4. If the ICJ hears the case, what additional judges would be appointed?	80
5. Is there any immediate response to the fighting the court could make?	30

Students with Active Learning Correctly Answered More Test Questions:

No. of Correct Answers	8 Cocounsel		22 Other Students		30 Students Total	
	No.	%	No.	%	No.	%
1	1	13	4	18	5	16
2	0	0	7	32	7	24
3	2	25	4	18	6	20
4	5	62	6	27	11	36
5	0	0	1	5	1	3
Total	8	100	22	100	30	100

Conclusion

In a culture dominated by television and computer games, can time spent before a monitor improve students' substantive knowledge and their cognitive and normative intelligence? Success requires programming and electronic communication that challenge students to think and exchange information rather than to have computers solve a problem. Whitehead cautioned: "[B]eware of 'inert ideas'—that is to say, ideas that are merely received into the mind without being utilized, or tested, or thrown into fresh combinations."[23] Well before the computer revolution, Dewey advised: "[T]eachers would find their own work less of a grind and strain if school conditions favored learning in the sense of discovery and not in that of storing away what others pour into them."[24]

Classical forms of active learning—the Socratic method, case-based teaching, and simulation—employ problem solving for intellectual and moral development. Dewey's 1916 prescription applies to the Internet as well as the school.[25] Preliminary assessment of the ICJ prototype problem reveals sufficient payoff to warrant continued development. Project THRO also offers a second interactive problem, "Terrorism and Human Rights in India."[26] Both problems are freely available for pilot testing; course instructors may obtain on-line teaching notes and are urged to provide feedback. Case authors may submit interactive problems for peer review that may be added to the THRO database.[27] Professors interested in arranging Internet and/or teleconference simulations of THRO cases with classes from other universities may contact the author for current information about the project. Instructors who use either THRO problem are urged to assist the teaching initiative by providing feedback on their students' experience with the exercises.

Since cyberspace is global, THRO could become a vehicle for transnational learning communities. Improved technology for online videoconferencing creates a unique opportunity for group-based problem-solving exercises beyond the classroom in cyberspace communication between students of different cultures. In a 1998 pilot teleconference, students from North Dakota and Ohio conducted a simulated world court hearing of Bosnia's claims against Yugoslavia. In 1999 an undergraduate class in Ohio exchanged live audio and video with students from Cape Town, South Africa, for a simulated ICJ hearing on Bosnia's claims. Preliminary contacts with prospective partner institutions in India and Turkey are being developed. By 2000 the project should have four additional interactive problems online presenting human rights issues related to women's rights and business ethics involving the United States and several other countries.

THRO cases will be further developed to provide asynchronous and synchronous text, audio, and video communication between students from different institutions and cultures. The prototype cases will remain freely available on the Web through 1999 and probably into 2000 as the project seeks feedback and solicits submissions from authors who wish to contribute interactive curriculum materials for peer review and inclusion in the electronic database.

Notes

1. Http://oz.uc.edu/thro/genocide/index.html.
2. Karen Mingst, ed. (1994), *A Special Issue of International Studies Notes: Case Teaching in International Relations* 19(2).
3. G. R. Shreve (1977), "Classroom Litigation in the First Semester of Law School—An Approach to Teaching Legal Method at Harvard," *Journal of Legal Education* 29(1): 95–105.
4. T. Romm and S. Mahler (1986), "A Three Dimensional Model for Using Case Studies in the Academic Classroom," *Higher Education* 15(6): 681.
5. Lincoln P. Bloomfield and Allen Moulton (1977), *Managing International Conflict: From Theory to Policy* (New York: St. Martin's), includes two CASCON software disks and User's Guide.
6. Since the 1980s the University of Maryland has operated a text conference on the Internet. ICONS now involves fifteen hundred students a

year at more than fifty-five colleges and universities. Students from eighteen countries compete in online international conferences simulating diplomatic negotiations to resolve foreign policy differences. For more information on ICONS, see http://www.bsos.umd.edu/icons/icons.html. See also Brigid Starkey and Jonathan Wilkenfeld (1966), "Project ICONS: Computer-Assisted Negotiations for the IR Classroom," *International Studies Notes* 21 (Winter):25–29.

7. Benjamin Bloom (1956), *Taxonomy of Educational Objectives. Handbook I: Cognitive Domain* (New York: McKay).

8. T. Romm and S. Mahler (1986), "A Three Dimensional Model," 681.

9. A U.S. Supreme Court interactive exercise created by Harvard professor of constitutional law Arthur Miller—"Courtroom Challenge"—served as the initial model. The seven landmark Supreme Court civil liberties decisions that Miller adapted include cases of particular interest to students on mandatory drug testing of a school athlete and a compulsory flag salute. As of June 1997, those exercises on the CourtroomTV Web site were no longer available.

10. W. G. Perry Jr. (1999), *Forms of Intellectual and Ethical Development in the College Years, A Scheme* (San Francisco: Jossey-Bass).

11. Pat Hutchings (1993), *Using Cases to Improve College Teaching* (Washington, DC: American Association of Higher Education).

12. Craig Nelson (1997), "Tools for Tampering with Teaching's Taboos," in *New Paradigms for College Teaching,* ed. William Campbell and Karl Smith (Edina, Minn.: Interaction Books).

13. "The ICJ Considers Genocide: Bosnia Versus Yugoslavia" was presented at the 1997 International Studies Association meeting as well as the World Affairs Case Research Association in 1998. The "Prime Minister's Dilemma" was selected after peer review for presentation to the 1997 North American Case Research Association.

14. With the end of training grants for Pew Faculty Fellows in 1995, professors seeking instruction in case writing can benefit from two interdisciplinary workshops. Lilly Conferences on College and University Teaching are offered by the International Alliance of Teacher Scholars, Inc., 414 S. Craig St., Suite 313, Pittsburgh, PA 15213 (800 718-4287; Alliance@IATS. com). Regional conferences in 1996–1997 were conducted in New Hampshire, Oregon, California, Ohio, Maryland, and Georgia. Pace University (previously in conjunction with the American Association of Higher Education) sponsors a summer workshop at the University of British Columbia in Vancouver. Rita Silverman and William Welty, Center for Case Studies in Education, School of Education, Pace University, 861 Bedford Rd., Pleasantville, NY 10570.

15. James R. Rest (1979) *Development in Judging Moral Issues* (Minneapolis: University of Minnesota Press).

16. Richard Lambert (1994), *Educational Exchange and Global Competence* (New York: Council on International Educational Exchange), 11–14.

17. John Dewey (1916), *Democracy and Education* (New York: Free Press).

18. G. Matthew Bonham and Jeffrey W. Seifert (1997). "Using the World Wide Web: Expanding the Classroom or a Virtual Distraction?" (paper presented at the annual meeting of the American Political Science Association, Computers and Multimedia Section, Washington, DC, August 28–31).

19. Deanna M. Raineri et al. (1997), "CyberProf[TM]—An Intelligent Human-Computer Interface for Interactive Instruction on the World Wide Web," *Journal of the Asynchronous Learning Network,* no. 2. Available on-line at http://www.aln.org/alnweb/journal/jaln.htm.

20. C. Manrique (1992), "Network Resources for Political Scientists," *PS: Political Science and Politics* 25(4):667.

21. For critical thinking, see S. Whitney (1990), "VAX Notes—Using a Computer Conference to Teach Critical Thinking," *Instructional Computing Update* University of Iowa: 3–5. For computer education, see B. Bergeron (1988), "Toward More Effective Learning Environments: Strategies for Computer Simulation Design," *Collegiate Microcomputer* 6(4):289–309. For research in other fields, see Paul Morris and Joan McNamara, eds. (1994), *Valuable Viable Software in Education: Cases and Analysis* (New York: McGraw-Hill).

22. Karen J. Hoelscher (1995), "It's Too Late to Dig the Well When Your House Is on Fire: Using Formative Evaluation to Increase the Educational Effectiveness of Technology Products," in Erwin Boschmann, ed., *The Electronic Classroom: A Handbook for Education in the Electronic Environment* (Medford, N.J.: Learned Information, Inc.), 205–214.

23. Alfred North Whitehead (1929), *The Aims of Education and Other Essays* (New York: Mentar Books), 2–3.

24. John Dewey (1916), *Democracy and Education* (New York: Macmillan), 179.

25. Ibid.

26. Howard Tolley Jr. (1999), "Terrorism and Human Rights in India: Teaching Human Rights On-Line," *International Studies Notes* 24(2):41–52.

27. THRO adds a curriculum component to the Urban Morgan Institute for Human Rights and DIANA, an electronic research database at the University of Cincinnati. Howard Tolley Jr. (1998), "Project THRO: Teaching Human Rights Online," *Human Rights Quarterly* 20(4):945–946.

16 | Learning About Foreign Policy at the Movies

Patrick Haney

The purpose of this chapter is to discuss ways to learn at the movies. Although the traditional medium through which students learn about political ideas, issues, and concepts may be reading texts and listening to lectures, it is not the only way. The effort to create an active learning environment in the classroom emphasizes the construction of avenues through which students can engage material and gain ownership over their own learning. The use of documentaries and news segments, and even movie clips, in class from time to time as a way to introduce or highlight a point or concept to students is not an uncommon practice. Video can be a useful instrument to help make something real to students and to engage them in an unintimidating way and thus can contribute to helping create an active learning environment.

What is perhaps less common is to use movies as one of the primary "texts" of a course.[1] I shall discuss some of the pedagogy behind "learning at the movies" and report on such a course that I constructed, focusing on issues and concepts in U.S. foreign and national security policy. I also discuss how the students and I have evaluated the course. The chapter appendix includes some additional movie ideas for U.S. foreign policy topics; it includes release dates and running times.

Educational Objectives

Movies can be a powerful tool to teach about politics or about any topic. They help bring to life abstract concepts, and they allow the student "vicariously to share experiences he or she might otherwise find remote and therefore puzzling."[2] Movies are an especially viable mode to create linkages between learning about concepts and placing them in a meaningful context for students. They are and become a part of the lived reality of students. The process of watching a film can transform abstract concepts and issues into a quasi-lived experience. A concept such as "deterrence" moves from existing on a page to the lived experience of students while watching *Dr. Strangelove,* for example.

Films also enliven the educational process.[3] Films dramatize the abstract and even the undramatic; they create bridges to past events and times, and they can help stimulate discussion and debate.[4] World War II, for example, is so far removed from many college students' point of reference that it is still unreal even after reading about it. But after watching *Patton*, the war and its politics become alive and real and thus a subject open for discussion and debate.

Chandler and Adams argued that movies can also serve as a leveling device between the instructor and the student. "Everyone knows how to watch a movie, right?" "The role played by the instructor can be in deepening discussion, increasing observational capacity, and, hopefully, helping students to become more thoughtful about not just the particular movie under discussion, but also about their overall role as moviegoers."[5] Using films can level the structures of hierarchy and power existing in some classrooms that can inhibit discussion. Students are used to talking openly about the movies they see. The use of movies tries to take advantage of the familiarity with movies to create a more lively discussion and debate.

The use of films in class thus fits within the emerging learning paradigm.[6] This view, which privileges *learning* in the classroom over *teaching,*

> requires instructors to frame pedagogic content in ways that enable students to discover the relationship of academic concepts to their own life experiences. To use movies and other popular art forms as tools for teaching, and to invite students to explore them as tools for learning, is a risky venture. It requires that we move away from the forms of communication at which we tend to excel to those where we also become students.[7]

Such a move is a real challenge for many of us. We may be used to—

and good at—lecturing. But there are sound pedagogic reasons for shifting from this mode, including thinking about how tools such as films can be brought to bear to increase learning in the classroom. We need to see our job not as to teach students (as the font of knowledge that is to be dispensed) but rather as to facilitate our students' learning. Movies can be a useful tool in this process, since most of us are used to being part of a discussion about movies, rather than lecturing about movies. The transition for us can be simpler here than with other media.

There are drawbacks to using films as learning devices. As Gregg discussed, films often do not use history very well. They leave some things out, make too much of other things, and often take license. They also tend to come from and can perpetuate a Western-centric bias.[8] It is also important to remember that although one of the ideas behind using films in class is to increase learning, some things in movies can hinder learning. It is impossible for instructors to know what emotional histories our students bring to class, and the themes in some movies can be very powerful. We do not want our experiment with films to backfire, so it is important to remember to make the classroom "safe," as Allen discussed.[9]

The instructor should give a sketch of what students are about to see in a movie and make it clear that students can leave if they become uncomfortable. It should also be made clear that there are other ways to learn the content that is contained in a movie, so that if a student does not watch a movie in the class the material can still be learned. In a foreign policy setting, movies about war, especially the U.S. experience in Vietnam, can be problematic on this count; it is impossible, however, to know or predict what might be counterproductive for a student to see in class. So we should always give a brief description of what the movie is about, warn students about tough scenes that might await them, and assure students that it is all right if they need to leave. We want our classrooms to be vibrant, provocative, and safe places for learning.

Course Design

Setting and Parameters

My first experience with offering a movie-based class came in the summer of 1997. If the theory that using movies could help students learn about politics was correct, then it seemed a worthwhile endeavor to see how well a course that primarily used movies to stimulate learning would work. It was safer to test this out in the summer when enrollments would be lower and the idea of such an experiment might fit in better. My basic objective for this experimental course was to try to attract student to politics by helping us all see the political issues and themes that are all around us—even in the popular movies that we watch. I wanted us to see how much we could learn in a structured environment that was still "at the movies."

Two opportunities came together at the right time to allow for this course to be constructed. First, the university wanted to experiment with its summer offerings to attract more students. Thus, the tide was favorable for trying out a course like this. Second, poll after poll reported that college students were losing interest in politics, and political science enrollments were dropping around the country, including in our department at Miami University. Although this may not seem like an ideal environment for a new political science class, it did provide an impetus for trying something new to develop student interest in politics courses. The idea was to take advantage of an interesting potential contradiction: students say they are not interested in politics, but they love good movies—even movies with political themes in them. Thus, the idea behind the movie course was to use good movies as a way to stimulate interest in politics.

Because one of the purposes of the course was to attract non-political science students, I approached the course as an introductory-level class. Also as a way to lower the cost of entry for students who liked the idea of a movie course but who were not sure they were very interested in politics, the course was offered "credit/no credit" only. This also made grading easier, since the most significant grading question was only whether someone's written work and participation were "satisfactory."

This course was thus designed as a 2-credit-hour course as a way to attract students and make the course look unintimidating. (Most of our courses are 3- or 4-credit-hour courses.) Our summer courses are six weeks long; such a class would need to meet for about 4 hours and 30 minutes per week over the six weeks. Thus, this course met for 2 hours and 15 minutes, twice per week. About twenty-five students took the course in summer 1998. This number may not seem high (and it would not be impressive during the regular school year), but this was a big draw as a summer class.[10]

Assignments in the course included attendance and participation in discussions that followed the films and on the days that were set aside as discussion days. We would always have some time to talk about the movies after watching them, but I also set most of three meetings aside so that we would have plenty of discussion time.[11] Each student was also required to write two short papers (three–four pages). In each paper students were required to comment in an analytic way on the political themes in a movie we had just seen and to integrate the issues raised in one of the readings that accompanied that movie. As a credit/no credit class assignment, these papers were evaluated as satisfactory or unsatisfactory.

Learning Goals

The course incorporated both procedural and conceptual learning goals. At a procedural level, the course was to provide a setting where ideas could be discussed and explored freely and openly. It should be a place where we all saw ourselves as students of politics with equal voice. Movies can be especially good at this because we all have experience watching movies; this helps level the field.[12] The course was not to feel burdensome or like a task that had to be performed. The learning here should seem enjoyable and accessible, especially since this was both a summer course and one of the first political science classes that many of the students would have taken.

The conceptual learning goals for the class included seeing the pervasiveness of politics in foreign and national security policy. I wanted to focus on the basic institutions and processes in this policy area, such as the president, Congress, the military, and the intelligence community. Also under examination would be the role of the public as an actor and as a group being acted upon in the Cold War. We would cover some Cold War and nuclear era history and the basics of deterrence theory and explore the role of the United States in world affairs during and after the Cold War.

Movies and Readings

With these learning goals in mind, I tried to match appropriate movies with each theme that was to be explored in the course; short readings were also matched with each movie and theme. The readings all came from the *Annual Editions* collection of readings on *American Foreign Policy 98/99*, which includes short essays on a variety of topics.[13] The themes, movies, and readings from the course are listed below.

Introduction. In the first class meeting we watched a fifteen-minute segment from the movie *Canadian Bacon* (1995; 90 minutes).[14] The clip shows U.S. policymakers trying to come up with a new "enemy" after the end of the Cold War, which includes their making an offer to the Russians to "mix things up a little" to get people's minds off their troubles. (The Russians turn down the offer and ask the Americans to stop being such bad winners.) U.S. policymakers then turn their attention to constructing an enemy out of Canada, and the clip shows how news and propaganda can be used to stir up strong anti-Canadian public sentiment in the United States. We then talked about the political themes in the clip. This clip was used as a way to give the students an example of how the course would proceed and how we would all be watching movies not just for entertainment but also with an eye toward the political themes that are embedded in them.

U.S. Global Leadership. To highlight this issue during and after the Cold War, we watched *The Mouse that Roared* (1959; 83 minutes), a very funny movie about a small country that declares war on the United States with the intention of losing immediately and thus gaining access to U.S. postwar aid. (The plan goes awry, of course.) The readings included a speech by Secretary of State Madeline Albright, an essay about U.S. values by George Kennan, and a provocative article about American leadership in world politics.[15]

The American Political Context. As a way to underscore the political context within which U.S. foreign and national security policy is made, we watched *The Candidate* (1972; 109 minutes), a very good movie in which the character played by Robert Redford runs for the U.S. Senate. This movie nicely shows the omnipresent connection between politics and policy. The readings for this movie included an essay about the politics in the U.S. Senate concerning the Chemical Weapons Convention and an essay about campaign contributions from the arms industry.[16]

The Intelligence Community. I wanted to show a movie about the intelligence community so we could bring that set of institutions into our discussion too and planned to show *Three Days of the Condor* (1975; 117 minutes).[17] I could not get a copy of the movie. Instead we watched *The Manchurian Candidate* (1962; 126 minutes; black and white), which is a classic conspiracy/political assassination film; its showing was also timely given the unfortunate death of Frank Sinatra at the same time. This movie is not as good at highlighting the Central Intelligence Agency (CIA) as *Condor*, but there is lots of political intrigue in it. The reading for this session was an essay about the CIA.[18]

The Space Race. In order to focus attention on the relation between the Cold War and U.S. society, I showed *The Right Stuff* (1983; 109 minutes), which is a good film for highlighting the space race and the Cold War and is amusing. Because of the length of the film, we watched it in two parts. The readings that accompanied the movie included an essay about trends in public opinion and foreign policy and essays about new arms races in the contemporary system.[19]

Deterrence. To introduce some basic concepts about deterrence and the nuclear age, we watched *Dr. Strangelove, or: How I Learned to Stop Worrying and Love the Bomb* (1964; 93 minutes; black and white). This is a great film that is as educational and scary as it is funny. To show that such issues do not exist only in movies, we watched part of the docudrama film, *The Missiles of October* (1974; 155 minutes). Readings for this week included essays on the White House situation room, arms reduction talks, and the history of the Doomsday Clock from *The Bulletin of the Atomic Scientists.*[20]

The United States in Latin America. I wanted to bring a substantive policy area into our discussions by showing a movie about U.S. policy in Latin America. There are a lot of good films for this. I intended to show *Romero* (1989; 102 minutes),[21] but it was unavailable. We watched the comedy *Moon over Parador* (1988; 105 minutes) instead, a movie about a U.S. actor who is able to fill in for a suddenly deceased Latin American dictator because the actor looks just like the dictator.[22] Readings for this movie included an essay about the U.S. operation in Somalia and articles about Islamic fundamentalism and pivot states.[23]

A World Transformed. As a way to talk about the end of the Cold War, we watched *Star Trek VI: The Undiscovered Country* (1991; 109 minutes), which is really a parable on the end of the Cold War. The readings focused on expansion of the North Atlantic Treaty Organization (NATO) after the end of the Cold War and the debate about Russia's reaction to the move.[24] We concluded with a discussion day that focused on the last few films we had seen and readings that reexamined the Gulf War and Bosnia as well as public reactions to the use of force in the post–Cold War era.[25]

Adjustments from the Original Experiment

I incorporated a couple of changes into the summer 1998 course based on the experience of the pilot course in 1997. First, the course included more time for discussion. Twenty minutes after a movie is not enough time, we found. For summer 1998 I planned discussion days so that we would have more time to talk about the movies and the readings. Second, readings were all in the *Annual Editions* reader, *American Foreign Policy 98/99,* so that the articles would be more accessible to students (a readings packet could serve the same purpose). Third, the course was evaluated more thoroughly. Last, I changed some of the movies that I showed, mostly for my own variety or theme changes. For example, I showed *Patton* (1970; 169 minutes) in 1997, which went well as a two-part movie. Rather than focus as much on World War II and civil-military relations, in 1998 I wanted to show more about life in the Cold War and so showed *The Right Stuff. Dr. Strangelove* stayed on the schedule because it worked so well and students liked it a lot.

Assessment

A couple of assessment mechanisms were used in the class. At the start of the class I used a presurvey that asked the students to rate their understanding of the basic issues, actors, and processes that would be covered in the course. This helped me know my audience and also would help track learning at the end of the class. It also helped make the students aware of the learning goals for the class. The survey asked them to rate on a seven-point scale how much they know about Congress, the presidency, the intelligence community, nuclear policy, the space race, U.S. policy toward Latin America, and the end of the Cold War. Most of the students rated their knowledge of U.S. institutions as fair to high but rated their substantive knowledge as low; especially low were nuclear policy and the space race.[26]

In our last meeting I distributed a postsurvey form. On this form the students were asked to rate on a scale of 0–100 percent how much of the assigned reading they did throughout the term. I also asked them to identify what movies they missed, if any. I then asked them to rate on a seven-point scale how much they thought they had learned about the role of Congress in foreign and security policy, the president, the intelligence community, the space race, nuclear policy, U.S. policy toward Latin America, and the end of the Cold War and debates about NATO expansion. I also asked them to rate on the scale how well the goal of "seeing" movies differently was attained in the class. Both surveys could have been anonymous, but many students put names on their forms.

Student responses to the postsurvey were interesting. The mean reading rate response was 77 percent, but it was bipolar with students either reported to have done nearly all of the reading or only about half of it. We can see the incentive problem with a credit/no-credit class here. Students reported having learned the most about nuclear policy, the space race, and the end of the Cold War; they reported having learned the least about U.S. policy in Latin America. I think we see the mixed effectiveness of the movies here. *Dr. Strangelove, The Right Stuff, and Star Trek* each worked well in this context. *Moon over Parador* really did not.[27] The mean rating on a scale of 0–6 (6 being high) on the question of how well the course achieved the goal of helping us see movies differently was 5. Students' written comments supported this rating.

The students also evaluated the class with a standard anonymous course evaluation form that the department uses to evaluate all courses every term. The form asks students to rate the course and the instructor on six questions, using a scale of 0 (poor) to 4 (excellent). The questions all really evaluate the instructor (overall effectiveness of the instructor, instructor enthusiasm, and so on). These evaluations were also very positive. The written comments on these evaluations noted that the combination of good movies, readings, and class discussions served to stimulate interest in politics. As one student put it, "I thought this class was very interesting—I thought about politics in a way I never had before. I also liked the fact the movies were all sort of tied to the Cold War theme. All the different aspects put the Cold War into a new dimension." Another student noted, "The movies helped reinforce the readings, and the discussion time helped [me] understand the concepts." Although people debate the utility of these evaluation instruments, these comments seemed to indicate that the learning goals set forth for the course were being met with some success.

My own evaluation of the course experience is that it is a useful experiment in learning, though it has some drawbacks. The course that I assembled fits well into a summer curriculum, and it can work well as an introductory course. Nevertheless, in a credit/no-credit course there is obviously a lack of incentive for students to do the reading. The readings are a key part of the course, so this lack of incentive is a weakness. On another mixed results issue, the learning curve was steep for students who did not know much about politics, but the political science majors who took the class learned less. Their written work was perhaps more informed and incisive, but they did not learn as much as the students taking the course as an introduction to these issues, which makes sense. I do not know how well it would work as a regular, graded, semester course, though some such courses are being offered.[28] My experience with this movie course suggests that it is possible to construct a movie-based course at an advanced undergraduate level for political science majors. Such a course would need to include clear evaluation criteria, since the course would be graded, and it would need to include readings at a more advanced level than the ones discussed here. A course at this level would likely include a component that pays more attention to the politics *of* movies as well as the politics depicted *in* movies.

The logistical problems involved are also worth noting. If your department or school does not have a large film library (most do not), you may have to rent these movies to show in class;[29] although doing so is cheap, this does represent a cost. Also, the movie you want to show might be out when you want it (this happened twice in summer 1998), so you may have to be a little flexible with the video schedule. Finally, you will want a room that is configured well to show movies, which can be difficult to find and in high demand. Still, with all these pluses and minuses, I evaluate the course as a success as a vehicle for drawing students to political issues.

Conclusion

There are a lot of ways to learn about U.S. foreign and national security policy or about any subject, for that matter. Learning about these issues through good movies and provocative readings has been an enjoyable and different experience from the usual classroom environment, no matter how active that classroom might be. Using movies can be particularly useful to introduce new concepts, and so the experiment worked fairly well at an introductory level. There were two main outcomes of the experimental course. First, the movies did help make abstract concepts real to the students. Movies such as *Dr. Strangelove* and *The Right Stuff* helped make sometimes difficult material accessible to new students of politics, and they did so in an entertaining way. Second, the experience changed the way the students in the class, and I, watch movies. The best example of this for the students was *Star Trek*. Many of the students had seen the movie before, but few had noticed the political issues in the movie. As the term went along, the ability of the students to see and discuss the political issues and concepts in the movies increased steadily—a real success.

Another benefit of the movie class that is worth mentioning is that for many students, college is the last time they will have the chance to sit in a class and learn. After graduation they will have to learn on their own. A class structured like the one described here can be a useful addition to the development of skills for lifelong learning. If a movie-based course on U.S. foreign and national security policy sparks interest in politics, and if the course shows how movies and readings in popular and scholarly outlets are a useful and accessible way to learn throughout one's life, this is an important contribution to learning. Although the course had some drawbacks, such as the incentive problem inherent in a credit/no-credit course, it has been a useful experiment in learning in a new and different way. I hope to go on learning at the movies.

Appendix: Some Additional Movie Ideas

The list in this appendix is by no means complete, but here are a few movies about U.S. foreign affairs that might be of use.[30] A classic movie about war is *Paths of Glory* (1957; 86 minutes; black and white). *The Ugly American* (1962; 120 minutes) is a good general-use movie about U.S. foreign affairs. *Invasion of the Body Snatchers* (1956; 80 minutes; black and white; 1978, 115 minutes) is a nice movie about anticommunism. *The Right Stuff* (1983; 193 minutes) is fun for showing the space race. For civil-military relations, these two would be good: *Patton* (1970; 169 minutes) and maybe *The Caine Mutiny* (1954; 125 minutes). *Three Days of the Condor* (1975; 117 minutes) and *Spies like Us* (1985; 109 minutes) can both be used to highlight intelligence community issues.

Great conspiracy movies certainly include *Seven Days in May* (1964; 118 minutes; black and white) and *The Manchurian Candidate* (1962; 126 minutes; black and white). Movies about the nuclear age include the classics *On The Beach* (1959; 133 minutes; black and white), *Fail Safe* (1964; 111 minutes; black and white), and *Dr. Strangelove* (1964; 93 minutes). More recent films include *Nightbreaker* (1989; 96 minutes; TV), *Atomic* Café (1982; 88 minutes), *The Day After* (1983; 120 minutes; TV), *Fat Man and Little*

Boy (1989; 126 minutes), *The Hunt for Red October* (1990; 135 minutes), *By Dawn's Early Light* (1990; 100 minutes; TV), and *Crimson Tide* (1995; 115 minutes).

There are far more movies about the U.S. experience in Vietnam than I could mention here, but the list would certainly include *The Green Berets* (1968; 141 minutes), *The Wild Bunch* (1969; 134 minutes), *Catch-22* (1970; 121 minutes), *M*A*S*H** (1970; 116 minutes), *Joe* (1970; 107 minutes), *Hearts and Minds* (1974; 110 minutes, documentary), *Taxi Driver* (1976; 113 minutes), *Coming Home* (1978; 127 minutes), *The Deer Hunter* (1978; 183 minutes), *Apocalypse Now* (1979; 150 minutes), *Platoon* (1986; 120 minutes), *Full Metal Jacket* (1987; 166 minutes), *Good Morning Vietnam* (1987; 120 minutes), *Gardens of Stone* (1987; 111 minutes), *Bat*21* (1988; 105 minutes), and *Born on the Fourth of July* (1989; 144 minutes). Also, *The Killing Fields* (1984; 141 minutes) focuses on Cambodia, and *The Year of Living Dangerously* (1983; 115 minutes) examines turmoil in Indonesia.

There are also some good movies about U.S. policy and Latin America, such as *Romero* (1989; 102 minutes), *Salvador* (1986; 123 minutes), and *Missing* (1982; 122 minutes). Some recent movies with political and foreign policy/national security themes are *Patriot Games* (1992; 116 minutes), *Clear and Present Danger* (1994; 141 minutes), and *Air Force One* (1997; 118 minutes).

Notes

I would like to thank John Boehrer, Sheila Croucher, Jeanne Hey, Mark Kemper, Lynn Kuzma, Jeff Lantis, Bill Mandel, Maureen Rada, Phil Russo, Keith Shimko, Walt Vanderbush, and the Miami University students who excitedly took the movie class in 1997 and 1998 for their help and suggestions. I would also like to acknowledge the financial support of the Miami University Political Science Department.

1. For examples of other courses that have used films as texts, see John Williams (1991), "Films and the Teaching of Foreign Policy—Part II," *Foreign Policy Analysis Notes* 17, nos. 1–2 (Spring and Summer): 11–13, and Deborah Gerner (1988–1989), "Films and the Teaching of Foreign Policy," *Foreign Policy Analysis Notes* 15, no. 3 (Winter): 3–6.

2. J. P. Lovell, ed. (1998), *Insights from Film into Violence and Oppression: Shattered Dreams of the Good Life* (Westport, CT: Praeger), p. ix.

3. R. C. Chandler and B.A.K. Adams (1997), "Let's Go to the Movies! Using Film to Illustrate Basic Concepts in Public Administration," *Public Voices* 8(2): 11.

4. R. W. Gregg (1998), *International Relations on Film* (Boulder: Lynne Rienner), pp. 2–6.

5. R. C. Chandler and B.A.K. Adams (1997), "Let's Go to the Movies!" p. 12.

6. See R. B. Barr and J. Tagg (1995), "From Teaching to Learning—A New Paradigm for Undergraduate Education," *Change* (November/ December): 13–25.

7. R. C. Chandler and B.A.K. Adams (1997), "Let's Go to the Movies!" p. 24.

8. R. W. Gregg (1998), *International Relations on Film,* pp. 8–15.

9. B. Allen (1998), "Making the Classroom a Safe Environment," in *Insights from Film into Violence and Oppression: Shattered Dreams of the Good Life,* ed. J. P. Lovell (Westport, CT: Praeger), pp. 105–125.

10. Seventeen students took the course in its first incarnation during summer 1997.

11. I did not do this the first time I offered the course, and as a result we did not have adequate time to talk through the issues in the movies.

12. Using movies in class will not automatically lead to such a dynamic, of course. Movies could still be used in a traditional lecture mode where the instructor interprets the movie to the students. It is also hard to get away from the professor's being seen as the "expert" no matter how hard you try. The effort here, though, was to try to construct a different kind of learning space than we typically inhabit.

13. Glenn P. Hastedt, ed. (1998), *Annual Editions American Foreign Policy 1998/99* (Guilford, Conn.: Dushkin/McGraw-Hill). The first time I offered this course I used fewer, longer articles on reserve at the library. For example, to highlight the issues of civil-military relations, I asked the students to read *Patton*: J. P. Lovell (1981), "From Defense Policy to National Security Policy," *Air University Review* 32(4): 42–54. Two other readings on civil-military relations that may be useful: R. J. Newman (1997), "Tell Us Your Name, Rank, and Sex Life," *U.S. News and World Report* (June 16): 34, and J. Kitfield (1998), "Standing Apart," *National Journal* (June 13): 1350–1358.

14. On the first day in summer 1997 I used the episode of *The Simpsons* in which Bart and his family have to travel to Australia because Bart has to apologize for his shenanigans, which led to a diplomatic incident. Bart is to be "caned" for his offenses. The episode has lots of diplomacy content.

15. M. Albright (1997), "Building a Bipartisan Foreign Policy: Diplomacy and Economics," *Vital Speeches of the Day* (April 15): 386–389; G. F. Kennan (1995), "On American Principles," *Foreign Affairs* 74 (March/April): 116–126; B. Schwartz (1996), "Why America Thinks It Has to Run the World," *Atlantic Monthly* (June): 92–102.

16. R. N. Haass (1997), "Starting Over: Foreign Policy Challenges for the Second Clinton Administration," *Brookings Review* (Spring): 4–7; S. Hoffman (1995), "The Crisis of Liberal Internationalism," *Foreign Policy* 98: 159–177; J. Washburn (1997), "When Money Talks, Congress Listens," *Bulletin of the Atomic Scientists* (July/August): 38–41; A. E. Smithson (1997), "Playing Politics with the Chemical Weapons Convention," *Current History* (April): 162–166.

17. This film worked very well when I showed it in 1997, although we could have done without the love-story portion of the script.

18. M. A. Goodman (1997), "Ending the CIA's Cold War Legacy," *Foreign Policy* 106: 128–143; cf. D. Corn (1997), "The Spy Who Shoved Me," *Nation* (May 19): 23–26.

19. J. Mueller (1997), "The Common Sense," *National Interest* (Spring): 81–88; S. Metz (1997), "Racing Toward the Future: The Revolution in Military Affairs," *Current History* (April): 184–188; and M. T. Klare (1997), "The New Arms Race: Light Weapons and International Security," *Current History* (April): 173–178.

20. M. Donley, C. O'Leary, and J. Montgomery (1997), "Inside the White House Situation Room," *Studies in Intelligence* 1: 7–13; F. von Hipple (1997), "Paring Down the Arsenal," *Bulletin of the Atomic Scientists* (May/June): 33–40; M. Moore (1995), "Midnight Never Came," *Bulletin of the Atomic Scientists* (November/December): 16–27.

21. I have shown this movie in my World Politics class with some success; in the movie class in summer 1997 I used the movie *Missing* (1982; 122 minutes) for this purpose.

22. An advantage of this movie is that a lot of students have seen the movie *Dave* (1993, 105 minutes), which has a similar plot.

23. R. S. Chase, E. B. Hill, and P. Kennedy (1996), "Pivotal States and U.S. Strategy," *Foreign Affairs* 75 (January/February): 33–51; S. G. Hajjar (1997), "The U.S. and Islamic Fundamentalists: The Need for Dialogue," *Strategic Review* (Winter): 48–54; D. Ignatius (1994), "The Curse of the Merit Class," *Washington Post* (February 27): C1, C4.

24. A. K. Pushkov (1997), "Don't Isolate Us: A Russian View of NATO Expansion," *National Interest* (Spring): 58–62; T. G. Carpenter (1997), "The Folly of NATO Enlargement," *The World and I* (July): 74–77.

25. C. M. Kelleher (1994), "Soldiering On: U.S. Public Opinion on the Use of Force," *Brookings Review* (Spring): 26–29; M. Sterner (1997), "Closing the Gate: The Persian Gulf War Revisited," *Current History* (January): 13–19; S. L. Woodward (1997), "Bosnia After Dayton: Year Two," *Current History* (March): 97–103.

26. Few indicated any knowledge of the National Security Act of 1947, by the way.

27. I still think it is a better movie than most people do; Leonard Maltin gave it 2 1/2 stars in his movie review book *Leonard Maltin's Movie and Video Guide* (1998) (New York: Plume).

28. For one example, see the syllabus by J. A. Kunkel (1997), *Political Science at the Movies* (Mankato, Minn.: Mankato State University, South Central Technical College). Http://www.mankato.msus.edu/depts/psle/fac/kunk/112.html.

29. Showing movies in class fits within the Face to Face Teaching Exemption to the Copyright Law of 1976. See K. R. Brancolini (1998), "A Bibliographic Essay on Using Film to Teach About Peace Studies and Structural Violence," in *Insights from Film into Violence and Oppression: Shattered Dreams of the Good Life*, ed. J. P. Lovell (Westport, CT: Praeger), pp. 141–160, esp. p. 154.

30. For other discussions and resources, see T. Christensen (1987),

Reel Politics: American Political Movies from Birth of a Nation *to* Platoon
(New York: Blackwell); R. Roberts (1993), "Film and the Vietnam War," in
The Vietnam War: Handbook of the Literature and Research, ed. J. S. Olson
(Westport, CT: Greenwood), pp. 401–425; P. L. Gianos (1998), *Politics and
Politicians in American Film* (Westport, CT: Praeger); R. W. Gregg (1998),
International Relations on Film; C. Hanterman (1998), http://www.sscf.
ucsb.edu/~hanterm/171videos.htm; and J. P. Lovell (1998), *Insights from
Film into Violence and Oppression.*

Part 4 | AFTERWORD

| 17 | # Reflections on Teaching and Active Learning |

Ole R. Holsti

Impressive common elements as well as considerable diversity mark the preceding chapters. The most important shared features are the imagination and enthusiasm that the authors bring to their seminars and classrooms. Although one of the world's worst-kept secrets is that the professional rewards for excellence in teaching pale in comparison to those for research, these chapters provide eloquent testimony to the creativity that the authors bring to their students.

The end of the Cold War no doubt played a role in stimulating new thinking about approaches to teaching international relations, but probably the effect was as often indirect as direct. When such events as the disintegration of the Soviet Union required a major overhauling of syllabi, assignments, and lectures—the familiar features of most traditional classes—they may also have made instructors more open to new ideas about approaches to teaching: as long as major changes in course *content* were required, why not go one step further and rethink *approaches* to teaching international relations and foreign policy? Overall, however, the driving force behind the innovative approaches discussed above appears to be as much an interest in the learning process as in the state of the international system. Thus, even had the Cold War not ended, the issues and approaches discussed in the preceding chapters would merit serious consideration.

Diversity is also evident, as these chapters span some of the oldest and newest approaches to instruction. Case-based teaching (Part 1) has been a staple approach in professional schools for many decades, but it is also clear that there are many different ways in which cases can be used in international relations courses. Simulations and games (Part 2) as instructional tools are largely the product of the half century since the end of World War II. In contrast, most of the approaches described in Part 3 were only made possible by development of fast and cheap computers, and these have been widely available only for a period that roughly corresponds to the post–Cold War era.

Before discussing my own experiences with active learning in the classroom—largely with case-based approaches—let me digress briefly with some general observations about teaching. These are neither original nor especially profound, but they may provide a useful background before turning more specifically to yet another approach to active learning.

Effective Teaching

The first prerequisite for effective teaching is a passion for the subject matter. Unless one can convey to students a genuine belief that the subject is important and interesting, it will be very hard to persuade them to put a maximum effort into their studies. If you do not really care very much, why should your students? In this respect, those who teach international relations have a huge advantage over their colleagues in many other departments. The "dramas of politics," to borrow a phrase from my friend and longtime collaborator, Jim Rosenau, have rarely been so graphically illustrated as during the past decade.[1] Imagine if twenty years ago a novelist or scriptwriter had submitted a prospectus to his or her publisher about a story that took place in a world featuring the existence of fifteen independent republics in the area once occupied by the Soviet Union, regular negotiations between Israeli and Palestinian leaders, creation of the European Union and a common currency, and the virtual collapse of the Japanese banking system. The prospectus would have been passed on to either the science fiction department or the local mental health authorities!

Our tasks are to help students analyze and understand these and other similarly fascinating and important events, their sources, and their consequences; to keep asking students to think about "of what class of events are these examples"; to weigh the relative merits of alternative theoretical explanations; and to assess critically the wide range of prescriptions for coping with such important problems as international conflict and cooperation, poverty, global environmental degradation, human rights, and the like. Moreover, hardly a month goes by during which the real world does not present, for better or worse, new intellectual puzzles with which to engage our students and with which they can grapple. There is thus every reason to believe that our advantage in focusing on topics of intrinsic importance and interest will persist.

Active learning approaches are especially useful for helping students to grapple with the issues arising from a world in flux. Indeed, games, simulations, debates, and case analyses can be effective tools in dealing with one of the central debates between realists and liberals about the post–Cold War era: What are the continuities and changes in the contemporary international system? Which recent events sustain the realist thesis that conflict arising from power relationships among major actors persists as the central source of dynamics in world affairs? Which ones provide support for the liberal thesis that self-interested actors can effectively use international institutions for cooperation and mutual gain?

A second important prerequisite for effective teaching is a genuine interest in students and their learning. This cannot be faked, because even the least discerning students will quickly pick up clues if an instructor regards them as a tolerable, but not necessarily welcome, feature of university life. Some years ago a dean produced multiple publications of a speech (necessitating the felling of several acres of Canadian forests) in which he announced that undergraduate students at a major research university should understand that the faculty do not have time to share a cup of coffee with them; indeed, he went on to say, these students should recognize that the faculty could do their important work without the presence of *any* undergraduates on campus. Ironically, this pronouncement coincided with an announcement from that university's trustees that undergraduate tuition in the following year would cross the $20,000 barrier. Another negative example is offered by Senator Phil Gramm, formerly an economics professor, who is reported to have regularly told colleagues as he left for class, "I'm off to slop the hogs."

An interest in students cannot be simulated by such gimmicks as dressing down to the level of the grungiest student in order to prove that one is a "regular guy." It is evidenced by going beyond the minimal requirements of meeting classes regularly, holding office hours, and turning in grades on time. The cliché that "the mind is not a vessel to be filled, but a fire to be ignited" is a relevant link between an interest in students and active learning approaches to teaching. In addition to engaging students in the various ways described in the previous chapters, active learning implies being readily available outside class for questions, discussions, consultation, and even "bull sessions"; being willing to provide advice about relevant academic matters, including such vital student concerns as postdegree career options; and engaging in other such activities. Compared to the traditional lecture course, active learning methods will require more of the instructor's time and energy, thereby inevitably cutting into time that might be used for research. They will also yield some of the richest and most satisfying experiences in an academic career.

A third general observation about teaching concerns the level of student performance and its relationship to teaching. There is a widespread conception, both on and off campus, that the present generation of students can be described as lazy, indifferent, career-obsessed grade grubbers whose interest in education lags far behind partying, sex, and obtaining a meal ticket with the least possible effort. Faculty are widely perceived as responding to the declining level of student performance by inflating grades.[2] There is no doubt some kernel of truth in this stereotype, but my own experience suggests a somewhat different and more optimistic generalization: student performance tends to be correlated to our expectations. If we set rather high standards, students will rise to meet them, whereas if our demands are very modest, the performance of all but a small fraction of the most highly motivated will decline in order to meet our expectations.[3] Setting high standards does not mean that mindlessly adding two books to the reading list or scheduling another midterm examination will automatically improve the level of student performance; there must be some rationale for the assigned workload. Expectations refer not only to the quantity of assignments but also—and more importantly—to the range of skills and understandings that students are encouraged to develop. But again it should be recognized that higher expectations in student performance will inevitably entail more work for instructors, whether because first drafts of papers are returned with extensive comments relating to both substance and the quality of writing or because the preparation for a simulation or case discussion takes more time than preparing a lecture.

Case-Based Teaching

Cases in the classroom are neither a panacea nor an easy way to overcome teaching problems for instructors with low expectations who are indifferent to their subject matter and students. Cases can, however, serve as a highly effective way of engaging students intellectually, introducing them to the complexities of international relations and foreign policy, and developing analytical skills that, it is hoped, will be useful long past the final examination.

Much of what follows has its origins in an intensive two-week period in June 1990 as a member of the first class of Pew Faculty Fellows in International Affairs at the Kennedy School. My U.S. foreign policy class had previously incorporated several mini case studies to illustrate some important theoretical points. One of these focused on the events of the winter of 1945–1946 to analyze how and why the optimistic premises that wartime cooperation between the Allies could serve as the foundations of a postwar international order—Franklin Roosevelt's conception of the Four Policemen— came to be viewed with increasing skepticism and, ultimately, discarded. Another examined the MX missile basing-mode controversy during the Carter and Reagan years to illustrate the interaction of deterrence policy, arms control, and domestic politics on issues relating to the acquisition and deployment of strategic weapons. However instructive these cases may have been, they were nevertheless presented as traditional lectures that involved student participation only to the extent that they may have raised questions about the events and my analyses during the time set aside for such queries and comments at the end of each lecture.

My first efforts at case-based teaching involved classes with enrollments ranging between 75 and 108 students. Although these weekly case analyses provided a very stimulating supplement to the twice-per-week lectures, and the discussions were usually lively and spirited, the experience during several semesters left me less than completely satisfied with this format. My concerns arose directly from constraints imposed by class size. It was too easy for some students to become spectators rather than active participants. Indeed, they could be even more passive than in a lecture because there was little need to take notes. "Cold calling" on the perpetually passive could only partly alleviate the problem. I also found it hard to evaluate with confidence the contributions of all but the most active participants. Requiring students to write and submit one-page analyses of each case prior to the discussion was a useful preparatory exercise, and it provided a more reliable basis for evaluation. Nevertheless, this assignment was only a partial remedy; it could not overcome the problem of trying to get widespread participation on complex issues from a very large class within a fifty-minute period.

Consequently, I broke up my foreign policy class into small groups of ten to fifteen students for weekly case discussions. These proved to be far more satisfactory. Student participation is much better, it is far easier to generate discussions and debates among students, and assessments of student performance can be made with a fairly high degree of confidence. My judgment is supported by confidential student evaluations, which consistently offer high marks for the case discussions.

Among the many virtues of cases in the classroom is that they can be used to address an almost infinitely wide range of questions. Because my courses generally adopt a decisionmaking perspective, cases have been especially helpful in exploring several central questions in foreign policy making, each of which receives greater or lesser attention depending on the specific case under discussion.

How did beliefs and assumptions affect the "definition of the situation" and the characterization of the goals, motives, and strategies of other nations? Were these largely the beliefs of individual policymakers, or were they more widely shared by the public? by special interests within society? by the Congress?

What U.S. national interests were involved in the case? If there were competing interests, were trade-offs between them adequately recognized and effectively resolved? These central questions often generate some of the best debates among students.

What role did morality and ethics play in defining national interests, assessing options, and coming to decisions? Cases with a human rights component are especially likely to give rise to spirited discussions of these questions. This is also a good point at which to make linkages back to the venerable debate between the realist and liberal conceptions of the appropriate foundations for conducting an effective foreign policy.

What was the proper balance between the executive branch and Congress on the issue? Corwin's stating that the U.S. Constitution offers an "invitation to struggle for the privilege of conducting foreign relations" aptly describes an issue that cuts across many cases.[4] The relevance of this question is largely confined to the United States, of course, and it would be of relatively little interest in foreign policy courses on most other nations.

Is there evidence that bureaucratic politics shaped decisionmaking in this case? Was it limited to the implementation of policy decisions? Alternatively, were policy preferences largely independent of positions within the government?

How effectively did policymakers monitor feedback from their decisions? Was evidence of impending difficulties overlooked? Why?

Whenever possible I have tried to pair cases in order to stimulate students to undertake comparative analyses. Pairing cases can also be an especially effective way to induce students to reexamine conclusions that they may have drawn from a single case. For example, England's perilous position during the summer of 1940 and the heinous nature of the Hitler regime in Germany make it likely that most students will sympathize with President Roosevelt's efforts to maneuver around a recalcitrant Congress to comply with Winston Churchill's pleas for the transfer of fifty desperately needed destroyers to Britain.[5] Indeed, they may come to the more general conclusion that, although the United States was a neutral nation in 1940, the president should always have broad powers to effect such weapons transfers to belligerents, even in the face of specific congressional prohibitions against doing so.

The Iran-contra episode during the Reagan administration provides a good case to pair with the destroyer deal because of some interesting surface similarities as well as some striking differences. On the one hand, both cases involve popular presidents who were determined to send weapons to belligerent nations in the face of explicit prior congressional disapproval of such actions. On the other hand, the international system had changed a good deal during the more than four decades between the two episodes; the U.S. interests in the recipients of the arms—Churchill's Britain, the Iran of the ayatollahs, and the contra rebels—may also have differed. This pair of cases may stimulate students to think more deeply about several aspects of foreign policy making, including the proper balance between the executive and legislature in foreign policy, competing views of the "national interest" and their effects on the policy process, the rights and obligations of neutral nations, and other such questions of enduring importance.

The Pew fellowship experience and the subsequent transformation of my foreign policy class led me to wonder whether it would be fruitful to extend case-based teaching beyond discussions of preexisting cases. Specifically, could undergraduate students become case *writers* as well as case *discussants*? More important, would adding such a significant new dimension to their assigned work enhance their analytical abilities and understanding of foreign policy making while providing an even more satisfying learning experience?

Several conversations with Pew colleagues appropriately pointed to the risks and possible pitfalls that needed to be faced. Nevertheless, the potential rewards struck me as worth the risks. Thus, for several years students in my senior seminar have not only been case analysts and discussants but have also been the authors of the cases that constitute a substantial part of the required reading list. They are told at the introductory meeting that, up to this point, they have been consumers of knowledge produced by others; it is now appropriate for them also to become producers of some of the knowledge for this class.

My senior seminar in international relations has been organized around the familiar passage in deTocqueville's *Democracy in America* in which he asserted that democracies are at a fundamental disadvantage in conducting foreign affairs:[6]

> As for myself, I do not hesitate to say, that it is especially in the conduct of their foreign relations that democracies appear to me decidedly inferior to other government. . . .
> Foreign politics demands scarcely any of those qualities which are peculiar to a democracy; they require, on the contrary, the perfect use of almost all those in which it is deficient. Democracy is favorable to the increase of the internal resources of a state; it diffuses wealth and comfort, promotes public spirit, and fortifies the respect for law in all relations which one people bears to another. But a democracy can only with great difficulty regulate the details of an important undertaking, persevere in a fixed design, and work out its execution in spite of serious obstacles. It cannot combine its measures with secrecy, or await their consequences with patience.

This diagnosis was written at a time when there were very few democracies. The growing number of democracies as well as the growing literature and lively debate on the "democratic peace" issue gives the "deTocqueville question" both timeliness and importance. In order to provide some evidence on the issue, each of the eighteen students in the seminar is asked to undertake a case study involving U.S. foreign policy.

The first four weeks of the seminar are devoted to discussions about the criteria for assessing the quality of decisions as well as to analysis of various writings on the relationship between democracy and foreign policy. A recently published book by a distinguished historian—Melvin Small's *Democracy and Diplomacy*—is an excellent initial reading that provides a good overview of some central issues as they are illustrated by two centuries of U.S. experience.[7] Briefer readings from deTocqueville, George Kennan, and Walter Lippmann represent the realist-skeptical view on the ability of democracies to conduct their foreign relations effectively. Articles by Elihu Root, Michael Doyle, and David Lake take the opposite position. Additional readings address various facets of U.S. foreign policy making, including the role of Congress and executive-legislative relations, interest groups, public opinion, and the like.

At this time we also engage in discussions about sources and methods. Available documentation varies widely by case. Those working on episodes prior to the 1960s have access to such important primary sources as the *Foreign Relations of the United States* series[8] as well as numerous memoirs, biographies, and monographic studies. Students who have selected more contemporary cases will need to place greater reliance on newspapers, the many sources available on Nexis-Lexis, and the like. We also discuss methodological issues— for example, how to make appropriate use of Gallup and other poll data in light of evidence that decisionmakers vary both in sensitivity to public opinion and in assessments of the most appropriate indicators of public sentiments.

During the initial month of the semester students are doing research and writing on their case studies. They are required to submit a draft of the case in two copies by the end of the fourth week. This initial draft is to be a detailed narrative of the events under analysis, focusing on such questions as: What individuals and organizations were involved in the decisionmaking process? How was the situation/issue defined? Were there differing definitions and interpretations of the interests at stake? If so, who represented them? How were trade-offs between competing interests resolved? In formulating options for dealing with the situation, what alternative courses of action were considered? Which were ruled out? What was the role, if any, of domestic political actors, including Congress, the media, major interest groups, and public opinion? What was their impact? What were the key decisions? How and by whom was the policy implemented? How was the effectiveness of the policy monitored? What were the policy outcomes?

One copy of each case is placed on reserve in the main library. These draft cases then serve as the primary reading for the next eighteen meetings of the seminar, each of which is devoted to an analysis of one case. The author briefly identifies some key issues for discussion, and two other students serve as discussants on each case. Assuming no more than five minutes for each of these preliminary presentations, this leaves a full hour for seminar discussion of the case and its relevance and contribution to our understanding of the "deTocqueville question." The discussions also provide the case authors with extensive feedback, supplementing my detailed written comments and suggestions on the draft.

The final draft of the paper includes not only a revised case narrative and analysis but also an analytical conclusion that addresses the central theoretical question of the seminar: To what extent did the evidence in this case support deTocqueville's pessimistic diagnosis about the ability of democracies to conduct foreign affairs effectively? The conclusion is to address at least two facets of the issue: (1) Were the decision processes in the case consistent with democratic/constitutional requirements? These criteria are not cast in concrete, of course, and are likely to vary according to issue and situation. (2) How did the processes contribute to or detract from the quality of the resulting decisions? Did the actions of such actors as Congress, the media, interest groups, and public opinion—or the anticipation by decisionmakers of their actions and reactions—favorably or adversely affect policy decisions? How?

The last seminar meeting is devoted to drawing generalizations from the eighteen case studies. At this point we also try to undertake multivariate analyses. Does the effectiveness of democracies in foreign affairs vary according to issue area? Type of situation? Nature of the administration and leadership qualities?

Assessment

To what extent has this experiment in case writing been a success? Although it is not a surefire formula for assuring the success of every seminar or for turning indifferent students into eager ones, this format has been an immensely rewarding teaching experience, and there is evidence that this judgment is shared by a majority of the students who have been in these seminars. This judgment is based on several specific outcomes.

The case studies have on balance been of very good quality. They compare very favorably with papers produced in my previous senior seminars. One possible explanation is that virtually all students have a higher motivation and work more diligently to produce high-quality papers when they know that their work will be read and analyzed not only by the instructor but also by their peers.

Students not only learn research skills working with diverse resources—ranging from primary diplomatic documentation to

Gallup polls—in preparing their own papers, but they also develop strong analytical skills in reading their classmates' case studies. The quality of case discussions has been exceptionally high. It appears that students who have written a case become more acute readers and analysts of other cases. Cross-case comparisons and generalizations seem to emerge quite naturally.

Comments on anonymous teacher-course evaluation questionnaires at the end of the semester indicate overwhelming approval for the seminar format. Students clearly seem to enjoy and gain considerable satisfaction from their roles as "producers of knowledge" as well as from reading and discussing their peers' papers. Some typical student comments are these:

Discussing case studies that the students have written is a great format.

I've never been in a class with such consistent student participation, stimulating discussions, etc.

Writing a case study is the best way to examine foreign policy.

I've enjoyed the case study format—reading papers done by my peers was always interesting.

I talked about this stuff outside of class.

One possible concern about this format—that a great deal of the work in the seminar is front-loaded because of the need to produce a first draft of the paper within a month—has been less of a problem than I had originally feared. One reason may be that most students are taking other courses in which a high proportion of the workload is back-loaded, with papers and final examinations coming at the end of the semester. The early deadline for the first drafts of papers also has one important benefit. Students receive extensive feedback, not only on substance but also on organization and the quality of writing, that can help in preparing a final draft. It is especially rewarding when a paper that had been rather mediocre in the initial draft has blossomed into a first-rate final draft.

The features of this seminar are not cast in concrete. The seminar has occasionally included sophomores of exceptional ability. I have used case studies produced in this senior seminar as teaching cases in a freshmen seminar. The freshmen were first surprised and then pleased to be reading student-produced papers. I suspect that a modified version of this seminar format could be used even with freshmen.

These experiences in using and experimenting with case-based teaching have convinced me that this is an extraordinarily valuable instructional tool that has increased my effectiveness in the classroom. The value of case-based teaching arises in large part from the fact that it requires the student to be an active rather than passive participant in the learning process. Case-based teaching does not offer a magic formula for all types of materials, but for courses in which the analysis of decisions—whether in foreign offices, bureaucracies, committees, courts, business firms, international organizations, or many other public or private venues—is central to the substantive and theoretical goals of the course, case-based teaching can be immensely valuable and rewarding. A well-crafted lecture can convey information, concepts, and theories, but in my experience, cases provide an even more effective means for examining and assessing how and to what extent these concepts and theories can help us to understand the processes and dilemmas of foreign policy decisionmaking.

Conclusion

The chapters in this book make it clear that there is a lively dialogue among those teaching international relations about ways of engaging students in their own education. Moreover, the chapters reveal a rich and diverse menu from which to choose. Finally, they leave readers with a clear impression that in their own teaching they have been effective in meeting the three criteria of effective teaching described earlier: a passion for the subject matter, a genuine interest in their students, and high expectations about student performance.

Notes

1. James N. Rosenau (1973), *The Dramas of Politics: An Introduction to the Joys of Inquiry* (Boston: Little, Brown).

2. In 1998, the *New York Times* published numerous stories, as well as letters to the editor, on the issue of grade inflation in universities, with such titles as "What's Trendy on Campus? Adjunct Faculty and Easy A's," "Grade Inflation Is Often a Cover for Bad Teaching," and "Why Colleges Shower Their Students with A's."

3. For a recent discussion of expectations in education, see Jay Matthews (1998), "Averaged Out," *New Republic* (December 29):20–21. Matthews, a *Washington Post* education reporter, focuses on high schools, but his observations are no less relevant for college teaching.

4. Edward S. Corwin, *The Constitution and What It Means Today,* Princeon, NJ: Princeton University Press, p. 42.

5. Ole R. Holsti (1993), *The 1940 Destroyer Deal with Great Britain,* Pew Case Studies in International Affairs 457 (Washington, DC: Institute for the Study of Diplomacy).

6. Alexis deTocqueville (1993), *Democracy in America* (1835; reprint, New York: A. Knopf and Random House), p. 243.

7. Melvin Small (1996), *Democracy and Diplomacy: The Impact of Domestic Politics on U.S. Foreign Policy, 1789–1994* (Baltimore: Johns Hopkins University Press).

8. See, for example, David Patterson (1996), *U.S. Department of State, Foreign Relations of the United States 1961–1963* (Washington, DC: U.S. Government Printing Office).

APPENDIX

This section presents a comprehensive collection of classic and contemporary active teaching resources in international studies. Materials are divided into the following categories for easy reference: The Case Method; International Studies Simulations, Role-Playing Exercises and Games; Instructional Technologies; General Active Learning Resources; Principles, Practices, and Assessment; and Active Learning and the Internet. Valuable related information on active teaching and learning—including course syllabi, teaching materials, case studies, and teaching tips—can be located through the official Web site of the Active Learning in International Affairs Section of the International Studies Association at http://csf.colorado.edu/isa/sections/alias/index.html.

The Case Method

Barnes, L. B., C. R. Christensen, and A. J. Hansen, eds. (1994). *Teaching and the Case Method*. 3d ed. Boston: Harvard Business School Press.
Boehrer, J. (1995). "How to Teach a Case." Cambridge: Case Program John F. Kennedy School of Government, Harvard University (N18-95-1285.0).
Boehrer, John (1994). "On Teaching a Case." In *A Special Issue of International Studies Notes: Case Teaching in International Relations*, edited by Karen Mingst. 19(2):14–20.
Boehrer, John (1994). "Teaching International Affairs with Cases." http://sfswww.georgetown.edu/sfs/programs/isd/files/cases/boehrer.html.
Boehrer, John (1991). "Spectators and Gladiators: Reconnecting the Students with the Problem." *Teaching Excellence* 2(7):1–12. New York:

The Professional and Organizational Development Network in Higher Education.

Boehrer, J., and M. Linsky (1990). "Teaching with Cases: Learning to Question." In *The Changing Face of College Teaching. New Directions for Teaching and Learning,* edited by M. D. Svinicki, 42:41–57. San Francisco: Jossey-Bass, pp. 41–57.

Carlson, J. A., and D. W. Schodt (1995). "Beyond the Lecture: Case Teaching and the Learning of Economic Theory." *Journal of Economic Education* 26(1):17–28.

Christensen, C. R., D. A. Garvin, and A. Sweet, eds. (1991). *Education for Judgment: The Artistry of Discussion Leadership.* Boston: Harvard Business School Press.

Clawson, J. G., and S. C. Frey (1986). "Mapping Case Pedagogy." *Organizational Behavior Teaching Review* 11:1–8.

Derek Bok Center for Teaching and Learning, Harvard University (1995). "The Art of Discussion Leading: A Class with Chris Christensen." Videotape. Bolton, MA: Anker Publishing.

Erskine, J. A., M. R. Leenders, and L. A. Mauffette-Leenders (1981). *Teaching with Cases.* London, Ontario: Research and Publications Division, School of Business Administration, University of Western Ontario.

Fratantuono, Michael J. (1994). "Evaluating the Case Method." In *A Special Issue of International Studies Notes: Case Teaching in International Relations,* edited by Karen Mingst. 19(2):34–39.

Frederick, Peter (1981). "The Dreaded Discussion: Ten Ways to Start." *Improving College and University Teaching* 29: 90–95.

Freie, John F. (1997). "A Dramaturgical Approach to Teaching Political Science." *PS: Political Science & Politics* 30(4):728–732.

Holsti, Ole (1994). "Case Teaching: Transforming Foreign Policy Courses with Cases." In *A Special Issue of International Studies Notes: Case Teaching in International Relations,* edited by Karen Mingst. 19(2):7–13.

Hunt, P. (1951). "The Case Method of Instruction." *Harvard Educational Review* 21:2–19.

Kasulis, Thomas P. (1986). "Questioning." In *The Art and Craft of Teaching,* edited by M. M. Gullette. Cambridge: Harvard University Press.

Kegley, Charles W., Jr., and Gregory A. Raymond (1999). *How Nations Make Peace.* New York: St. Martin's Press/Worth Publishers.

Klein, Hans E., ed. (1995). *The Art of Interactive Teaching with Cases, Simulations, Games, and Other Interactive Methods.* Madison, WI: Omni Press.

Klinger, Janeen (1992). "The Use of History in Teaching International Politics." *International Studies Notes* 2:39–44.

Lang, Anthony F., and James M. Lang (1998). "Between Theory and History: *The Remains of the Day* in the International Relations Classroom." *PS: Political Science & Politics* 31(2):209–214.

Lang, C. (1986). *Case Method Teaching in the Community College: A Guide for Teaching and Faculty Development.* Newton, MA: Education Development Center.

Laurence, E., Jr. (1999). *Teaching and Learning with Cases: A Guide Book*. New York: Chatham House

Long, William J. (1993). "The Pew Initiative: Case Teaching in International Affairs." *International Studies Notes* 18(3):36–40.

Mansbach, Richard W., and Edward Rhodes, eds. (1999). *Global Politics in a Changing World: A Reader*. Boston: Houghton Mifflin.

Mingst, Karen (1994). "Cases and the Interactive Classroom." In *A Special Issue of International Studies Notes: Case Teaching in International Relations*, edited by Karen Mingst. 19(2):1–6.

Mingst, Karen, ed. (1994). *A Special Issue of International Studies Notes: Case Teaching in International Relations* 19(2).

Mingst, Karen A., and Katsuhiko Mori, eds. (1997). *Teaching International Affairs with Cases: Cross-National Perspectives*. Boulder, CO: Westview.

Ortmayer, Louis L. (1994). "Decisions and Dilemmas: Writing Case Studies in International Affairs." In *A Special Issue of International Studies Notes: Case Teaching in International Relations*, edited by Karen Mingst. 19(2):28–33.

Paraschos, Peter E. (1997). "Good Teaching Cases and Bad: The Institute for the Study of Diplomacy's Point of View." Paper presented at the Annual Meeting of the International Studies Association. Toronto, Canada.

Robyn, Dorothy (1986). "What Makes a Good Case?" Cambridge: Case Program, John F. Kennedy School of Government, Harvard University (N15-86-673).

Skidmore, David (1993). "Group Projects and Teaching International Relations." *International Studies Notes* 18(2):49–53.

Sykes, Gary (1990). "Learning to Teach with Cases." *Journal of Policy Analysis and Management* 9(2):297–302.

Velenchik, Ann D. (1995). "The Case Method as a Strategy for Teaching Policy Analysis to Non-Majors." *Journal of Economic Education* 26(1): 29–38.

Wasserman, Selma (1994). *Introduction to Case Method Teaching: A Guide to the Galaxy*. New York: Teachers College Press.

Welty, William M. (1989). "Discussion Method Teaching." *Change: The Magazine of Higher Learning* 21(4):41–49.

Wrage, Stephen D. (1994). "Best Case Analysis: What Makes a Good Case and Where to Find the One You Need." In *A Special Issue of International Studies Notes: Case Teaching in International Relations*, edited by Karen Mingst. 19(2):21–27.

International Studies Simulations, Role-Playing Exercises, and Games

Abu-Nimer, Mohammed (1998). "Conflict Resolution Training in the Middle East: Lessons to Be Learned." *International Negotiation: A Journal of Theory and Practice* 3(1):99–116.

Alger, Chadwick F. (1963). "Use of the Inter-Nation Simulation in Undergraduate Teaching." In *Simulation in International Relations: Developments for Research and Teaching*, edited by Harold Guetzkow, Chadwick F. Alger, Richard A. Brody, Robert C. Noel, and Richard C. Snyder. Englewood Cliffs, NJ: Prentice-Hall.

Alker, Hayward R. (1968). "Decision Makers' Environments in the Inter-Nation Simulation." In *Simulation in the Study of Politics*, edited by William D. Coplin. Chicago: Markham.

Applegate, John S., and Douglas J. Sarno (1997). "FUTURESITE: An Environmental Remediation Game Simulation." *Simulation & Gaming* 28(1):13–27.

Armstrong, Robert, Fred Percival, and Danny Saunders, eds. (1994). *The Simulation and Gaming Yearbook*. Volume 2: *Interactive Learning*. London: The Society for Interactive Learning.

Baba, Nancy, Hariachi Sukida, and Yoshi Sawaragi (1984). "A Game Approach to the Acid Rain Problem." *Simulation & Gaming* 15(3): 305–314.

Babbus, Sylvia, Kathryn Hodges, and Erik Kjonnerod (1997). "Simulations and Institutional Change: Training U.S. Government Professionals for Improved Management of Complex Emergencies Abroad." In a Special Issue of *The Journal of Contingencies and Crisis Management*, edited by Martha Cottam and Thomas Preston. 5(4):231–240.

Benson, Oliver (1969). "A Simple Diplomatic Game." In *International Politics and Foreign Policy*, edited by James N. Rosenau. New York: The Free Press.

Beriker, Nimet, and Daniel Druckman (1996). "Simulating the Lausanne Peace Negotiations, 1922–1923: Power Asymmetries in Bargaining." *Simulation & Gaming* 27(2):162–183.

Bock, Joseph G., and D. Dean Dunham Jr. (1992). "An Active Approach to Teaching the Political Economy of Development." *PS: Political Science & Politics* 25(3): 538–541.

Boocock, Sarane S. (1970). "Using Simulation Games in College Courses." *Simulation & Gaming* 1(2):67–79.

Boocock, Sarane S., and Erling O. Schild, eds. (1968). *Simulation Games and Learning*. Beverly Hills, CA: Sage.

Boocock, Sarane S., Erling O. Schild, and Clarice Stoll (1967). *Simulation Games and Control Beliefs*. Baltimore, MD: John Hopkins University Press.

Butler, John K., Jr. (1996). "After NAFTA: A Cross-Cultural Negotiation Exercise." *Simulation & Gaming* 27(4):507–516.

Caldwell, Daniel (1991). "The 1990 Middle East Crisis: A Role Playing Simulation." *Foreign Policy Analysis Notes* 2:13–15.

Cavanagh, T. K. (June 1994). "From SIMGAMES to Africa and Back: A Retrospective from Canada." *Simulation & Gaming* 25(2):185–192.

Chapin, Wesley D. (1998). "The Balance of Power Game." *Simulation & Gaming* 29(1):105–112.

Charles, Cheryl L., and Ronald Stadsklev (1973). *Learning with Games: An Analysis of Social Studies Educational Games and Simulations*. Boulder, CO: Social Science Education Consortium.

Collins, Edward, Jr., and Martin A. Rogoff (1991). "The Use of an Interscholastic Moot Court Competition in the Teaching of International Law." *PS: Political Science & Politics* 24(3):516–520.

Coplin, William (1968). *Simulation in the Study of Politics.* Chicago: Markham.

Cottam, Martha, and Thomas Preston (1997). "An Overview of the Value and Use of Simulations in the Academic, Business, and Policy Communities." In a Special Issue of *The Journal of Contingencies and Crisis Management,* edited by Martha Cottam and Thomas Preston. 5(4):195–198.

Crookall, David (1995). "A Guide to the Literature of Simulation/Gaming." In *Simulation and Gaming Across Disciplines and Cultures,* edited by David Crookall and Karen Arai. Thousand Oaks, CA: Sage.

Crookall, David (1995). "Learning More About Simulation/Games." In *Simulation, Gaming, and Language Learning,* edited by David Crookall and Robert Oxford. New York: Harper and Row.

Crookall, David, and Kiyoshi Arai, eds. (1992). *Global Interdependence: Simulation and Gaming Perspectives.* Tokyo, Japan: Springer-Verlag.

Crookall, David, and Jonathan Wilkenfeld (1985). "ICONS: Communications Technologies and International Relations." *System* 13(3):253–258.

Cusack, R. R., and R. J. Stoll (1990). *Exploring Realpolitik: Probing International Relations Theory with Computer Simulation.* Boulder: Lynne Rienner.

de Vries, Benjamim (1995). *SUSCLIME: A Simulation/Game on Population and Development in a Resource-and-Climate-Constrained Two-Country World.* Bilthoven, Netherlands: GESPE.

Diehl, Barbara J. (1991). "Crisis: A Process Evaluation." *Simulation & Gaming* 22(3):293–307.

Dodge, Dorothy R. (1983). "Domestic Politics and Simulations: An Evaluation." In *The Guide to Simulations/Games for Education and Training,* edited by Robert Horn and Anne Cleaves. Beverly Hills, CA: Sage, pp. 61–68.

Druckman, Daniel (1994). "Tools for Discovery: Experimenting with Simulations." *Simulation & Gaming* 25(4):446–455.

Druckman, Daniel, and Victor Robinson (1998). "From Research to Application: Utilizing Research Findings in Negotiation Training Programs." *International Negotiation: A Journal of Theory and Practice* 3(1):7–38.

Dukes, Richard A. (1983). "SIMSOC: An Evaluation." In *The Guide to Simulations/Games for Education and Training,* edited by Robert Horn and Anne Cleaves. Beverly Hills, CA: Sage.

Greenblatt, Charles S. (1988). *Designing Games and Simulations: An Illustrated Handbook.* London: Sage.

Guetzkow, Harold S. (1995). "Recollections About the Inter-Nation Simulation (INS) and Some Derivatives in Global Modeling." *Simulation & Gaming* 26(4):453–470.

Guetzkow, Harold S., ed. (1962). *Simulation in Social Science.* Englewood Cliffs, NJ: Prentice-Hall.

Guetzkow, Harold S., and Philip Kotler (1970). *Simulation in Social and Administrative Science.* Englewood Cliffs, NJ: Prentice-Hall.

Guetzkow, Harold S., Chadwick F. Alger, Richard A. Brody, Robert C. Noel, and Richard C. Snyder (1963). *Simulation in International Relations: Developments for Research and Teaching.* Englewood Cliffs, NJ: Prentice-Hall.

Gump, W. Robert, and James R. Woodworth (1994). *Atlantis: Role Playing Simulations for the Study of American Politics.* Chicago: Nelson-Hall.

Heitzmann, William R. (1974). *Educational Games and Simulations.* Washington, DC: National Education Association.

Helsing, Jeffrey W. (1997). *One Step at a Time: The Derry March and Prospects for Peace: A Simulation on Northern Ireland.* Washington, DC: United States Institute for Peace.

Hermann, Charles F., and Margaret G. Hermann (1967). "An Attempt to Simulate the Outbreak of World War I." *American Political Science Review* 61(2):400–416.

Horn, Robert E. (1995). "The Story of *The Guide to Simulations/Games for Education and Training.*" *Simulation & Gaming* 26(4):471–479.

Horn, Robert, and Anne Cleaves (1983). *The Guide to Simulations/Games for Education and Training.* Beverly Hills, CA: Sage.

Houseman, Gerald L. (1989). "Simulating the Nuclear Threat in the Classroom." *The Political Science Teacher* 2:10–11.

Inbar, Michael, and Clarice Stoll (1972). *Simulation and Gaming in Social Science.* New York: The Free Press.

Inbar, Michael, and Clarice Stoll (1970). "Games in Learning." *Interchange* 1:53–61.

Jones, Kenneth (1998). "Simulations: Hidden Damages to Facilitators and Participants." *Simulation & Gaming* 29(2):165–172.

Jones, Kenneth (1991). *Imaginative Events: A Sourcebook of Innovative Simulations, Exercises, Puzzles and Games* (2 vols.). Maidenhead, UK: McGraw-Hill.

Jones, Kenneth (1987). *Simulations: A Handbook for Teachers and Trainers.* London: Kogan Page.

Jones, Kenneth (1985). *Designing Your Own Simulations.* New York: Routlege.

Jones, Kenneth (1980). *Simulations: A Handbook for Teachers.* London: Kogan Page.

Kaarbo, Juliet, and Jeffrey S. Lantis (1997). "Coalition Theory in Praxis: A Role-Playing Simulation of the Cabinet Formation Process." *PS: Political Science & Politics* 30(3):501–506.

Kaufman, Joyce P. (1998). "Using Simulation as a Tool to Teach About International Negotiation." *International Negotiation. A Journal of Theory and Practice* 3(1):59–75.

Kaufman, Joyce P., ed. (1998). "Special Issue on the Teaching of International Negotiation." *International Negotiation. A Journal of Theory and Practice* 3(1).

Keys, Louise, and Bernard Keys (1992). "ISAGA '91: Global Modeling for Solving Global Problems." *Simulation & Gaming* 23(3):212–214.

Kraus, S., J. Wilkenfeld, M. A. Harris, and E. Blake (1992). "The Hostage Crisis Simulation." *Simulation & Gaming* 23(4):398–416.

Lamy, Steven W. (1994). *Teaching Global Awareness with Simulations and Games: An Experimental Unit.* Denver, CO: Center for Teaching International Relations at the University of Denver.

Lamy, Steven W. (1990). "Simulation in Foreign Policy Instruction." *Foreign Policy Analysis Notes* 1:13–15.

Lantis, Jeffrey S. (1998). "Simulations and Experiential Learning in the International Relations Classroom." *International Negotiation. A Journal of Theory and Practice* 3(1):39–57.

Lantis, Jeffrey S. (1996). "Simulations as Teaching Tools: Designing the Global Problems Summit." *International Studies Notes* 21(1):30–38.

Lederman, Linda C. (1992). "Debriefing: Toward a Systematic Assessment of Theory and Practice." *Simulation & Gaming* 23(2):145–160.

Licklider, Roy (1990). "Simulation in Foreign Policy Instruction." *Foreign Policy Analysis Notes* 1:9–11.

Maidment, Robert, and Richard Bronstein (1973). *Simulation Games, Design, and Implementation.* Columbus, OH: Merril.

Moreno, Dario (1992). "Potential U.S. Intervention in Peru: A Simulation." *Foreign Policy Analysis Notes* 2:4–5.

Muldoon, James P., Jr. (1995). "The Model United Nations Revisited." *Simulation & Gaming* 26(2):27–35.

Muldoon, James P. Jr., ed. (1991). *A Guide to Delegate Preparation.* New York: United Nations Association.

Nesbitt, William A. (1968). *Simulation Games for the Social Studies Classroom.* New York: Foreign Policy Association.

Newkirk, M. Glenn (1978). "Simulations in Political Science and International Studies." In *Learning with Simulation Games,* edited by Richard Dukes and Constance Seidner. Beverly Hills, CA: Sage.

Noel, Robert C. (1963). "Inter-Nation Simulation Participants' Manual." In *Simulation in International Relations: Developments for Research and Teaching,* edited by Harold Guetzkow, Chadwick F. Alger, Richard A. Brody, Robert C. Noel, and Richard C. Snyder. Englewood Cliffs, NJ: Prentice-Hall.

Petranek, Charles F., Susan Corey, and Rebecca Black (1992). "Three Levels of Learning in Simulations: Participating, Debriefing, and Journal Writing." *Simulation & Gaming* 23(2):174–185.

Pimentel, Florosito Q. (1995). "Gaming and Simulation: A Third World Experience." *Simulation & Gaming* 26(4):480–488.

Powers, Richard B. (1993). "Visit to an Alien Planet: A Cultural Diversity Game." *Simulation & Gaming* 24(4):509–518.

Preston, Thomas, and Martha Cottam (1997). "Simulating U.S. Foreign Policy Crises: Uses and Limits in Education and Training." In a Special Issue of the *Journal of Contingencies and Crisis Management,* edited by Martha Cottam and Thomas Preston. 5(4):224–230.

Randel, Josephine M., Barbara A. Morris, C. Douglas Wetzel, and Betty V. Whitehill (1992). "The Effectiveness of Games for Educational Purposes: A Review of Recent Research." *Simulation & Gaming* 23(3):261–276.

Robinson, J. A., L. F. Anderson, R. C. Snyder, and Margaret G. Hermann (1966). "Teaching with Inter-Nation Simulation and Case Studies." *American Political Science Review* 60(1):53–65.

Rockler, Michael J. (1983). "Social Studies Games and Simulations: An Evaluation." In *The Guide to Simulations/Games for Education and Training,* edited by Robert Horn and Anne Cleaves. Beverly Hills, CA: Sage.

Rosenthal, U., and B. Pijnenburg. eds. (1991). *Crisis Management and Descision Making: Simulation-Oriented Scenarios.* Dordrecht, The Netherlands: Kluwer.

Rybalskiy, Victor (1994). "Recollections from a Country Where Freedom Was Simulated." *Simulation & Gaming* 25(2):236–244.

Sadow, Jeffrey D. (1991). "Pedagogical Problems in Playing Planetary Politics." *Simulation & Gaming* 22(3):373–381.

Schaefer, Larry, Harry O. Haakonsen, and Orah Elron (1983). "Ecology/LandUse/Population Games and Simulations." In *The Guide to Simulations/Games for Education and Training,* edited by Robert Horn and Anne Cleaves. Beverly Hills, CA: Sage.

Schrodt, Philip A. (1988). "PWORLD: A Precedent-Based Global Simulation." *Social Science Computer Review* 6(1):27–42.

Seidner, Constance, and Richard R. Dukes (1978). *Learning with Simulation Games.* Beverly Hills, CA: Sage.

Sharrock, W. W., and D. R. Watson (1987). "Power and Realism in Simulation and Gaming, Some Pedagogic and Analytical Observations." In *Simulation-Gaming in the late 1980s,* edited by David S. Crookall, C. S. Greenblat, A. Coote, and J.H.G. Klabbers. Oxford: Pergamon.

Smith, Elizabeth T., and Mark A. Boyer (1996). "Designing In-Class Simulations." *PS: Political Science & Politics* 29(4):690–694.

Starky, Brigid, and J. Wilkenfeld (1996). "Project ICONS: Computer-Assisted Negotiations for the IR Classroom." *International Studies Notes* 21(1):25–29.

Starky, Brigid A. (1994). "Negotiation Training Through Simulation: The ICONS International Negotiation Seminars." *Educators Technology Exchange* (2):6–11.

Steinwachs, Barbara (1992). "How to Facilitate a Debriefing." *Simulation & Gaming* 23(2):186–195.

Steward, Lea P. (1992). "Ethical Issues in Postexperimental and Postexperiential Debriefing." *Simulation & Gaming* 23(2):196–211.

Suleiman, R., and I. Fischer (1996). "The Evolution of Cooperation in a Simulated Inter-Group Conflict." In *Frontiers in Social Research,* edited by W.B.G. Liebrand and D. M. Messick. New York: Springer-Verlag.

Suransky, Leonard (1983). "International Relations Games and Simulations." In *The Guide to Simulations/Games for Education and Training,* edited by Robert Horn and Anne Cleaves. Beverly Hills, CA: Sage.

Theobald, David M., Steven Hal Huntsman, and John R. Supra Jr. (1995). "World System Simulation: A Generational Perspective on Global Systems." *Simulation & Gaming* 26(2):249–260.

Thiagarajan, Sivasailam (1994). "How I Designed a Game—And Discovered the Meaning of Life." *Simulation & Gaming* 25(4):529–535.

Thiagarajan, Sivasailam (1992). "Using Games for Debriefing." *Simulation & Gaming* 23(2):161–173.

Towne, Douglas M. (1995). *Learning and Instruction in Simulation Environments.* Englewood Cliffs, NJ: Educational Technology Publications.

Van Ments, M. (1989). *The Effective Use of Role Play: A Handbook for Teachers and Trainers.* London: Kogan Page.

Walcott, Charles (1980). *Simple Simulations 2.* Washington, DC: American Political Science Association.

Ward, Michael D., ed. (1985). *Theories, Models, and Simulations in International Relations: Essays in Honor of Harold Guetzkow.* Boulder, CO: Westview Press.

Wilkenfeld, Jonathan, Richard D. Brecht, et al. (1988). *ICONS User Manual.* College Park: University of Maryland Press.

Wilkenfeld, Jonathan, and Joyce Kaufmann (1993). "Political Science: Network Simulation in International Politics." *Social Science Computer Review* 11:464–476.

Willis, Jerry, Larry Hovey, and Kathleen Gartelos Hovey (1987). *Computer Simulations: A Source Book to Learning in an Electronic Environment.* New York: Garland Publishing.

Wolfe, Joseph, and David Crookall (1998). "Developing a Scientific Knowledge of Simulation/Gaming." *Simulation & Gaming* 29(1):7–19.

Woodworth, James R., and W. Robert Gump (1994). *Camelot: A Role Playing Simulation for Political Decision Making.* Belmont, CA: Wadsworth Publishing.

Instructional Technologies

Alley, Lee R., and Philip C. Repp (1996). "Technology Precipitates Reflective Teaching: An Instructional Epiphany and the Evolution of a Red Square." *Change* 28(2):48.

Anderson, Ronald E. (1983). "Computer Simulation Games: Exemplars." In *The Guide to Simulations/Games for Education and Training*, edited by Robert Horn and Anne Cleaves. Beverly Hills, CA: Sage.

Bailey, Martha (1995). "USENET Discussion Groups in Political Science Courses." *PS: Political Science & Politics* 28(4):721–722.

Ball, William (1995). "Symposium: Using the Internet in the Political Science Classroom." *PS: Political Science & Politics* 28(4):718–730.

Bane, Adele F. (1994). *Technology and Adult Learning: A Selected Bibliography.* Englewood Cliffs, NJ: Educational Technology Publications.

Bates, A. W., ed. (1984). *The Role of Technology in Distance Education.* New York: St. Martin's.

Batson, Trent, and Randy Bass (1996). "Teaching and Learning in the Computer Age: Primacy of Process." *Change* 28(2):42–49.

Bowers, David A., Jr. (1994). "Using Prodigy and Other Online Services in the Political Science Classroom." *PS: Political Science & Politics* 27(4):708–710.

Branch, Robert M., and Barbara B. Minor, eds. (1997). *Educational Media and Technology Yearbook*. Englewood, CO: Libraries Unlimited.

Brecke, Peter (1995). "The Soviet Global Model: SIM/GDP." *Simulation & Gaming* 26(1):17–26.

Bremer, Stuart A., ed. (1987). *The GLOBUS Model; Computer Simulation of Worldwide Political and Economic Developments*. Boulder, CO: Westview Press.

Brown, John Seely, and Paul Duguid (1996). "Universities in the Digital Age." *Change* 28(4):10.

Bruffee, Kenneth A. (1995). "Sharing Our Toys." *Change* 27(1):12.

Daniel, Sir John S. (1997). "Why Universities Need Technology Strategies." *Change* 29(4):10.

Ellsworth, J. H. (1994). *Education on the Internet*. Englewood Cliffs, NJ: Educational Technology Publications.

Ely, Donald P., and Plomp Tjeerd, eds. (1995). *Classic Writings on Instructional Technology*. Englewood, CO: Libraries Unlimited.

Eraut, Michael, ed. (1989). *The International Encyclopedia of Educational Technology*. Oxford: Pergamon Press.

Falk, Dennis R., and Helen L. Carlson (1995). *Multimedia in Higher Education: A Practical Guide to New Tools for Interactive Teaching and Learning*. Medford, NJ: Learned Information.

Fisher, Francis (1989). "The Electronic Lumberyard and Builders' Rights: Technology, Copyrights, Patents, and Academe." *Change* 21(3):12–21.

Forsyth, Ian (1996). *Teaching and Learning Materials and the Internet*. London: Kogan Page.

Fowler, Sandra M. (1994). "Two Decades of Using Simulation Games for Cross-Cultural Training." *Simulation & Gaming* 25(4):464–476.

Garson, David (1994). "Computerized Simulation in Social Science: A Personal Retrospective." *Simulation & Gaming* 25(4):477–486.

Gayeski, Diane M., ed. (1993). *Multimedia for Learning: Development, Application, Evaluation*. Englewood Cliffs, NJ: Educational Technology Publications.

Gilbert, Steven W. (1996). "Making the Most of a Slow Revolution." *Change* 28(2):10–11.

Green, Kenneth C. (1996). "The Coming Ubiquity of Information Technology." *Change* 28(2):24.

Green, Kenneth (1996). "The 1995 National Survey of Desktop Computing in Higher Education." http://ericir.syr.edu/Projects/Campus_computing/index.html.

Green, Kenneth C., and Steven W. Gilbert (1995). "Great Expectations." *Change* 27(2):8.

Hall, Barbara Welling (1995). "Electronic News Groups in the Liberal Arts Classroom." *International Studies Notes* 20(1):9–15.

Hall, Barbara Welling (1993). "Using E-Mail to Enhance Class Participation." *PS: Political Science & Politics* 26(4):757–759.

Harasim, Linda M., ed. (1990). *Online Education: Perspectives on a New Environment*. Westport, CT: Praeger.

Harknett, Richard J., and Craig T. Cobane (1997). "Introducing Instructional Technology to International Relations." *PS: Political Science & Politics* 3:496–500.

Hebenstreit, Jacques, ed. (1992). *Education and Informatics Worldwide: The State of the Art and Beyond.* Paris: Jessica Kingsley Publishers.

Heide, Ann, and Linda Stilborne (1996). *The Teacher's Complete and Easy Guide to the Internet.* Toronto, Canada: Trifolium Books.

Heinich, Robert, Michael Molenda, and James D. Russell (1989). *Instructional Media and the New Technologies of Instruction.* New York, NY: Macmillan.

Hughes, Barry B. (1993). *International Futures: Choices in the Creation of New World Orders.* Boulder, CO: Westview.

Hughes, Kay (1994). *Entering the World Wide Web: A Guide to Cyberspace.* New York: Enterprise Integration Technologies.

Janda, Kenneth (1992). "Multimedia in Political Science: Sobering Lessons from a Teaching Experiment." *Journal of Educational Multimedia and Hypermedia* 1:341–354.

Janda, Kenneth (1990). "Theory of the Laser Class: Using Video Disc." Paper delivered at the Annual Meeting of the American Political Science Association, San Francisco, CA.

Johnstone, Sally M., and Barbara Krauth (1996). "The Visual University: Principles of Good Practice Balancing Quality and Access." *Change* 28(2):38.

Jonsen, Richard W., and Sally M. Johnstone (1991). "The Future of Information Technology in Higher Education: The State Perspective." *Change* 23(1):42–46.

Jordan, Donald L., and Peter M. Sanchez (1994). "Traditional Versus Technology-Aided Instruction: The Effects of Visual Stimulus in the Classroom." *PS: Political Science & Politics* 27(1):64–67.

Joseph, Lawrence C. (1995). *World Link: An Internet Guide for Educators, Parents, and Students.* Columbus, OH: Greyden Press.

Kozma, Robert B., and Jerome Johnston (1991). "The Technological Revolution Comes to the Classroom." *Change* 23(1):10–23.

Kuzma, Lynn M. (1998). "The World Wide Web and Active Learning in the International Relations Classroom." *PS: Political Science & Politics* 31(3):578–583.

Lamb, Annette C. (1991). *Emerging Technologies and Instruction: Hypertext, Hypermedia, and Interactive Multimedia.* Englewood Cliffs, NJ: Educational Technology Publications.

Laurillard, Diana M. (1993). *Rethinking University Teaching: A Framework for the Effective Use of Educational Technology.* London: Routledge.

Laurillard, Diana M. (1984). "Interactive Video and the Control of Learning." *Educational Technology* 24(6):7–15.

Laurillard, Diana M., Brian Swift, and Jane Darby (1993). "Academics' Use of Courseware Materials: A Survey." *Association of Learning Technology Journal* 1(1):12–17.

Lawler, Robert W., and Masoud Yazdani, eds. (1987). *Artificial Intelligence and Education.* Norwood, NJ: Ablex Publishing.

Luna, Carl J., and Joe Mac McKenzie (1997). "Beyond the Chalkboard:

Multimedia Sources for Instruction in Political Science." *PS: Political Science & Politics* 30(1):60–68.

McHaney, R. W. (1991). *Computer Simulation: A Practical Perspective.* San Diego, CA: Academic Press.

Permaloff, Anne, and Carl Grafton (1991). "Using the Microcomputer in the Classroom: Initial Considerations." *PS: Political Science & Politics* 24(4):689–694.

Pike, Matthew A. (1995). *Using the Internet.* Indianapolis, IN: Que Corporation.

Poole, Bernard J. (1997). *Education for an Information Age: Teaching in the Computerized Classroom.* New York: McGraw Hill.

Rada, Roy. (1995). *Developing Educational Hypermedia: Coordination and Reuse.* Norwood, NJ: Ablex Publishing.

Rosenberg, Mark B. (1992). "AMERICAS: New Video and Print Resources for Teaching About Latin America and the Caribbean." *PS: Political Science & Politics* 25(3):546.

Rowntree, Derek (1982). *Educational Technology in Curriculum Development.* London: Harper & Row.

Scanlon, Eileen, and Timothy O'Shea (1992). *New Directions in Educational Technology—Proceedings of the NATO Advanced Research Workshop on New Directions in Advanced Educational Technology.* New York: Springer-Verlag.

Schwier, Richard. (1993). *Interactive Multimedia Instruction.* Englewood Cliffs, NJ: Educational Technology Publications.

Seels, Barbara B., and Rita C. Richey (1994). *Instructional Technology: The Definition and Domains of the Field.* Washington, DC: Association for Educational Communications and Technology.

Thompson, Ann D., Michael R. Simonson, and Constance P. Hargrave (1996). *Educational Technology: A Review of the Research.* Washington, DC: Association for Educational Communications and Technology.

Ward, Art, et al. (1996). "Multimedia in the Political Science Classroom: Smoke and Mirrors or a Legitimate New Pedagogy?" Paper presented at the Annual Meeting of the American Political Science Association, San Francisco, CA.

Weisberg, Herbert F., and Leo V. Hennessy III (1991). "Teaching Data Analysis in an Interactive Graphics Environment." *PS: Political Science & Politics* 24(3):505–510.

Willis, Barry, ed. (1994). *Distance Education: Strategies and Tools.* Englewood Cliffs, NJ: Educational Technology Publications.

Winders, Ray (1988). *Information Technology in the Delivery of Distance Education and Training.* London: Peter Francis Publishers.

General Active Learning Resources

Bean, J. C. (1996). *Engaging Ideas: The Professor's Guide to Integrating Writing, Critical Thinking, and Active Learning in the Classroom.* San Francisco: Jossey-Bass.

Belenky, M. F., B. McV. Clinchy, N. R. Goldberger, and J. M. Tarule (1986). *Women's Ways of Knowing: The Development of Self, Mind, and Voice*. New York: Basic Books.

Bell, Chris, Mandy Woden, and Andrew Trott, eds. (1997). *Implementing Flexible Learning*. London: Kogan Page.

Bonwell, Charles C., and James A. Eison (1991). *Active Learning: Creating Excitement in the Classroom*. ASHE-ERIC Higher Education Report No. 1. Washington, DC: The George Washington University School of Education and Human Development.

Bonwell, Charles C., and Tracey Sutherland (1996). *Using Active Learning in College Classrooms: A Range of Options for Faculty*. San Francisco: Jossey-Bass.

Brookfield, Stephen D. (1990). *The Skillful Teacher: On Technique, Trust, and Responsiveness in the Classroom*. San Francisco: Jossey-Bass.

Burns, Alvin C., and James W. Gentry (1998). "Motivating Students to Engage in Experiential Learning: A Tension-to-Learn Theory." *Simulation & Gaming* 29(2):133–151.

Carr, William (1986). *Becoming Critical: Education, Knowledge, and Action Research*. London: Falmer Press.

Christensen, C. Roland, David A. Garvin, and Ann Sweet (1991). *Education for Judgment: The Artistry of Discussion Leadership*. Cambridge: Harvard Business School Press.

Cooper, James, S. Prescott, L. Cook, L. Smith, R. Mueck, and James Cuseo (1990). *Cooperative Learning and College Instruction: Effective Use of Student Learning Teams*. Long Beach: The California State University Foundation.

Cuseo, James (1992). "Collaborative and Cooperative Learning in Higher Education: A Proposed Taxonomy." *Cooperative Learning and College Teaching* 2(2):2–4.

Elbow, Peter (1986). *Embracing Contraries: Explorations in Learning and Teaching*. New York: Oxford University Press.

Freire, Paulo (1970). *The Pedagogy of the Oppressed*. New York: Herder & Herder.

Gamson, Zelda F. (1994). "Collaborative Learning Comes of Age." *Change* 26(5):44.

Kagan, Steven (1989). *Cooperative Learning Resources for Teachers*. San Juan Capistrano, CA: Resources for Teachers.

Katz, Joseph, and Mildred Henry (1988). *Turning Professors into Teachers: A New Approach to Faculty Development and Student Learning*. New York: American Council on Education/Macmillan Publishing.

Kolb, D. A. (1984). *Experiential Learning: Experience as the Source of Learning and Development*. Englewood Cliffs, NJ: Prentice-Hall.

Light, Richard J. (1990). *The Harvard Assessment Seminars: Explorations with Students and Faculty About Teaching, Learning and Student Life*. Cambridge: Harvard Graduate School of Education and Kennedy School of Government.

Matthews, Roberta S., James L. Cooper, Neil Davidson, and Peter Hawkes (1995). "Building Bridges Between Cooperative and Collaborative Learning." *Change* 27(4):34.

Millis, Barbara J., and Philip G. Cottell Jr. (1998). *Cooperative Learning for Higher Education Faculty*. Phoenix, AZ: Oryx Press.

Oliver, Arnold J. (1995). "Enhancing International Studies with Undergraduate Academic Conferences." *International Studies Notes* 20(1):16–20.

Perry, William G. (1970). *Forms of Intellectual and Ethical Development in the College Years: A Scheme.* New York: Holt-Rinehart.

Schon, Donald A. (1987). *Educating the Reflective Practitioner: Toward a New Design for Teaching and Learning in the Professions.* San Francisco: Jossey-Bass.

Summers, Jerry A. (1991). "Effect of Interactivity upon Student Achievement, Completion Intervals, and Affective Perceptions." *Journal of Educational Technology Systems* 19:53–57.

Principles, Practices, and Assessment

American Association of Higher Education (1987). *Principles for Good Practice in Undergraduate Education.* Racine, WI: The Johnson Foundation.

Angelo, Thomas A., and K. Patricia Cross (1993). *Classroom Assessment Techniques: A Handbook for College Teachers.* San Francisco: Jossey-Bass.

Ashcroft, K., and David Palacio (1996). *Researching into Assessment and Evaluation in Colleges and Universities.* London: Kogan Page.

Astin, A. W. (1993). *What Matters in College: Four Critical Years Revisited.* San Francisco: Jossey-Bass.

Baiocco, Sharon A., and Jamie N. DeWaters (1998). *Successful College Teaching: Problem-Solving Strategies of Distinguished Professors.* Des Moines, IA: Longwood.

Banner, James M., and Harold C. Cannon (1997). "The Personal Qualities of Teaching: What Teachers Do Cannot Be Distinguished from Who They Are." *Change* 29(6):40.

Barr, Robert B., and John Tagg (1995). "From Teaching to Learning—A New Paradigm for Undergraduate Education." *Change* 27(6):13–25.

Bennett, Clinton, Francis Foreman-Peck, and Charles Higgins (1996). *Researching into Teaching Methods in Colleges and Universities.* London: Kogan Page.

Bower, George H., and Ervin Milgred (1981). *Theories of Learning.* Englewood Cliffs, NJ: Prentice-Hall.

Boyer, Ernest L. (1990). *Scholarship Reconsidered: Priorities of the Professoriate.* Princeton, NJ: Princeton University Press.

Chickering, Arthur W., and Zelda F. Gamson, eds. (1991). *Applying the Seven Principles for Good Practice in Undergraduate Education.* San Francisco: Jossey-Bass.

Cronin, Thomas (1991). "On Celebrating College Teaching." *PS: Political Science & Politics* 24(3):282–291.

Douglas, George H. (1992). *Education Without Impact: How Our Universities Fail the Young.* New York: Birch Lane Press.

Eble, Kenneth (1988). *The Craft of Teaching: A Guide to Mastering the Professor's Art*. San Francisco: Jossey-Bass.

Elton, Lawrence (1994). *Management of Teaching and Learning: Towards Change in Universities*. London: CVCP/SRHE.

Entwistle, Nancy (1981). *Styles of Learning and Teaching*. New York: John Wiley and Sons.

Fairweather, James S. (1996). *Faculty Work and Public Trust: Restoring the Value of Teaching and Public Service in American Academic Life*. Des Moines, IA: Longwood.

Fink, L. Dee (1984). *The First Year of College Teaching: New Directions for Teaching and Learning*. San Francisco: Jossey-Bass.

Flood, Barbara, and Joy K. Moll (1990). *The Professor Business: A Teaching Primer for Faculty*. Medford, NJ: Learned Information.

Gibbs, G., ed. (1995). *Improving Student Learning Through Assessment and Evaluation*. Oxford: The Oxford Centre for Staff Development at Oxford Brookes University.

Gibbs, G., and Anne Jenkins (1992). *Teaching Large Classes in Higher Education*. London: Kogan Page.

Hativa, Nira, and Michele Marincovich, eds. (1995). *New Directions for Experiential Learning: Disciplinary Differences in Teaching and Learning: Implications for Practice*. San Francisco: Jossey-Bass.

Haworth, Jennifer G., and Clifton F. Conrad (1997). *Emblems of Quality in Higher Education: Developing and Sustaining High-Quality Programs*. Des Moines, IA: Longwood.

Heginbotham, Stanley J. (1994). "Shifting the Focus of International Programs." *The Chronicle of Higher Education* 10(19):A68.

Higgins, C., Jane Reading, and Paul Taylor (1996). *Researching into Learning Resources in Colleges and Universities*. London: Kogan Page.

Hoey, Ross, ed. (1994). *Designing for Learning: Effectiveness with Efficiency*. London: Kogan Page.

Hutchings, Pat, and Ted Marchese (1990). "A Special Report—Watching Assessment: Questions, Stories, Prospects." *Change* 22(5):12–43.

Iannuzzi, Patricia, Stephen S. Strichart, and Charles T. Magnum, II (1998). *Teaching Study Skills and Strategies in College*. Des Moines, IA: Longwood.

Jones-Shoemaker, Cynthia C. (1998). *Leadership in Continuing and Distance Education in Higher Education*. Des Moines, IA: Longwood.

Lambert, Richard D. (1989). *International Studies and the Undergraduate*. Washington, DC: American Council on Education.

Loacker, Georgine, and Ernest G. Palola, eds. (1981). *New Directions for Experiential Learning: Clarifying Learning Outcomes in the Liberal Arts*. San Francisco: Jossey-Bass.

Lovell-Troy, Larry, and Paul Eickmann (1992). *Course Design for College Teachers*. Englewood Cliffs, NJ: Educational Technology Publications.

McCall, W. A. (1923). *How to Experiment in Education*. New York: Macmillan.

McKeachie, Wilbert J., Paul R. Pintrich, Yi Guang Lin, David A.F. Smith, and Rajeev Sharma (1986). *Teaching and Learning in the College*

Classroom: A Review of the Literature. Ann Arbor, MI: National Center for Research to Improve Postsecondary Teaching and Learning.

Merrill, M. David (1994). *Instructional Design Theory.* Englewood Cliffs, NJ: Educational Technology Publications.

Morris, Michael A. (1993). "Teaching Political Science in a Foreign Language." *PS: Political Science & Politics,* 26(1):72–75.

Myers, Christopher, and T. B. Jones (1993). *Promoting Active Learning: Strategies for the College Classroom.* San Francisco, CA: Jossey-Bass.

Palmer, Parker J. (1990). "Good Teaching: A Matter of Living the Mystery." *Change* 22(1):10–16.

Robson, Carl (1993). *Real World Research: A Resource for Social Scientists and Practitioner Researchers.* Oxford: Blackwell.

Shea, Christopher (1997). "Political Scientists Clash over Value of Area Studies." *Chronicle of Higher Education* 1(10):A13–14.

Smist, Frank J. (1992). "International Education in an Age of Transition." In a Special Issue of *International Studies Notes: International Studies— The State of the Discipline,* edited by Llewellyn D. Howell. 17(4):43–46.

Spencer, Ken. (1991). "Modes, Media, and Methods: The Search for Educational Effectiveness." *British Journal of Educational Technology* 22:12–22.

Stark, Joan S., and Lisa R. Lattuca (1997). *Shaping the College Curriculum: Academic Plans in Action.* Des Moines, IA: Longwood.

Stimpson, Catherine R. (1988). "Is There a Core in This Curriculum? And Is It Really Necessary?" *Change* 20(2):26–42.

Tennyson, Robert D., and Sanne Dykstra, eds. (1997). *Instructional Design: International Perspectives.* Mahwak, NJ: L. Erlbaum Associates.

Torney-Purta, Judith (1998). "Evaluating Programs Designed to Teach International Content and Negotiation Skills." *International Negotiation. A Journal of Theory and Practice* 3(1):77–97.

Vavrina, Vernon J. (1992). "From Poughkeepsie to Peoria to the Persian Gulf." *PS: Political Science & Politics* 25(4):700–702.

Walters, G. A., and T. E. Marks (1981). *Experiential Learning and Change.* New York: John Wiley.

Active Learning and the Internet

Another way to teach and learn actively about international studies is to explore interesting sites on the World Wide Web. The Web is becoming more valuable and more popular as a source of information every day, but one must always approach its use as a research tool carefully and with a critical eye. What follows is a list of interesting (and authoritative) Web sites that relate well to exercises in this book and that are active at the time of writing.

Active Learning in International Affairs Section
http://csf.colorado.edu/isa/sections/alias/index.html
> This is the official Web site of the Active Learning in International Affairs Section of the International Studies Association, the largest professional organization dedicated to teaching and research in international studies. This site supports the section's mission to "provide a forum for exploring active learning approaches to teaching international affairs" and currently features valuable materials on case teaching, simulations, and active teaching tips.

American Diplomacy
http://www.unc.edu/depts/diplomat
> A terrific collection of journal articles and a running commentary on U.S. foreign policy. This Web site includes inside information on the content and conduct of foreign affairs.

ArabNet
http://www.arab.net
> Proclaimed as "the online resource for the Arab World in the Middle East and North Africa," this site is well organized and offers an A-to-Z directory of Arab organizations, people, companies, and views as well as information on each of the Arab nations. Local news stories from the region are also available.

ASEAN Web
http://www.asean.or.id/
> The most complete Web site for the Association of Southeast Asian Nations offers information about their policies as well as links to other pages on the member nations. Be sure to check out the online newspapers for information from this region.

The Bulletin of the Atomic Scientists
http://www.bullatomsci.org/
> This site contains the latest information concerning nuclear weapons, energy technology, and proliferation. Read about new discoveries in current (or past) issues of the *Bulletin* online and see the famous Doomsday Clock.

Central Intelligence Agency
http://www.odci.gov/cia/ciahome.html
> This is the main page for the CIA and contains many interesting links that allow one to retrieve basic statistical information on many subjects and nations. This page could be used as a quick reference for statistical information.

Demography and Population
http://coombs.anu.edu.au/ ResFacilities/DemographyPage.html
> This site provides demographic information from around the world. It is quite comprehensive and contains many links on related global concerns such as population growth and world hunger.

DiploNet
http://www.clark.net/pub/diplonet/DiploNet.html
> This site focuses on diplomacy and negotiation. Use it to research negotiation and diplomacy or find out more about current issues in world politics.

Europa—European Union
http://europa.eu.int/
> This site will take you on a virtual visit to the European Union (EU) headquarters in Brussels as well as provide information on the history, policies, and institutions of the EU.

Federation of American Scientists (FAS)
http://www.fas.org/
> This site is packed full of interesting information on a wide variety of topics from government security to space policy to arms sales monitoring.

Foreign Affairs (FA)
http://www.foreignaffairs.org/
> This journal home page provides valuable research assistance on themes related to U.S. foreign policy. It includes an archive of *FA* and other respected foreign affairs journals and links to many interesting Web sites on foreign affairs.

Friends of the Earth (FOE)
http://www.foe.co.uk/index.html
> This is a very interesting site for any environmentally conscious citizen. Read about the environmental campaigns FOE undertakes as well as press releases and environmental hot topics. This page is a strong example of grassroots mobilization and action.

Government Servers and Information
http://www.eff.org/govt.html
> This site offers the addresses of hundreds of Web sites. Find out about the governmental information on an entire continent or a small neighborhood. One can also conduct research on international organizations such as the United Nations and European Union as well as on many multinational corporations.

The Hunger Project
http://www.thp.org/
> This site is dedicated to reporting on efforts by this nongovernmental organization to combat hunger locally, nationally, and around the world.

IISDnet
http://iisd1.iisd.ca/
> This site is well organized into five themes of sustainable development. Find out how to turn sustainability into a competitive advantage under the Business and Sustainable Development link or read up-to-date information under the Hot Topics link.

Inside China Today
http://www.insidechina.com/
> This Web site is dedicated to current news events from China. The site covers domestic and international affairs of concern in Asia.

InterAction
http://www.interaction.org/advocacy/advocacy.html
> Use this site as a springboard to connect to other sites that detail current advocacy issues and international organizations such as the World Bank and the North Atlantic Treaty Organization. Find out the latest news by connecting to CNN or C-Span or let the president know how you feel by e-mailing him through a mail link that is also offered on this page.

International Studies Association (ISA)
http://www.isanet.org/
> This is the official Web site of the International Studies Association, the world's largest professional organization dedicated to research and teaching in international affairs. This site includes many important links to ISA publications, sections, professional conference information, and international relations research areas.

ISN International Relations and Security Network
http://www.isn.ethz.ch/
> This site proclaims itself to be "your one-stop information network for security and defense studies, peace and conflict research, and international relations"—and it certainly is. It offers countless amounts of information on all regions, countries, and subjects.

NAFTA Border Home Page
http://www.iep.doc.gov/border/nafta.htm/
> This site offers an interesting and extensive collection of information on the North American Free Trade Agreement, including many government documents and trade bank data for Canada, Mexico, and the United States.

National Geographic Society
http://www.nationalgeographic.com
> This list allows you to access all the resources available from the National Geographic Society online. Link after link references useful information in the form of statistics, articles, pictures, maps, and other Web sites.

National Oceanic and Atmospheric Administration
http://www.noaa.gov/
> This site is full of information on the conditions of our oceans and the changes in our climate. The research and environmental links will lead you to material that covers many environmental concerns.

Penn Library
http://www.library.upenn.edu/resources/websitest.html
> This is a direct connection to the University of Pennsylvania library home page—containing a virtual treasure trove of international relations subjects and links. This is a terrific resource for international relations research.

Social Influence
http://www.public.asu.edu/~kelton/
> This Web site describes the complicated relationship among public opinion, social pressures, and policymakers. It includes interesting public attitude survey information and explores the role of the media in foreign affairs.

The Henry L. Stimson Center
http.//www.stimson.org/
> This page is devoted to public policy research. One can find information on projects from the elimination of weapons of mass destruction to confidence-building measures in regions of tension.

U.S. Information Agency
http://www.usia.gov/usis.html
> This government agency Web site promotes awareness of current events and concerns on topics including foreign policy, global issues, and human rights.

U.S. Institute of Peace
http://www.usip.org/
This U.S. government agency was created by Congress to promote nonviolent conflict resolution and cross-national communication. The Web site describes many programs available for research and education about peace, and it provides links to a number of related organizations.

World Bank
http://www.worldbank.org/
This is an interesting Web site that one can explore for hours. The Topics in Development link offers especially good information on agriculture, environmental issues, trade, infrastructure development, and poverty.

World Wide Web Virtual Library
http://info.pitt.edu/~ian/ianres.html
This is a Web page of pages. All links are organized into three main categories: Type (news, country, statistics), Source (think tanks, international organizations), and Topics (international trade, conflict resolution, and proliferation).

World Wildlife Federation (WWF)
http://www.wwf.org
This well-organized and intriguing Web site allows you to read about current actions and dilemmas of the WWF as well as to find out about all the functions of the organization. This site details many environmental problems and offers you information on many subjects, from the effects of water pollution on whale migration patterns to global warming.

THE CONTRIBUTORS

John Boehrer is a lecturer at the Daniel J. Evans School of Public Affairs, University of Washington, and director of Teaching Resources for the Electronic Hallway (www.hallway.org), an Internet resource on case teaching and active learning in public affairs. He was formerly director of Teaching Development at the John F. Kennedy School of Government, Harvard University, where he directed the Pew Faculty Fellowship in International Affairs. He was involved in creating the Web site CaseNet: Active Learning in International Affairs (csf.colorado.EDU/CaseNet) and the Active Learning in International Affairs Section (ALIAS) of the International Studies Association (ISA) and continues to serve on the ALIAS Executive Committee. He has published several articles on the use of cases and has led case teaching and writing workshops in North America, Europe, Asia, and Africa.

G. Matthew Bonham is chair of International Relations and director of Global Programs at the Maxwell School of Citizenship and Public Affairs, Syracuse University. His research, which involves information technology and the development of computer simulation models of foreign policy decisionmaking, has been funded by three grants from the National Science Foundation. He has published three monographs, fourteen refereed journal articles, and ten chapters in anthologies. He offers courses on international relations theory and the analysis of political texts as well as workshops on writing hypertext, policy advocacy through the World Wide Web and videoconferencing, and expert systems for economic forecasting.

Mark A. Boyer is associate professor of political science at the University of Connecticut and director of the Connecticut Project in International Negotiation (http://spirit.lib.uconn.edu/~mboyer/). He is the author of *International Cooperation and Public Goods* (Johns Hopkins University Press, 1993) and numerous journal articles, and coauthor (with John T. Rourke) of *World Politics* (Dushkin/McGraw-Hill, 1998).

Patrick Callahan is professor of political science at DePaul University. His primary research interest is the place of moral norms in international affairs, with special attention to Roman Catholic social teaching.

Maryann Cusimano is an assistant professor of politics at The Catholic University of America in Washington, D.C. She teaches graduate and undergraduate courses at both Catholic University and the Pentagon, including courses on globalization, sovereignty, post–Cold War interventions, international relations theory, the media and foreign policy, U.S. foreign policy, and political psychology. Her recent publications include *Beyond Sovereignty: Issues for a Global Agenda* (St. Martin's Press, 1999) and *Unplugging the Cold War Machine: Rethinking U.S. Foreign Policy Organizations* (Sage Publications, forthcoming).

Lev Gonick is university dean for Instructional Technology and Academic Computing at the California State Polytechnic University in Pomona. He was a Pew Faculty Fellow in International Affairs (1990–1995) and cofounded and currently manages the CaseNet initiative based at the Kennedy School of Government at Harvard University. He established the International Political Economy Network at Communications for a Sustainable Future, which is a project of the International Political Economy Section of the ISA. Gonick also developed the first Web presence of the ISA. He is actively engaged in consulting and education work on information technology.

Joe D. Hagan is professor of political science and associate director of the International Studies Program at West Virginia University. He teaches and conducts research in the fields of international relations, U.S. foreign policy, and comparative foreign policy. He is the author of *Political Opposition and Foreign Policy in Comparative Perspective* (Lynne Rienner Publishers, 1993) and coeditor of *Foreign Policy Restructuring: How Governments Respond to Global Change* (University of South Carolina Press, 1994). He has received the two top teaching and research awards at West Virginia University and was the recipient of a Pew Faculty Fellowship at Harvard University.

Patrick Haney is associate professor of political science at Miami University in Oxford, Ohio. He teaches courses in world politics and U.S. foreign and national security policy. His recent publications include *Organizing for Foreign Policy Crises: Presidents, Advisers, and the Management of Decision-Making* (University of Michigan Press, 1997) and articles on U.S. policy toward Cuba with Walt Vanderbush in *International Studies Quarterly* and *Political Science Quarterly.* He currently serves as president of the Active Learning in International Affairs Section (ALIAS) of the International Studies Association.

Jeanne A. K. Hey is an associate professor of political science and international studies at Miami University in Oxford, Ohio. Her teaching and research interests focus on foreign policy behavior, especially in small and less developed countries. Her research has been published in *Comparative Political Studies, Third World Quarterly, International Interactions,* and the *Journal of Latin American Studies.* She teaches courses on international politics, comparative foreign policy, and the developing world. She is currently in residence at Miami University's European Center in Luxembourg.

Heidi Hobbs is currently visiting assistant professor in the Department of Political Science at North Carolina State University, having previously held faculty positions at Florida International University and Illinois State University. Her teaching experience includes courses in international relations, foreign policy, international law, and international organizations. She is the author of *City Hall Goes Abroad: The Foreign Policy of Local Politics* (Sage Publications, 1994) and editor of *Pondering Postinternationalism: A Paradigm for the 21st Century?* (SUNY Press, forthcoming).

Ole R. Holsti is George V. Allen Professor of International Affairs in the Political Science Department at Duke University. Recently his teaching has focused on theories of international relations at the graduate level, U.S. foreign policy, and various seminars in international relations, including Democracy and American Foreign Policy and New World Orders. His recent publications include *Public Opinion and American Foreign Policy* (University of Michigan Press, 1996) and "A Widening Gap Between the U.S. Military and Civilian Society: Some Evidence, 1976-96," *International Security* (winter 1998/1999). He is a former president of the Active Learning in International Affairs Section (ALIAS) of the International Studies Association.

Lynn M. Kuzma is assistant professor of political science and director of international studies at the University of Southern Maine. She teaches classes on U.S. foreign policy, conflict and security, international organizations, international relations, and political theory. Her most recent publication is "The World Wide Web and Active Learning in the International Relations Classroom," *PS: Political Science and Politics* 31(3):578–584. She is a former president of the Active Learning in International Affairs Section (ALIAS) of the International Studies Association, and she has given numerous presentations on the applications of information technology to pedagogy.

Steven Lamy is an associate professor in the School of International Relations at the University of Southern California and director of the Teaching International Relations Program. His current research and teaching interests focus on the analysis of foreign policy in Western nation-states and on alternatives to realist thinking in international relations theory. His major publications include *Contemporary International Issues: Contending Perspectives* (Lynne Rienner Publishers, 1988) and *International Relations for the Twenty-First Century: A Rough Guide for Participants in Global Communities* (McGraw-Hill, forthcoming). The recipient of numerous teaching awards, he has directed the University of Southern California's Center for Excellence in Teaching and the Center for Public Education in International Affairs and was a master teacher in Harvard University's Pew Faculty Fellowship program. He is currently vice president/program chair of the Active Learning in International Affairs Section (ALIAS) of the International Studies Association.

Jeffrey S. Lantis is an assistant professor of political science and chair of the International Relations Program at The College of Wooster. He is also secretary of the Active Learning in International Affairs Section (ALIAS) of the International Studies Association. He has taught a variety of international studies courses on global issues, U.S. and comparative foreign policy, and international security. Recent publications include *Domestic Constraints and the Breakdown of International Agreements* (Praeger, 1997); "Simulations and Experiential Learning in the International Relations Classroom," *International Negotiation* (March 1998); and, with Matthew Queen, "Negotiating Neutrality: The Double-Edged Diplomacy of Austrian Accession to the European Union," *Cooperation and Conflict* (June 1998).

Michael McIntyre is assistant professor of international studies at DePaul University. His research is oriented around a Gramscian perspective that cuts across the fields of international relations and historical sociology. He is currently at work on a manuscript comparing British imperialism in India and Brazil from 1850 to 1930.

Dario Moreno is associate professor of political science at Florida International University and chairman of the board of One Nation, Inc. He was a Fulbright Scholar in Costa Rica in 1990 and a Pew Faculty Fellow at Harvard's John F. Kennedy School of Government in 1992. His areas of teaching and research specialization are Cuban-American politics and U.S.–Latin American relations. He has published two books, *U.S. Policy in Central America: The Endless Debate* (University Press of Florida, 1990) and *The Struggle for Peace in Central America* (University Press of Florida, 1994). Moreno has also written numerous articles and book chapters on Cuban-American politics in Miami, and he has commented extensively on Miami politics in the national media.

Thomas Preston is an assistant professor of international relations in the Department of Political Science at Washington State University. He teaches undergraduate and graduate courses involving political psychology, international affairs, and U.S. public policy. His research interests include presidential leadership style and decision-making, group dynamics, foreign and defense policy, and nuclear proliferation. His recent publications include "'From Lambs to Lions': Nuclear Proliferation's Grand Reshuffling of Interstate Security Relationships," *Cooperation and Conflict: Nordic Journal of International Studies* 32(1) (March 1997); "Following the Leader: The Impact of U.S. Presidential Style upon Advisory Group Dynamics, Structure, and Decision," in B. Sundelius, P. 't Hart, and E. Stern, eds., *Beyond Groupthink: Group Decision Making in Foreign Policy* (University of Michigan Press, 1997); and *The President and His Inner Circle: Leadership Style and the Advisory Process in Foreign Policy Making* (Columbia University Press, forthcoming).

David Schodt is professor of economics and director of the Hispanic Studies Program at St. Olaf College in Northfield, Minnesota, where he teaches courses on microeconomic theory, economic development, and the economies of Asia and Latin America. He is the author of several cases on economic development and has conducted case teaching and writing workshops for the World Bank's Economic Development Institute. He has published articles on case teaching and learning, including, with John Carlson of Purdue University, "Beyond the Lecture: Case Teaching and the Learning of Economic Theory," *Journal of Economic Education*. He has been active in fostering case writing in international affairs and is a former president of the Active Learning in International Affairs Section (ALIAS) of the International Studies Association.

Jeffrey W. Seifert is a Ph.D. candidate in political science at the Maxwell School of Citizenship and Public Affairs at Syracuse University. While a research assistant at the Global Affairs Institute, he coordinated Phase II of the Early Adopters Project and organized the Teaching Technologies Workshop Series. He has also served as the online Web master for Syracuse University's University College's initiative to offer distance education via the Internet. His research interests include the effect of technology on states' powers, policy decisionmaking, and the use of computer technology in teaching.

Howard Tolley Jr. is professor of political science at the University of Cincinnati (UC) and director of the Teaching Human Rights Online project for the UC College of Law's Morgan Institute for Human Rights. His major published works include *The International Commission of Jurists: Global Advocates for Human Rights* (University of Pennsylvania Press, 1994) and "Project THRO: Teaching Human Rights Online" (*Human Rights Quarterly*).

INDEX

ABOUT THE BOOK

This innovative volume effectively combines curricular themes and teaching methods to provide practical teaching tools for international studies faculty.

The broad range of substantive issues addressed in the book reflects the diversity of actors—national, regional, and international—that respond to global problems. The authors explore new techniques for covering these issues, focusing on the case method, games, simulations, role-play exercises, and uses of technology. Emphasizing linkages between theory and practice, each chapter features classroom activities designed to engage students and encourage critical thinking. A comprehensive list of active teaching and learning resources, submitted by members of the International Studies Association, complete this distinctive handbook.

Jeffrey S. Lantis is assistant professor of political science at The College of Wooster. **Lynn M. Kuzma** is assistant professor of political science at the University of Southern Maine. **John Boehrer** is lecturer at the Daniel J. Evans School of Public Affairs at the University of Washington.